GOODNESS OF FIT:
CLINICAL APPLICATIONS FROM
INFANCY THROUGH ADULT LIFE

GOODNESS OF FIT: CLINICAL APPLICATIONS FROM INFANCY THROUGH ADULT LIFE

Stella Chess, M.D.
Professor of Child Psychiatry
N.Y.U. Medical Center
and
Alexander Thomas, M.D.
Professor of Psychiatry
N.Y.U. Medical Center

BRUNNER/MAZEL
· Taylor & Francis Group ·

616.891
C524g
1999

USA	Publishing Office:	BRUNNER/MAZEL *A member of the Taylor & Francis Group* 325 Chestnut Street, Suite 800 Philadelphia, PA 19106 Tel: (215) 625-8900 Fax: (215) 625-2940
	Distribution Center:	BRUNNER/MAZEL *A member of the Taylor & Francis Group* 47 Runway Road, Suite G Levittown, PA 19057-4700 Tel: (215) 269-0400 Fax: (215) 269-0363
UK		BRUNNER/MAZEL *A member of the Taylor & Francis Group* 1 Gunpowder Square London EC4A 3DE Tel: 171 583 0490 Fax: 171 583 0581

GOODNESS OF FIT: Clinical Applications From Infancy Through Adult Life

1 2 3 4 5 6 7 8 9 0

Printed by Edwards Brothers, Ann Arbor, MI, 1999.

A CIP catalog record for this book is available from the British Library.
  ∞ The paper in this publication meets the requirements of the ANSI Standard Z39.48-1984 (Permanence of Paper)

Library of Congress Cataloging-in-Publication Data

Chess, Stella.
        Goodness of fit: clinical applications from infancy through
adult life / Stella Chess and Alexander Thomas.
        p. cm.
    Includes bibliographical references and index.
    ISBN 0-87630-893-0 (alk. paper)
    1. Personality disorders -- Treatment. 2. Temperament -- Physiology.
  3. Behavior therapy. 4. Personality development. I. Thomas,
  Alexander, 1914- II. Title.
    RC554 .C476 1999
    616.89'1 -- ddc21   98-43420
ISBN: 0-87630-893-0 (hardcover)   CIP

Dedicated to Miriam Rosenberg
April 21, 1919 to September 15, 1998

To our good friend and invaluable colleague of forty years. Her dedication, integrity and intelligence were an integral element of our research and clinical functioning.

CONTENTS

FOREWORD

It was at least 40 years ago, when I was being mentored by Dr. Stella Chess, that she taught me to distinguish between "reactive" behavior disorders and other disorders of behavior and mentation in children. She argued then that the reactive disorders tended to have their genesis in specific life conditions and situations and that these disorders tended to recede or to be self-correcting when the situation was corrected or removed. A few years later she and Dr. Alexander Thomas began their studies of temperamental individuality. In their research and their practice they continued to be sensitive to behavioral/contextual variations and especially to the interactions between patterned individual human responsivity and characteristics of the environments in which or to which the response occurred. Their observations led them to conclude that when the response is judged to be psychologically or socially inappropriate, it is considered to be disordered or dysfunctional. When the disordered response can be associated with conditions or factors specific to the contexts in which it has been expressed, we have Dr. Chess's reactive behavior disorder. When the interaction between the response capacities of the organism and the effective context or environment results in behavior considered to be appropriate or functional we conclude that the behavior is normal or, in the language of this text, that there has been a goodness of fit between the behavior of the individual and circumstances which surround it.

Drs. Chess and Thomas are psychiatrists and this book is written with a strong clinical psychiatric emphasis. However, this work, while not self-consciously theoretical is by no means atheoretical. The very common sense notion of "goodness of fit" is grounded in two systems of thought. Fundamental to the construct is the notion that the genesis of all behavior is to be found in the dialectical interactions between whatever is given in the organism and the environment in which it exists and functions. Genetic material comes to be expressed in phenotypic phenomena, and phenotype is the product of whatever is in the genes in interaction with whatever is provided by the effective environment. The characteristics of the organism or individual are developed and expressed through interactions with these environments of which they both are a part. Debate continues concerning the privileging of endogenous or exogenous phenomena as causal factors but there is wide agreement concerning the interactive involvement of both. For Chess and Thomas, if primacy must be assigned, it is assigned to the interaction. The notion "goodness of fit" assumes such interaction.

It is not only the origins of behavior that are explained by interactionist conceptions, but the continuing expressions of behavior as well. When interactionist and epigenetic perspectives are combined, three conclusions may be drawn concerning the causes of behavior: 1) Behavior arises from both biological and social origins; 2) The interactions between biological and social phenomena that cause behavior are complex and multiple; and 3) These interactions result in bi-directional transformations, which influence both the social environments and the bio-social behaviors. Behavior—normal and abnormal, adaptive and maladaptive—is the product of these interactions. According to Chess and Thomas those adaptive and normal behavioral responses reflect a high degree of goodness of fit, while those mal-adaptive and abnormal behaviors generally reflect a poorness of fit. In all of these processes interactions are the constant. Goodness of fit is a judgement based on empirical evidence and sometimes on aesthetic value.

Also central to the Chess and Thomas goodness of fit construct is the concept of behavioral individuality. Individual differences in the behavior of humans has long been a subject of study but it was in the middle of the twentieth century that we came to more fully appreciate the facts and importance of differences in affective and cognitive response tendencies. By the latter quarter of the twentieth century we had begun to recognize situative response tendencies—the inclination for certain situations to evoke particular kinds of responses. The pioneering work of Chess, Thomas and Birch concerning nine dimensions of temperament established the fact of important and persistent differences in patterns affective behavior comparable to those differences in cognitive behavior described by Anastasie, Witkin, Kagen and Messick. The works of these scientists helped us understand that while humans have many characteristics in common and even though individual human beings share some characteristics with members of the groups to which they belong, there exist considerable variation between the behavior of one individual and that of another. Not only is there such variance between individuals, there is also consistency within individuals. Persons tend to persist in the expression of the traits with which they have become associated, so long as there is situational consistency. Such that temperament and cognitive style are often thought to be associated with aspects of personality.

It is the relationship between manifestations of behavioral individuality in interaction with specific life conditions and circumstances that Chess and Thomas reference when they write of "goodness of fit." In numerous clinical cases they illustrate how the dynamics of this construct can be used both diagnostically and therapeutically to understand patient's behavior and to intervene in its correction and management. They wisely caution against the mechanical application of the goodness of fit construct. In the use of rich clinical material they remind the reader, and illustrate with case material, that the construct does not always work. They end the book with clinicians' guidelines for the application of the goodness of fit concept, and a reflective look at the future of the construct.

In the early chapters of this book Chess and Thomas offer a critique of some of the major systems of developmental thought. In the closing chapter the authors return to these theorists to call attention to points at which there is complementarity with the goodness of fit construct as well as to other points of utility in these ideas. Attention is also called to ways in which the authors' own work can be extended and combined with the ideas of other scholars to further advance our understanding of human behavior. They modestly suggest that this future work must be left to scholars younger than they.

These two prolific scholars of psychiatric practice and developmental theory can take heart in the fact that their challenge is being assumed by a variety of younger scholars. Some are extending investigations and theorizing concerning behavioral individualities in temperament and their conditional correlation with adaptive and mal-adaptive behavior. Others are examining the relationships between other expressions of individuality in responses to situational variance and the impact of these interactions on adaptive behavior. Still others are using J. McV. Hunt's problem of the match and the Chess/Thomas concept of goodness of fit to examine the "dynamic blending" or "orchestration" of phenomena intrinsic to the person with that which is intrinsic to the environment to better understand, to pedagogically and therapeutically intervene and to make predictions concerning human behavior. In all of this work and more, I see the long reach of the Chess and Thomas perspective which is but extended and clinically applied in this book. "Goodness of fit results when the properties of the environment and its expectations and demands are in accord with the organism's own capacities, characteristics, and style of behaving." (Chess and Thomas 1999, p.3)

Edmund W. Gordon
John M. Musser Professor of Psychology, Emeritus, Yale University

PREFACE

Over the last forty years, we have been absorbed in our studies of the theory and practice of the important variable of temperament (see Appendix for Temperament Definitions, Categories, and Ratings). We can place the early 1970s as the time when our concepts and practical applications of temperament became formalized and systematized and began to be accepted in the mainstream of developmental and clinical psychiatric and psychologic thought. Since the 1970s, a stream, even a flood, of talented students and workers have explored and pursued the many implications of the significance of temperament (Chess & Thomas, 1996, p. 82). Dr. Leon Eisenberg, Professor of Psychiatry, Emeritus, at Harvard has commented that, "our insights concerning temperament have been so thoroughly incorporated into the mainstream of theory and clinical practice in psychiatry and pediatrics that it may be difficult for students to recognize how revolutionary they were 36 years ago" (1994, p. 285).

In the many professional publications on temperament, we and others have noted one of its significant theoretical and practical implications, the concept of *goodness of fit* (Chess & Thomas, 1984; Kohnstamm, Bates, & Rothbart, 1989; Carey & McDevitt, 1995). However, in the literature, no formulation, including our own, has been represented, nor given more attention than a paragraph or, in a few, a portion of a chapter. As to the clinical applications of the concept of goodness of fit, they have been restricted to a modest number of community parent guidance temperament programs such as the Kaiser-Permanente H.M.O. system, community centers in LaGrande, Oregon, and Vancouver, Canada, and at parent–child programs in a number of school districts in Minnesota (Chess & Thomas, 1996; Carey & McDevitt, 1995).

As to ourselves, we started the active application of the goodness of fit concept in the treatment of childhood behavior problems of the subjects in our longitudinal studies and our clinic and office practices. In these first cases, we concentrated on parent guidance with the dissonance or poorness of fit of the child temperament–parent functioning interactional process.

As our clinical experiences expanded, we were increasingly struck by the expression of the usefulness of the goodness of fit concept, beyond the application of the issues of temperament–parent poorness of fit. Our panoply of clinical cases have included all age-periods—infancy, toddler and preschool periods, school age and middle childhood, adolescence, and adulthood. A wide variety of environmental expectations and demands—parental and other caregivers' child practices and goals, peer group judgements, special community values, cultural and ethnic diversity—has been considered. Educational rules and expectations, career stresses, sexual issues, and marital problems have been addressed.

The range of diagnostic categories applicable to the goodness of fit concept extended from the adjustment disorders, to the anxiety and mood disorders, to the personality disorders Diagnostic and Statistical Manual of Mental Disorders, fourth revision (DSM-IV), and from the mild to the severe. The severe mental illnesses and panic disorders that included a primary or major biological causation could not be expected to, and could not, utilize the application of goodness of fit as a primary therapeutic strategy. However, even in such cases as schizophrenia, autism, severe depression, manic-depressive illness, mental retardation, and special brain dysfunction, the application of the goodness of fit paradigm often could be useful as an adjunctive and secondary therapeutic amelioration.

In addition to expanding the clinical data from our case histories, we developed a clinical system. In addition, the clinical data has stimulated us to extend the theoretical basis of the goodness of fit concept. The extensive data on the theory and practice of the implications of this concept spurred us on to organize and report these data. This has required the writing of a comprehensive systematic volume and we have undertaken it with this manuscript.

In writing this book, we have kept several objectives in mind. Our audience should comprise the researchers and clinicians of mental health professionals, pediatricians, and educators. The dominant theme of the book appears most important for the clinical usefulness of the application of the goodness of fit concept. Hence, we have offered a large number of illustrative clinical vignettes in almost all the chapters, and have also spelled out specific guidelines (Chapter 19). All of the case reports come from real life cases we have treated and followed-up over the years. The only change made in the cases has been to prevent the personal identification of the patients or families, by pseudonyms and alteration of their career status in many cases.

While the volume has been designed as a clinical text, we have not ignored the discussion of pertinent and theoretical issues. These considerations require a strengthening and solidification of our clinical formulations, as is true in any substantial clinical system.

We are indebted to the many valuable suggestions and criticisms of our manuscript given by our friends and colleagues, Drs. James Cameron, Edmund Gordon, William Carey, Sidney Thomas, and Leland Hays. Their contributions have been thoughtful and pertinent, and enhanced the strength of our manuscript.

I

EVOLUTION OF THE GOODNESS OF FIT CONCEPT

1

Goodness of Fit: A Special Developmental Concept and Its Clinical Applications

☐ **What is Goodness of Fit?**

It is a specific definitive and comprehensive concept of normal and deviant psychological development. The concept also has extensive clinical applications.

Our Definition

Goodness of fit results when the properties of the environment and its expectations and demands are in accord with the organism's own capacities, characteristics, and style of behaving. When consonance between organism and environment is present, optimal development in a progressive direction is possible. Conversely, poorness of fit involves discrepancies and dissonances between environmental opportunities and demands and the capacities of the organism, so that distorted development and maladaptive functioning occur. Goodness of fit is never an abstraction, but is always goodness of fit in terms of the values and demands of a given culture or socioeconomic group (Thomas & Chess, 1977, pp. 11–12).

☐ In What Way is the Goodness of Fit Concept "Special"?

Psychological Development

Utilization of a goodness of fit paradigm demands first that the study of psychological development at any age-period assemble the specific hard facts of the individual's behavior, motivations, temperament, cognitive level, and special talents. At the same time, the factual nature of the environmental expectations and demands, as well as any unusual or unexpected events, is also gathered. Then, according to our definition, the student of development can examine these comprehensive data and select the pertinent aspects of the individual's characteristics and the relevant items of the environmental status. The data can then be organized to develop an interactional individual–environmental process. If the process is manifested as a goodness of fit at that age-period, the individual will be functioning on a healthy level, with a potential for a positive life course. If the interactional process is manifested as a poorness of fit at that age-period, the individual will be functioning on an unhealthy level, with potentially unfavorable and even pathogenic consequences.

At sequential age-periods, the psychological development, whether with goodness or poorness of fit, may be consistent. On the other hand, at different age-periods there may be change, such as goodness of fit altering to a poorness of fit. It may then remain consistent or may shift back to goodness of fit. Or a similar pattern of variability may change from a poorness of fit, etcetera. The consistency or change of goodness/poorness of fit over time is determined by the constancy versus the variability in the individual and his or her environment at sequential age-periods.

To orient the reader, the pertinent factors of the development of individual and environmental characteristics are spelled out in each chapter. Infancy (Chapter 5), Toddler and Preschool Periods (Chapter 6), School Age and Middle Childhood (Chapter 7), Adolescence (Chapter 8), and Adulthood (Chapter 9). An additional chapter discusses the dynamics of continuity and change of personality development (Chapter 10).

Clinical Applications

Secondly, a clinician's use of the goodness of fit concept also requires that the clinical history assemble the specific hard facts of the patient's characteristics, and the details of the expression of symptoms including their origin, developmental course, and current state. At the same time, the history of the factual nature of the previous and current environmental status should be included.

Once this history is obtained, a clinician has the first diagnostic responsibility. Does the data indicate that the patient may be suffering from a psychotic mental illness, such as schizophrenia, manic-depressive illness, severe depression, or any other physiological system affecting the brain and producing a mental illness? If so, the therapeutic program for such a case would require the use of the effective psychotropic drugs and other special programs provided by specialized therapists or treatment institutes.

If the diagnostic evaluation eliminates the possibility of a substantial psychiatric illness, a therapist can turn his/her attention to the patient's symptoms. We are now confronting psychiatric disorders such as anxiety disorders, adjustment disorders, personality disorders, sexual disorders, social anxiety disorders, and relational problems such as marital dysfunction. This list conforms to the DSM-IV. Other symptomatic disorders such as educational, marital, or vocational problems may also be responsible.

It has now been established that the symptoms are due to a lesser psychiatric disorder, or alternatively to a dysfunctional episode in the life course. The likelihood is that the patient has come to the therapist asking for help with symptoms, which are the consequences of the poorness of fit in the individual–environment interactional process. It is quite possible that the data a therapist has gained from the detailed factual history will be sufficient to formulate the patient's poorness of fit and its symptomatic consequences. In some cases, these data may provide significant clues for understanding the structure of this particular poorness of fit, but not sufficient to validate the hypothesis. In those cases, additional factual information from family, friends, or other sources invited by the patient may be required to fill out the necessary details of the unfavorable interactional process.

Once a therapist has formulated the clear poorness of fit elements responsible for the patient's psychological symptoms, the next crucial step is the transformation of the poorness of fit to a goodness of fit. This is achieved by starting with a carefully detailed factual scrutiny of the unfavorable interactional process. Through such a scrutiny, the therapist can identify what specific *change* or *changes* in the patient's functioning and/or the environment's influence is required. Such a metamorphosis is the basic therapeutic process essential to alter a poorness to a goodness of fit. In most cases, patients are willing to embrace a program to alter their actions—sometimes fearfully, sometimes reluctantly, and sometimes with enthusiasm.

However, if a therapist has succeeded in identifying the pivotal change, the therapy will be successful. Once the goodness of fit is achieved it is desirable to arrange several follow-up discussions—one after several weeks, others after six months or a year—to make sure the achievement of goodness of fit has become, in fact, an essential and automatic manner of functioning.

A most important chapter (Chapter 19), entitled Guidelines for the Clinician, has been devoted to a detailed description of successive steps for the management and treatment of a patient, starting from the referral and first session. From that, the logical sequence of steps one-by-one are spelled out to analyze the dynamic evolution of a poorness of fit, and therapeutic strategies are described that will advance the therapeutic process so as to ameliorate or cure the person's psychological disturbances.

☐ Fact versus Myth

In this chapter we have made it clear that in the developmental concept and research strategies of goodness of fit and its clinical applications, facts are the keystone for a human being. Facts include behavior, emotions, motivations, ideas, goals, and values. However, they do not include speculations, unverified assumptions, or generalizations regarding a person's characteristics.

In Chapter 3 we have formulated brief but meaningful critiques of several current major theoretical concepts and their clinical applications in the psychological and psychiatric fields. But, at this point, it is desirable to contrast the factual sina qua non of the goodness of fit with the opposite approach of data collection within psychoanalytic theory, research, and clinical applications. Psychoanalysis remains an influential field for clinicians and a number of other mental health professionals, as well as for academicians in the arts and literature. They have utilized Freud's highly complex structure of the developmental life-course and elaborated techniques in psychoanalytically-oriented treatment of patients and in erudite but questionable reconstruction of the influences on the lives of real artists such as Shakespeare, and fictional characters such as Hamlet.

Freud has emphasized the crucial importance of early life determinism, to wit, "The events of the first years are of paramount importance . . . a (child's) whole subsequent life" (1949, p. 83). With this edict, psychoanalysts, and other professionals, have searched for those particular presumed traumatic events of "paramount importance" in the infant's life. Various techniques have been employed in the older child or adult, especially by probing to reveal repressed infantile memories. These methods and their presumed findings have been subjected to a number of scholarly critiques (see Chapter 3).

In 1996, Dr. Peter Wolff, Professor of Psychiatry at Harvard, who has been dedicated to an examination of child development for decades, published a challenging paper, "The Irrelevance of Infant Observations for Psychoanalysis." With the many very dubious methods attempting to discover the infantile memories of older children and adults, Wolff has observed that, "the current consensus among psychoanalysts holds that direct infant observations are one means for testing the developmental propositions of psychoanalytic theory." He critically reviewed a number of these psychoanalytic early childhood researchers and concluded that, "psychoanalytically informed infant observations may be the sources for new theories of social–environmental development, but that they are essentially irrelevant for psychoanalysis as a psychology of meanings, unconscious ideas, and hidden motives" (p. 369).

A very recent statement of one experienced and thoughtful psychiatrist and psychoanalyst confirms Wolff's devastating critique of psychoanalytic research on infant observers. At a meeting of a large group of psychoanalysts in New York in March 1998, Dr. Robert Michels, Professor of Psychiatry at Cornell University, was quoted as stating that, "We are experts not in helping learn facts but in helping them construct useful myths. We are fantasy doctors, not reality doctors. We don't help patients decide what is true." From the newspaper reporter at the meeting, it appears that most of the psychoanalysts at the meeting agreed with Dr. Michels' statement (Boxer, N.Y. Times, 1998).

Thoughtful psychoanalysts, such as Cooper, Kernberg, and Person (1989) are faced with a serious dilemma. In their volume, they refer to a number of Freud's contradictions and inconsistencies among his theories. But they contend that the current generation of analysts have developed "newer ideas out of our own data and intellectual climate" but admit that "these views have yet to be integrated into a single overarching analytic theory" (1989, p. 2). However, Wolff and Michels have emphatically asserted that the infantile theories based on a central structure of psychoanalysis are founded on invalid factual data, even constructed into a "comfortable myth." Confronted with this reality, how can psychoanalysts hope to even achieve a "single overarching analytic theory"?

The chapter on Infancy (Chapter 5), reviewing the non-analytic research studies of the last 30 years, demonstrates changes in this view of the neonate's functioning. In one study after another, based on the classical scientific criteria, researchers have found *valid factual data* on infantile abilities and functions of perception, temperament, learning, social communication, and neural plasticity.

☐ Poorness of Fit: Normalcy and Vulnerability

Our definition of the goodness/poorness of fit concept involves another significant theoretical aspect of poorness of fit called *vulnerability*.

In goodness of fit the consonance between organism and environment is present and indicates that the organism's own capacities, characteristics, and style of behaving are basically normal. Also, that the properties of the environment and its expectations and demands are in accord indicates that the environment is benign.

For a poorness of fit, the issue is different. The characteristics and capacities of the organism are not clearly specified. Neither are the discrepancies and dissonances of the environment clarified. A poorness of fit leads to pathological functioning. Does this mean that the person's capacities and characteristics are pathological, and/or that the environment is excessively stressful? We have studied the dynamics of the person–environment interaction in a number of cases with poorness of fit. The result of this study has led us to a specific postulation. A person's pathological symptoms resulting from the development of a poorness of fit do not necessarily reflect his/her abnormal capacities and characteristics. The individual suffering from a poorness of fit is not bedeviled from some unconscious pathological pattern. Nor is a person's development of a poorness of fit based on some basic pathology. Rather, the individual is normal, but suffers from a distinct *vulnerability*.

Webster's New World Dictionary defines vulnerable as, "open to, or easily hurt by criticism or attacked," or "affected by a specified influence." In other words, an individual does not have an intrinsic liability but rather a characteristic that is "easily hurt by criticism or attacked" if "affected by a specified influence." For a typical example, Norman (see Chapter 10) started life as a normal infant and would probably have continued to develop without major problems throughout his life-course except for one vulnerability, his distractibility and low attention span. Moreover, this vulnerability need not have distressed him and could have been at most a minor interference with his functioning from time to time. However, his temperamental characteristics became a serious vulnerability because he was "affected by a specific influence," namely his father's persistent derogation, criticism, and sniping at his characteristic behavior. We postulate that this youngster's severe vulnerability with its disastrous consequences was due to his father's frequent negative pronouncements. This temperament–environment interactional process started with the boy's normal, but inconvenient (to the father) style of functioning, and the pathological development occurred during the process of the interaction. This leads to the formulation of the concept: *the pathology is in the interaction*.

This paradigm, the evolution of poorness of fit with its pathological consequences, was due to the interaction of an individual with a specific vulnerability created by the environmental outside influence and stress. This vulnerability–environmental stress generated increasing dysfunction of the individual. To repeat, the pathology was generated in the interaction.

The reader can apply this paradigm, with the vulnerability and the pathology in the interaction, in one case after another, as will be described in succeeding chapters. Chapter 18, entitled "Normalcy and Vulnerability vs. Pathology" discusses this paradigm in detail, with many case examples and their clinical implications.

The Origins of the Goodness of Fit Concept

In the early 1950s, as therapists working with children and adult patients, we were troubled at the dominant child–parent relationship theory of the times. To put it simply, if a child had a behavior problem it was presumed to have been caused by a pathogenic mother's behavior. In our clinical experience, some disturbed mothers did have disturbed children. However, some healthy mothers had disturbed children, and other disturbed mothers had healthy children. Something was wrong with the prevalent theory. We puzzled, searched the literature, and came to an idea that might be the key to explaining the contradicting factors of our clinical experiences. An extensive literature written by a number of developmental psychologists and psychiatrists had mentioned the many behavioral differences they noticed in individual children in the same family. Experienced mothers and baby nurses were aware of these differences in their young children. This was also true with our own children. With these extensive observations, we thought that the individual behavioral differences of children might be the explanation for the inadequacy of the dominant theory of the child-parent relationship. But no one, in spite of all of these observations, had pursued a systematic study of the possible significance of the children's behavioral individuality for the variations in child-parent relationship.

☐ The First Phase of the New York Longitudinal Study (NYLS)

We were troubled enough to decide to examine this hypothesis through systematic study. Such a project required a longitudinal study with an adequate sample of cooperative parents with newborn and very young infants. A satisfactory methodology for gathering and analyzing the pertinent data of the successive age-periods of the subjects was also essential. We gathered a group of cooperative parents either expecting a child or with healthy newborn or young infants and developed a methodology for obtaining appropriate data, launched the project in 1956, and entitled it the New York Longitudinal Study (NYLS).

After gathering the first wave of pertinent data, we enlisted the collaboration of a colleague, Dr. Herbert Birch. Herb was a sophisticated and experienced developmental researcher who could categorize and rate the data we were accumulating. He succeeded in solving this task quickly and accurately (Thomas, Chess, Birch, Hertzig, & Korn, 1963) and named the categories as temperamental characteristics. (In Appendix we have described the definitions, categories, and ratings of temperament).

☐ The Confluence of Ideas Flowing into the Goodness of Fit Concept

We had completed the first NYLS task of naming and categorizing the specific temperamental characteristics of each child at succeeding ages. With that, we came to our next fundamental step. The NYLS was based on the hypothesis that the behavioral individuality of children, now called temperament, would constitute a significant factor in shaping the development of normal and deviant psychological functioning. By the time the subjects had reached the toddler age-period, we had accumulated a mass of data on each child: the temperamental characteristics as identified and rated at each age, the details of the parental child-care practices and attitudes, contemporaneous recording of the occurrence of special events, such as a move to a new home, the beginning attendance at nursery school, or a physical illness, as well as the details of the reactions of the child and parent to such an occurrence.

The next crucial element of data collection comprised the identification of any children suffering with specific symptoms of behavioral disturbance. For each such case, I (S. C.) performed a careful clinical evaluation, as reported in my textbook (Chess & Hassibi, 1978).

With that done, I was faced with reviewing the data in terms of the basic hypothesis of our study. Now I had completed the clinical evaluation of each referred child and, in addition, had documented the data of the child's behavioral characteristics, for each year from birth to the time of clinical evaluation. From this information, I sought a meaningful dynamic of the behavioral disturbance in the context of each child–parent relationship.

I read the complete file of each case together with the clinical examination and evaluation. As I absorbed the data, I pondered and found myself formulating my considerations in terms of goodness of fit. This concept did not come to me as a flash of inspiration, or a bolt of epiphany. It came to me, rather, by the confluence of ideas that had converged into a central concept. Those ideas had been utilized from the onset of the NYLS.

☐ What Were These Concepts?

Interactionism

First and foremost, has been the formulation and the developmental model of *interactionism*.

In the past, ideas of development were dominated by Aristotelian concepts, in which opposites were mutually exclusive. Behavioral phenomena were ascribed either to heredity or to environmental influences, depending on which theory was dominant at the time. It was presumed that the contribution of each category could be parceled out—so much for heredity and so much for environment.

By this mid-century, this model has been posited to be an inadequate theoretical framework. In 1957, Theodore Schneirla, then director of the animal behavior research unit of the American Museum of Natural History, in New York City, stated, "For an adequate perspective in the methodology of research and theory, we cannot accept an a priori definition of behavioral development either as an unfolding of the innate, . . . or as a continuum expanding mainly through the presence of environmental forces, with the genes merely contributing an initial push to the process. Rather, a defensible generalization is that a species' genetic constitution contributes in some manner to the development of all behavior in *all* organisms, as does milieu, developmental context, or environment" (1957, p. 79). René Dubos, research biologist at Rockefeller Institute, reaffirmed the same principle, "Whether the organism be microbe, corn plant, fruit fly, or man, all its characteristics are heredity, and all are also determined by the environment. This apparent paradox applies to human health and disease as well as to all manifestations of life" (1965, p. 10).

Thus, development becomes a dialectical process of interactionism, in which opposites interact with each other to produce an organic unity of opposites. We, ourselves, have adopted this principle from the beginning of our research studies. Thus, in one of our first papers, in 1961, reporting our goals for the NYLS, we spelled out this approach definitively: "Behavioral phenomena are considered to be the expression of a continuous organism-environment interaction from their very first manifestations in the life of the individual. This overall approach may be designated as interactionist" (Thomas, Chess, Birch, & Hertzig, 1961, p. 723).

A number of developmental research psychologists and psychiatrists in the late 1960s and 1970s have contributed to bringing a dynamic interactionist viewpoint into the mainstream of psychological and psychiatric theory. These many references are cited in our volume (Thomas & Chess, 1980, p. 83).

Individualization: Variability and Flexibility in Individual Children

Another idea that fed the formulation of goodness of fit was *individualization*. Normal children show a wide variety of variability in their psychophysiological, perceptual, and cognitive attributes. Individual differences in temperament are striking and functionally significant. The time of emergence of motor capacities and skills and the effective use of language varies widely from one normal child to another. Children from different social classes and cultural backgrounds can show conspicuous differences in terms of behavior, speech, and values. This individual variability has vital evolutionary advantages for humankind. The geneticist, Dobzhansky put it well, "The sociologically as well as the biologically most advantageous traits is a developmental plasticity of behavior. In any culture, a person meets in his lifetime a variety of challenges and a variety of opportunities. To be able to respond successfully to various challenges is better than to be specialized for just one. To be able to acquire competence in any one of several functions or professions is more useful than to be fit for the single one" (1966, p.14).

Maternal Overprotection: David Levy's Research

Dr. David Levy was a pioneer in the field of child psychiatry. I (S.C.) was fortunate to have been one of his students. He had done a unique study with stimulating findings as far back as 1943. To summarize, Levy had developed a new concept of *maternal overprotection,* and elaborated this formulation by identifying and studying a number of mothers who fit his criteria for overprotection. He found that the children of these over-protective mothers fell into two contrasting clusters, domineering or submissive. The mothers also fell into two groups, domineering, or sub-missive and highly indulgent of the child's desires. He then found a striking correlation: the children who were domineering had submissive mothers, while the passive and submissive children had domineering mothers. (The details of his studies are described in Chapter 4). To our knowledge, David Levy's study was the first substantial report that the mother–child relationship could be a two-way street, actually an inter-actional process, though he did not use that term (Levy, 1943).

☐ The Birth of the Goodness of Fit Concept

As I pondered over the data of the clinical case records, one aspect of the mass of information stimulated me with the idea of interactionism, an-other, with the idea of individualization, and another, with the implica-tions of Dr. Levy's provocative findings. With this confluence of data and ideas, a coherent formulation shaped in my mind. Optimal develop-ment occurs when there is consonance between environmental oppor-tunities and expectations and the organism's capacities. Should there be dissonance between organism and environment, the postulated out-comes are distorted development and maladaptive functioning. In addi-tion, it occurred to me that this concept might be appropriate to be labeled goodness of fit and poorness of fit.

I brought this formulation and label to Alex Thomas and Herb Birch for discussion in one of our early morning conferences, and they imme-diately responded with enthusiasm.

We pulled out at random from our NYLS records, one group with well-functioning subjects, then one group with behavioral disturbance cases. The three of us sat down and reviewed each record, analyzing the nature of the interactional process in the healthy children versus the clinical cases. The analysis of a goodness of fit with the healthy children, and by contrast, a poorness of fit with the disturbed children confirmed usefulness of the concept for every subject. With these findings, we refined the definitive formulation that is explicated in the beginning pages of Chapter 1.

☐ The Applications of the Goodness of Fit Concept

Impressed with the power of goodness of fit as an organizing principle, we began to realize the value of this principle with the children of our three other longitudinal studies. We had developed these other projects for our special interests in the cross-cultural influences of temperament, and the psychiatric issues of children with physical and/or psychological handicaps.

These three additional studies included:

1. Ninety-five children of working class Puerto Rican parents, who were followed from early infancy to adolescence (Thomas, Chess, Sillen, & Mendez, 1974).
2. Fifty-six children with mildly retarded intellectual levels were traced from ages 5 to 11 years through adolescence (Chess & Korn, 1970).
3. A population of 243 children with congenital rubella resulting from the maternal rubella epidemic of 1964, who were studied from age 2.5 to 5 initially and were followed through adolescence. This last group has been of special interest because of the large numbers and diversity of physical, neurological and intellectual handicaps (Chess, Korn & Fernandez, 1971).

Data gathered on the children and parents of these three groups utilized the same methodological procedures as with the NYLS subjects (Thomas, Chess & Birch, 1968, pp. 14–19, pp. 31–35).

All these populations included children with both healthy and problem developmental courses. The selection of the children of the NYLS was made before their birth. Those of Puerto Rican working class parentage were identified in the public health well-baby clinics of two housing projects in Spanish Harlem in New York City. The two other populations were selected specifically because of their problem natures. The mildly retarded youngsters were selected from the rolls of special classes in public schools initially and subsequently by parental word-of-mouth. The children with congenital rubella were part of a public health study of children born to mothers infected by the rubella virus in pregnancy during the worldwide epidemic of 1964. It was in the course of pondering the complex data of the children's physical and temperamental individuality as well as of their environments, that the theoretical structure of the goodness of fit concept was further formulated. As an example of the complexity, we can look at just the educational element of their environment. The middle class children (NYLS) as a group had access to the most favorable educational circumstances. Many attended private schools. Those who enrolled in neighborhood public schools did so because their parents found the schools satisfactory in accordance with their own standards. If achievement problems occurred, their causes were investigated promptly and remedial measures were undertaken. In contrast, the children of working class Puerto Rican families (WCPR) were dependent on neighborhood public schools, except for the few who were sent to religious schools. Unable, because of their own educational status, to help their children with class assignments or to judge the quality of the educational experience, few parents challenged school decisions. During middle childhood, we found an unexpected number of children to have been placed in special classes where little was taught, because of poor achievement and school psychological assessments showing mental retardation. Our own I.Q. testing, done at ages 3 and 6, according to our protocol, by Puerto Rican psychologists with no time pressures, had indicated normal intelligence. Repeat testing by our staff in middle childhood showed normal intelligence despite the retarded achievement. We were able to tutor the youngsters, restore them to regular classes, and have them reclassified as normal intellectually. Other Puerto Rican children in similar circumstances, having no knowledgeable advocates, continued in these inadequate special educational settings.

The mildly retarded children, having been selected because of their special class placements, were in fact within appropriate educational settings. The parental willingness to enroll in our research was one element of their child-oriented attitude. These youngsters' educational experience was a goodness of fit.

The congenital rubella youngsters' educations were obtained in such varied environments as regular public schools, schools for the deaf, for the visually impaired, for the deaf–blind, and schools having accommodations for motorically handicapped children. Placements depended upon the presence or absence of physical and intellectual sequellae of congenital rubella. If present, the nature, severity, and multiplicity of handicap were crucial to school choice. There were further divisions, such as boarding versus day schools.

This general itemization of the school environments encountered by the children is a much-simplified example of the many environments to be taken into account. With the organizing principle of goodness of fit, we were able to better comprehend the elements favoring the constructive mastery of the environment and the obverse.

There were children in all of our research groups who had problem development. The disorders that were present during the child and adolescent periods included, in terms of the DSM-IV (1994). Diagnosis of some behaviors that fulfilled DSM-IV diagnostic criteria for a disorder require special scrutiny.

For children with degrees of blindness, for example, it would not be a good fit to employ the usual visual route for judging the presence and strength of affectionate bonds, as is the practice with visually intact babies. Neither would it be good diagnostic strategy to ignore blindness in a mother when assessing the health of attachment in terms of eye contact. While this statement seems absurd and unnecessary, there was a period in which visual regard was believed to be an essential route to healthy attachment formation. There are myriad ways in which babies and caregivers form attachments to each other, and the diagnostician must take into account which are available in a particular home.

☐ Findings of the Four Longitudinal Studies

As expected, these four groups of children showed a great variety of children with a goodness of fit, who had the ability to cope successfully with the stresses and expectations of their environment. Some of them, especially those with cognitive or other handicaps, struggled with a poorness of fit and developed one or another mild or severe behavior problem. The clarification of a poorness of fit indicated the therapeutic processes that could be useful in eliminating or ameliorating a behavior problem. In the NYLS and Puerto Rican children, the strategies for the treatment of the problem cases were relatively simple. For the handicapped children, some were spontaneously successful in coping with their environmental demands, and produced a goodness of fit with the promise of an adaptive life course. For others, especially those with severe and multiple handicaps, the achievement analysis of the basic child–environment interaction could devise opportunities or procedures to ameliorate the extent of their handicaps.

Our experiences with the usefulness of the application of the goodness of fit model in all kinds of children, and even adults, made it clear that this principle was not a panacea, nor a global model. No goodness/poorness of fit is compatible with concepts of linear, unidirectional continuity.

Goodness of fit should never be applied as a Procrustian bed. Its application should be fitted to the specific situation with a specific individual interacting with a specific environment.

Critique of Other Major Developmental Concepts and Clinical Applications

A young actress, Joyce H., was referred to me (A.T.) because of her increasing anxiety and difficulties with her work.

At our first appointment, Joyce introduced herself with a charming smile. She was 23, physically very attractive, but clearly very tense, as shown in her facial appearance and the tightness of her body movements. Her voice was melodious and modulated, and each word was very clearly pronounced as she gestured with her hands toward me. Her voice and manner were those of a trained actress.

Joyce had a major but not leading role in a good bi-weekly TV serial daytime program. This was her first professional job in New York, which she had started about two months prior, unsure of herself, but at the same time basically self-confident of her theatrical training, and prior success in amateur shows in the Midwest. In this assignment in the TV program she had started well, optimistic, but with each show she was criticized by the director, and given contradictory signals from the leading actor. As each week passed she became confused and began to lose her self-confidence: "By now, I am convinced I'm becoming a failure, thinking I should choose another career, but I can't figure out how I can improve myself. It gets worse every week, every time I step on the stage, I make one mistake after another, and by now I am demoralized."

Joyce was born in a Midwestern City, in a prosperous, functional family, of a normal gestation and delivery, and developed normally through her childhood and adolescence, always healthy, good in school, made friends easily, and never had any physical or psychological problems that she remembered.

Her mother was affectionate and close to her. She had worked as a teacher until their first child was born, and since then she had been a housewife. Her father ran a successful business of medium size, was always helpful to the children, but quite reserved and hard to get close to.

In high school, Joyce participated in a play, directed by one of the English teachers. The play was a very modest success, but Joyce was excited and thrilled even with her small part, felt inspired, and immediately was sure she would become an actress. She went several times to all the plays of the local stock company and read all the books she could find on techniques of acting.

When she was a senior, picking her choices for college, Joyce announced to her family that she wanted to become an actress, and researched all the good colleges in the area until she found one with a good drama department, and that was her choice. Her parents were startled—no one in the community had made that particular college selection. Her mother was dubious, but when she saw that Joyce was determined, she gave her her blessing. Her father was distressed. He knew that actors had a hard life, and that only a few could be successful. He looked at her sister, two years older, who was on the way to becoming a lawyer, "How," he asked, "can you compare that to a life as an actress?" At first he was adamant, but when it was clear that his arguments had no effect on Joyce's resolution, and that her mother had accepted Joyce's desires, he relented. He summed up his attitude: "If Joyce is determined we just have to let her have her choice. She's always been a reasonable person and we should trust her."

Joyce went through college "in a breeze." The drama department was good, and she threw herself into its curriculum with a total commitment. The director, recognizing her talent and dedication, became a mentor. He gave her his time and encouragement, and picked her for increasingly difficult roles in the various classical plays. When she graduated with honors, he arranged an acting position in the local stock company where she functioned well and got considerable experience.

After a year, her mentor said, "Joyce, it is time for you to go to New York. It's tough there, but you have to do it if you want to develop as a successful professional actor. I have spoken to one of my good friends who is a prominent theatrical agent in New York. With my praise about you he is ready to give you an appointment." Two months later she received an acting position in the TV series company. This was her chance. She started with trepidation, but with basic self-confidence and determination to succeed. "But it has turned into a disaster, and I keep saying to myself, Why?"

"That's my story," Joyce said, and looked at me expectantly. "You have given me a clear picture of your life story," I told her. "I don't have a miraculous answer for you now, but I know how to proceed for us together. The next performance of the TV program will be tomorrow. I will give you the next appointment for the day after that, and then you will give me a detailed account, hour by hour, of everything that happened in the TV performance."

Joyce stared at me, looking very confused. "But, I thought you would go on to an analysis of my childhood years. In college, I had a course in psychology, and the professor, a good one, told us that a person's psychological problems were caused by his or her special experiences in the first few years of life. I thought you would try to analyze that, and now you tell me you're concentrating on what will happen to me tomorrow." I spoke to Joyce seriously, "Your professor was correct in presenting the theory of most psychiatrists. I've listened to you carefully, couldn't find the hint of any pathologic clue in your childhood, but the fact is you had a perfectly normal life until you started with your acting job on the TV program. Therefore, it is probable that your problems have occurred in some interactions on that theatrical stage. At least, when we meet next time, in two days, we can examine that possibility." Joyce looked uncertain, then said, "Alright, I'll do what you want me to do."

Joyce reported two days later that, "everything that happened yesterday was routine, I can tell you that hour by hour, and what then?" "Think back now to the very initial week on your job for any interaction that bothered you and continues to occur each week, so that now it seems routine" I suggested. "Try your best to think back at that." Joyce began to shake her head no, and then suddenly her whole face changed, as with a vision. "When I acted in other plays in the stock company, I always experimented with some new motion gesture, or changed my voice, to make the action more vivid. It usually worked, and my director congratulated me.

"On my new job, on a professional level, I started by sticking to the fixed script. After the first week, I had confidence, and would try to experiment as I used to do. The second week, I tried something new during the rehearsal and the leading actor, Bob R., the star, hit me with a ton of bricks, 'You are doing something wrong and stupid, stick to the script!' Who was I to argue with him. Bob is an experienced, talented actor, well-known in the field, so I stuck to the script. After the performance, the director nodded, but said, 'I hope you get greater depth to your role!' The same thing happened the following week, when I tried something else new during rehearsal and Bob was enraged. After that, I just kept to the script, and the director began to tell me that I was too dull. He was disappointed with me, especially since his friend, my mentor, had given him a glowing account of my innovative acting. So here I am, hit by both star and the director. They are the experts. I am just a beginner. I thought I would become a good actress, but it looks as if I fooled myself, I'll never be an actress, and I'm in despair."

As we reviewed the events it seemed more and more evident that Joyce, unable to express her individual style of acting that had previously brought praise, was becoming demoralized. I suggested a risky gamble: "Study the script for the performance three days from now. When you start the rehearsal I'm sure you will have some specific ideas of how your acting can change to enliven your performance. Bob will shriek and demand that you stick to the script. But, in action, in front of the TV camera, boldly go through with your ideas in spite of Bob." Joyce was shocked, "Bob will damn me, I'll be fired." "Yes," I said, "You could be fired, but you might also get the director's approval. It is a gamble. If you don't take the chance, you're becoming demoralized, and almost ready to quit acting. If you take the gamble, it may be worth it for your future acting career." A kaleidoscope of different expressions went over Joyce's face, and finally she said, "I understand what you've said, it is a big gamble, but somehow it seems right to me. I will do it."

I waited the next two days keeping my fingers crossed, and the next day at her appointed time, Joyce rushed in, laughing and crying, "I did it, it worked, it was wonderful." She did exactly as I had suggested and played her part with her new ideas. At the end there was a hushed silence, and Bob exploded, "How dare you, you ruined the whole session," he looked at the director, pointed to me, and shouted, "Fire her!" The director lifted his arms, said "Bob, you are wrong. For the first time Joyce has given a splendid performance. Joyce, I always had a feeling you had the capacity to be a talented actor. Now you've done it, congratulations, keep it up. The whole company crowded around me, cheering me, and Bob just sulked."

I sighed with relief and delight. Then she asked me, "I'm on my seventh cloud, but I'm also bewildered, why did Bob act that way?" I replied, "There must be some real explanation. For some reason, when you started working, you may have insulted Bob, so that he became hostile and angry with you, and was determined to put you down in revenge. Can you think of any incident that could explain how you might have insulted him?"

Joyce sat quietly and thoughtfully for a few minutes, then her face lit up, and, with a peal of laughter, she recounted the tale. "It was so silly!" Ever since she was 16 she had been physically attractive to many men of all ages. All of these men, she explained, tried to make a pass at her, even seduce her, and it was a nuisance, because she was not interested in them. So she worked it out, over time, statements given in good humor, giving each man the notice that while she was flattered, she was not interested; he should look for someone else. She had to do this so often it became practically automatic. Now, she remembered that in the first week of the TV program, Bob had made a pass at her. She does not recall what she said or did, it was so automatic. But she recognizes now that Bob, a handsome celebrity, egomaniac, and a successful woman-izer, must have been outraged that this little meek young actress on her first job made fun of his sexual overtures instead of falling at his feet. "I forgot the incident completely. But now I realize Bob must have been outraged by my rejecting him and interpreted it as my making fun of him, and had to get back at me. It's so sad, for a talented mature man to act that way."

I was sure Joyce's explanation was correct. "Your gamble worked out perfectly, your self-confidence is restored, you know what to do."

At the next appointed time, she came in beaming, reporting, "Every-thing is fine. I tried new ideas whenever they came to me, I did them, Bob started to shriek, but the director cut him short and congratulated me. He tried to upstage me when we were acting together, but the di-rector warned Bob to stop that after the first incident, and if he tried again Bob would be fired. For the director, who was tough and ethical, Bob was not a real star. When we passed each other by chance, Bob al-ways had a nasty comment for me, I just laughed at him, which only made him more furious." She looked at me with a little wicked smile.

I laughed with Joyce, told her she didn't need any further appoint-ments, unless some new unexpected problem came up, and I would al-ways be available. "But you have to promise to call me once or more a year, just to tell me how you have been progressing." She agreed, and we said good-bye.

She kept her promise, and over the years her acting career has been successful and happy. She never became a star, but was always in demand for acting positions in TV series, and in several movies. She married in her late twenties, had three children, and she and the family prospered.

☐ Discussion

How in Joyce's situation, did the goodness of fit concept help to concep-tualize her problem? First we had to define Joyce's abilities and status at the time of her dysfunction. A neophyte professional actor, Joyce was facing her initial high level expectations. She had been well trained and had proved her competence in her functioning in regional drama com-panies, enough to have been highly recommended by her mentor to her current director of a new television series. Her functioning included her personal technique of achieving an interpretation of the character she was portraying. Her techniques included spontaneous experimentation during filming, of gestures and speech patterns to bring depth and interest to her character.

In the goodness of fit conceptualization, we then had to consider the environment. As reported by Joyce, her acting environment was favorable with one important exception. The leading man, the star of the series, Bob, was incensed by her improvisations. He defined these as "departures" from the script. Whenever she moved spontaneously into such action, he would become angry, order her to "stick to the script." Deprived of her usual individual acting style, Joyce felt her characterization becoming dull and uninteresting. The director of the show was critical of her work and ended each filming session with a negative critical analysis, one with which Joyce concurred. This had become a threatening poorness of fit.

This, then, is a brief summary of the organism–environment interaction. In order to change the poorness of fit, it was necessary to identify the point at which action could be taken. We may have speculated at the reasons for Bob's behavior. He may have been convinced that Joyce was misinterpreting the character of the TV role. He may have felt threatened at the excellence of her acting. He may simply have been an arrogant person whose routine functioning included putting his colleagues into an inferior position. He might have had any number of reasons for his action. Under these circumstance we, Joyce and I (A.T.), agreed that the only course was for her to defy Bob and pursue her own acting style. As has been reported, she did so, and found that this was what the director had, in fact, been waiting for.

Having achieved freedom to act, it was then possible to find an explanation of sexual harassment for Bob's actions. Without such understanding, there would be the possibility that another situation with similar elements might arise in the future and be unrecognized. We spelled this out in a final discussion with her, and, predictably, she learned the lesson and applied it successfully in her subsequent career.

☐ Clinical Applications of Other Major Developmental Theories

We have summarized the case of Joyce H. She had no evidence of deviant psychological symptoms in any of her age-periods. But, finally, in her first demanding work situation in her highly motivated career path, within six weeks she developed a severe adjustment disorder, with increasing destructive symptoms of excessive stress and anxiety to the point of demoralization. Her acting career might have ended at its very beginning.

Using the concept of the goodness of fit, the analysis of her problem shifted to an examination of her interaction with the staff in her work situation. Joyce's disturbed behavior, inhibited acting, and anxiety were not the cause but the result of her problem. With that, I (A.T.) concentrated on gathering the details of her current life behavior. The cause of her poorness of fit became clear, the change in her work function followed decisively, and a healthy goodness of fit quickly established itself. With this there followed disappearance of her pathogenic behavior and symptoms.

We asked the question: If Joyce had been referred to a therapist committed to one of the alternative developmental concepts and therapeutic approaches, what course of treatment and its outcome would have been likely?

Firstly, we have reviewed the primary concepts of other major developmental theories. All of them, psychoanalysis, behaviorism, attachment theory, and Piaget's concepts, have advocated the decisive importance of early life experience in shaping normal and/or pathological development in successive age-periods. These theories may vary in the specific origins and dynamics of the foundation for later years, but all agree on its basic importance. We will spell out briefly the critique of each theory. Also critiqued is a fifth model, the cognitive-behavioral therapy of Dr. Aaron Beck.

Psychoanalysis

Freud's theories were based on the evaluation of the preschool years in the form of oral, anal, or genital characteristics, depending on the vicissitudes of instinctual development. The environment was important, but primarily in terms of reinforcing or shaping this development of instincts and of creating points at which they become fixated (Freud, 1949). Based on his theories, he succinctly stated, "Neuroses are only acquired during early childhood (up to the age of six) even though their symptoms may not make their appearance until much later . . . the events of the first years are of paramount importance for . . . (a child's) whole subsequent life" (1949, p. 83).

In recent years a number of scholarly and cogent critiques of psychoanalysis have been published such as those by Grunbaum (1984), Webster (1995) and others. Some rigid orthodox psychoanalysts have clung to Freud's basic concepts and therapeutic practices. Other flexible psychoanalysts have acknowledged "some of the more glaring contradictions and problematics in Freud's work" (Cooper, Kernberg & Person, 1984, p. 3), and affirmed that "Since Freud's death there have been advances in ego psychology, object-relations theory, self psychology and interpersonal psychology, to mention a few of the many currents in contemporary psychoanalysis. But these views have yet to be integrated into a single overarching analytic theory" (p. 2). These modifications in psychoanalytic theory are welcome, but, to our knowledge, have not repudiated the thesis of the decisive importance of early life.

Behaviorism

John Watson, the father of the theory of behaviorism, was influenced by the conditioning studies of Pavlov. Watson, whose formulation became a popular concept in the 1920s, applied it to a set of rules for child-care practices, and pronounced that "at three years of life the child's whole emotional life has been laid down, his emotional life set" (1928, p. 3). This behaviorist concept speculated that the internal processes of the mind were "a black box"—unknowable scientifically, and in any case unimportant. This formulation was untenable, and after the 1930s most behaviorists divorced themselves from Watson's system. Instead, they developed a "social learning theory" (Bandura, 1978, p. 348). But, "By the 1950s efforts to apply more sophisticated learning theories to psychopathology became widespread. However, rather than attempting to change problem behavior, these efforts mainly translated the clinical theory and lore of psychoanalysis into learning theory terms" (Achenbach, p. 569).

Attachment Theory

John Bowlby, the British psychiatrist, studied the deleterious effects of the mental health of homeless children (Bowlby, 1951). He continued to pursue this issue and in his volume in 1969 reaffirmed his conviction that the loss of the mother figure in early life is capable of "generating responses and processes that are of the greatest interest in psychopathology and that continues in its adult life" (1969, p. xiii).

Bowlby's emphasis on the basic importance of the mother's influence stimulated him and a number of developmental psychologists and psychiatrists to develop the concept of the secure or insecure attachment of the infant to the mother. This characterization gradually blossomed to an extensive belief that the quality of the infant's attachment was a key issue to the determination of the child's future psychological development (Karen, 1994). Furthermore, a very simple test, taking twenty minutes, called the Strange Situation test, was devised with the claim that this procedure could conclusively predict that the child was secure or insecure. With such an easy, quick procedure, innumerable psychologists then applied this test to a host of mental health issues of children. Some of us protested the absurdity of the virtue of the Strange Situation test (Thomas & Chess, 1982). Jerome Kagan, Professor of Psychology at Harvard, pointed out, "is it reasonable that a history of interaction between mother and infant comprising over a half-million minutes in the home would be revealed in twenty minutes in an unfamiliar room?" (1984, pp. 62–63).

In addition, earlier, Michael Rutter, the most respected international researcher and theoretician (Rutter has been knighted in England for his professional contributions), had written a critique of the concept of "maternal deprivation" in 1972. In his volume he summarized the extensive literature and emphatically concluded "it would be a mistake to seek all connections between relationships in terms of attachment qualities" (p. 505). In his conclusion, Rutter commented that, "if knowledge is to advance . . . it will be necessary that we pay attention to one of the first features of attachment theory, namely that attachment is not the whole of relationships" (p. 563).

Piagetism

Jean Piaget became famous for his imaginative and painstaking studies and findings of the development of children's thinking and intelligence at sequential age-periods. In his definitive American book, *The Developmental Theory of Jean Piaget* (Flavell, 1963), Flavell summarized Piaget's studies, ideas and theories. This useful volume has given us the opportunity to compare Piaget's theories and implications with those of the goodness of fit concept. Flavell formulated Piaget's basic developmental studies, stating that Piaget "described in considerable detail a general conception about the nature of intellectual *functioning*. He had tried to uncover the basic and irreducible properties of cognitive adaptation which holds true at all developmental levels" (p. 41). Piaget postulated that two specific basic factors that the child–environment interacted and adapted. One he labeled *assimilation*, the "function of living matter is that of incorporating into its structure nutrition—providing elements from the outside" (p. 45). The other, *accommodation*, is "its functioning to the specific contours of the object it is trying to assimilate" (p. 45). Flavell then interpreted as Piaget's concept that "assimilation and accommodation constitute the most fundamental ingredients of intellectual functioning. Both functions are present in every intellectual act, of whatever type and developmental level" (p. 58). With this fundamental thesis the process of cognition was organized at sequential age periods. Sensory motor intelligence (0–2 years), concrete operations (2–11 years), and formal operations (Chess & Hassibi, 1978, pp. 63–68).

To conclude, Piaget's work has been monumental, but his contributions have been almost exclusively in the area of cognition and epistemology. Basically, Piaget's concepts and implications have been excluded from the fields of behavioral development, psychopathology, and the prevention or treatment of deviant development. A few groups of psychologists have attempted to apply Piaget's concepts of assimilation and accommodation to child–environment interaction and the dynamics of behavioral development (Cameron, 1997, personal communication). Their discussions are intriguing, but as yet are not convincing.

Cognitive-Behavioral Therapy

This active therapeutic system and its originator are defined in a comprehensive textbook, as "Aaron Beck, the originator of cognitive-behavioral therapy, developed a comprehensive, structured theory of depression. According to the theory, depression is associated with negative thought patterns, specific distorted schemas and cognitive errors or faulty information processing" (Merikangas & Kupfer, 1995, p. 1183). Beck, in a recent paper (1997) has verified the basic cognitive theory in the textbook definition above, to quote, "The cognitive model stipulates that dysfunctional thinking is the essence, is the case, not the cause of psychological disorder" (p. 57). In addition, he states, quite correctly, that "we don't really know exactly what causes depression" (p. 57). Beck cites a number of clinical cases suffering from a wide variety of negative personality characteristics, but considers them as consequences of depression. The improvement with his structured cognitive-behavioral therapeutic system is not impressive. Candidly, Beck states that "In the National Institute of Mental Health Collaborative Study of the treatment of depression, the results of the follow-up study were not significantly different between cognitive therapy and anti-depressant medication" (p. 63).

Probably, Beck's therapeutic approach is helpful for a limited number of patients. In his paper, there is no recognition of any dynamic environmental influence for depressive cases, and the study of the comparable value of antidepressants raises the question of the value of Beck's elaborate psychotherapeutic system (pp. 55–64).

Other Advocates of the Decisiveness of Early Life

Beyond the discussions of the five major concepts above, there is a flood, almost epidemic, of the mid-century articles asserting the ideology of the ontogenesis by early childhood life, in one way or another. We have cited just a sample: schizophrenia, (Ackerman, 1958; Lidz, Fleck, & Cornelison, 1965; Wynne & Singer, 1963); cultural deprivation (Hess, 1970); the "culture of poverty" (Lewis, 1966); "imprinting" (Lorenz, 1952); and the all-importance of cognitive development (Bloom, 1964; White, 1975).

☐ The Challenge to Early Life Determinism

By the 1970s, which witnessed a progressive shift in the thesis of early life determination, Rutter (1972), reassessed the whole issue of maternal deprivation through a masterly comprehensive review of the entire literature and concluded that "it is now evident that the experiences included under the term maternal deprivation are too heterogeneous and the effects too varied for it to continue to have any usefulness" (p. 128).

Then, in 1977, Alan and Ann Clarke, Professors of psychology at Hull University in England, published a most important book, entitled, *Early Experience, Myth and Evidence*. In their volume, they gathered over 50 studies, emphasizing that early experiences did *not* predict their outcome in later years. They concluded, "What then are the main implications? First and foremost, the whole of development is important, not merely the early years. There is as yet no indication that a given stage is clearly more formative than others, in the long-term all may be important" (p. 272).

And there are our own experiences, from our NYLS cases and clinical practice (representative cases presented through various chapters of the book). In our judgment, these challenges have stemmed the tide of the ideology of early life determinism. But all too many mental health professionals are still committed to their ideology.

☐ Why is this Early Life Determinism Harmful?

The story of the case of Joyce H., detailed at the beginning of this chapter, gives the answer. She came to me asking for help urgently and correctly. She had developed a severe acute anxiety state, starting about six weeks previously which became worse over the weeks, and was now demoralized. Further, she was realistically threatened by the possibility of the disastrous loss of her job, her first professional position. Her entire career was literally hanging by a thread.

What would have happened if Joyce had been referred, by chance, to a competent therapist who was committed to the theory of early life determinism? The therapist presumably would have expertly launched a search for significant childhood experiences—conflict with her father and sibling rivalry appeared obvious in her life story in a first interview, and perhaps other issues might also be probed by free associations and dreams. The therapist might have been a helpful, empathic, warm, and supportive personality in his/her sessions with Joyce. But no matter his/her expertise and positive personality, probing into Joyce's childhood life and reassuring her would take many weeks or months. But, inevitably, within a month Joyce would have lost her first professional job, lost her self-confidence as an actor, and even ruined her career. By luck, she might have found another acting position in a benign atmosphere, and restored her self-confidence and reputation, but such luck rarely occurs.

Review of the Literature: Clarification and Evolution of the Goodness of Fit Concept

Our formulation of the concept of Goodness of Fit evolved from the analysis of the first ten years of data from our New York Longitudinal Study (Thomas, Chess, & Birch, 1968). The definition is spelled out in Chapter 1.

As our subjects moved into further developmental periods, our analyses of their fit with the ever-complex environment become more demanding. It is now useful to examine some antecedents of the goodness of fit concept in the psychologic and psychiatric literature. We will start with an important study written in 1943.

Dr. David Levy, a psychoanalyst, was a pioneer in the newly forming specialty of child psychiatry and author of a number of papers in child psychoanalysis from the 1920s on. He opened a new theoretical direction in his 1943 book, *Maternal Overprotection*. The head of the Institute for Child Guidance in New York City, over several years at the clinic he noticed the phenomenon of overprotectiveness in some mothers, who voiced diverse complaints of their children. Using a staff team, he organized a search of the 2,000 plus mother records and identified 20 mothers who fit his criteria for overprotection. He has documented and catalogued the behaviors, which summed to explain maternal attempts to prolong the infants' dependence, excessive caretaking, and exaggerated protection against the children's trauma or illness.

Levy then tabulated the nature of the complaints about their children by the 20 overprotective mothers. These children were 19 boys and 1 girl ranging in age from 5 to 16. These complaints fell into 2 contrasting clusters. One group of children was domineering. They ruled at home, by their tantrums they determined bedtime, mealtime and menu, recreational and other daily activities. When angry, some struck their mothers physically and verbally. The second group of children had sharply contrasting complaints and behavior. These were highly obedient children, submissive to a fault, little automatons. For both groups, the father's involvement was peripheral.

In examining the characterization of the mothers' overprotection, Levy found them also to fall into two groups. One type of maternal behavior was dominating in attitude. Contrasting sharply, the second type of overprotecting behavior was submissive and indulgent with the child's desires. Levy also found a striking correlation: The children who were domineering had submissive mothers, while the passive and over-obedient children had domineering mothers. Of interest in these data was the lack of school problems for both groups of children. Data on teachers' reports failed to indicate misbehavior at school, and both groups heeded rules. Academic achievement was satisfactory.

We are indebted to David Levy for this first substantial report by an influential clinician that the mother–child interaction is a two-way street. Of even more importance is that Levy recognized that the nature of this interaction was an area needing further clarification. In his concluding summation he commented, "the question remains, is the type of maternal overprotection determined primarily by maternal attitude or by the response of her offspring?" (p. 39).

We now relate Levy's contribution to the emerging history of a goodness of fit concept. Such children's behavior was poorly fitted to the developmental expectations of the environment, that is the unhealthy caregiving of the overprotective mothers. The ages of referral, from 5 to 16, show that, within the family the mutual behaviors of mother to child and child to mother were tolerated up to a point. What that point was in individual situations, as to the nature of the interactions, required the answer of Dr. Levy's challenging question. It could only be answered by a prospective study of a longitudinal nature.

Jerome Kagan, in 1971, studied perceptual schemata in infants and their interaction with new environmental stimuli. He emphasized that "excessive stress and distress will depend on a discrepancy from an established schema and not from the novelty or change in stimulation as such. The emphasis is placed on the relation between his schemata and the events in the new environment, not on the absolute variability or intensity of the new situation . . . If disruption is seen as a product of lack of congruence between schema and environment, one examines the distinctive qualities of the environment" (p. 11). Thus, Kagan's formulation that excessive stress in the infant's experience of new stimuli depended on the nature of the congruence between schema and environment, is an analogous concept to goodness or poorness of fit in the consonance or dissonance of the organism–environment interaction in infants.

David Stern spelled out a concept similar to that of Kagan. Stern wrote, "Very slight degrees of discrepancy provide very slight stimulation and provide low levels of attention. Increasing degrees of discrepancy produce progressively more attention up to some maximum threshold beyond which the infant finds the experience unpleasant and avoids it" (1977, p. 68).

In 1976, Lawrence Pervin reported an extensive survey of the psychological literature from the 1930s through the 1960s, with the interesting title "Performance and Satisfaction as a Function of Individual-Environment Fit in the Volume edited by Endler and Magnusson" (1976). Unfortunately, the review was diffuse and fragmented and did not report any significant findings relating to the goodness of fit concept and failed to shed light on his title.

☐ The 1980s and 1990s

By the 1980s a number of developmental psychiatrists, psychologists, and educators began to crystallize the goodness of fit concept.

Lois Murphy (1981) in discussing the data of the Topeka Longitudinal Study, spoke of "interesting examples of misfit and fit between mothers and babies" (p. 168). Jacqueline Lerner (1984) assessed the expectations for behavioral style, in an eighth-grade classroom, of each subject's classroom teacher and peer group. Those subjects whose temperament best matched each set of demands had more favorable teaching ratings of adjustment and ability, better grades, more positive peer relations, and more positive self-esteem than did subjects whose temperaments were less well matched with teachers and/or peer demands. On the cognitive level, Hunt (1980) emphasized what he called "the problem of the match" between the child's cognitive capacity and the demands made on him. If the demand was dissonant with his cognitive level, the child showed "withdrawal and distress, and often tears," if consonant, the task was performed with "interest and joyful excitement" (pp. 34–35).

The paragraph above has cited only a few examples of the flood of observations in the evaluation in terms analogous to goodness of fit in the 1980s.

Now, in the current decade, the 1990s, the clarification of goodness of fit has been further expanded. Dr. Jerome Frank, Professor of Psychiatry at Johns Hopkins Medical School, has dedicated his clinical and research studies to "more than fifty years of studying and practicing psychotherapy" (p. 301). In the last edition (1991) of his authoritative volume "Persuasion and Healing" and in his previous edition (1974) he critically reviewed and analyzed most of the various types of psychotherapy: psychoanalytic, psychodynamic, behavioral, cognitive, group and family, and milieu. In both editions, in his last chapter, he has formulated his long, thoughtful chapter on "A Conceptual Framework for Psychotherapy." Following that chapter, the 1974 summary had a relatively simple and short discussion. But in his 1991 edition, his thoughtful summary is as follows: "All illness can be viewed as a failure of adaptation, an imbalance between environmental stress and coping capacity. The ability to cope is determined by constitutional vulnerabilities and strengths on the one hand, and by the favorable or unfavorable meanings persons attribute to events on the other . . . Healthy assumptive systems are internally harmonious and correspond clearly to actual environmental conditions . . . [and] lead to reliable, satisfactory social interactions and feelings of competence, inner security and well-being . . . Unhealthy assumptive systems are internally conflictual and do not accurately correspond to circumstances. They lead to experiences of frustration, failure, and alienation that paradoxically increase a person's resistance to changing in response to new experiences such as those provided by psychotherapy" (Frank & Frank, 1991, pp. 50–51). This statement elaborates an elegant formulation of the goodness and poorness of fit, though he has not used that term.

Richard Lerner, Director, Institute for Children, Youth and Families, Michigan State University, and Jacqueline Lerner, his wife and co-worker, Professor of Psychology at the same university, have jointly, with several of their research fellows, tested the goodness of fit concept with several studies. These studies were of short longitude with approximately 150 young adolescents. In three tests, their findings found positive results of the application of the goodness of fit formulation (Nitz, Lerner, Lerner, & Talwar, 1988; Talwar, Nitz, & Lerner 1990; East et al., 1992). The Lerners concluded that the goodness of fit concept "leads to an integrated, multi level concept of development, one in which the focus of inquiry is the person–environment dynamic interaction. Furthermore, such an orientation places an emphasis on the potential for individual change in structure and function—for plasticity—across the life span" (Lerner & Lerner, 1994, pp. 166–167).

There is a current of thought in child psychiatry which suggests that some syndromes subsumed as pathogenic in the DSM-IV might be better considered as adaptation of the organism to the environment. This trend is indicated in a recent paper, "Evolution and Revolution in Child Psychiatry: ADHD as a Disorder of Adaptation" by Jensen and colleagues in the *Journal of the American Academy of Child and Adolescent Psychiatry,* 36:12, December, 1997, pp. 1672–1681. ADHD is the acronym for Attention Deficit Hyperactivity Disorder and has been increasingly prominent in the professional literature for its diagnosis and treatment but controversial as to its actual meaning. It is thought by many, including us, that ADHD is over diagnosed. In a leading textbook, *Child and Adolescent Psychiatry: A Comprehensive Textbook,* edited by Melvin Lewis, Gabrielle Weiss's (1996) chapter defines this disorder as a clinical syndrome in which "Hyperactive children have a short attention span, difficulties with inhibitory control manifested by behavioral and cognitive impulsive and inappropriate restlessness . . . These traits lead to their being frequently in trouble with adults and unpopular with peers. They underachieve in school . . . the etiology of the syndrome is not known" (p. 544–550).

The six authors of the article by Jensen et al. are professors of psychiatry and psychology in medical schools in this country and write as members of the Child Psychiatry Committee of the Group for the Advancement of Psychiatry (GAP). The link of their presentation with goodness of fit (a term that is used in their discussion) is in the thesis that "for an organism to adapt successfully, it must constantly explore the environment of threats and opportunities." They then postulate that behaviors now considered symptoms of ADHD must have been adaptive in primitive societies in which vigilance and "response-ready" characteristics aided survival.

The authors are to be commended on their presentation, which is counter to the dominant view. We welcome them to this orientation which had been a constant in our temperament and goodness of fit theory since its inception. We join Dr. William Carey, a developmental pediatrician who has pioneered in clinical application of temperament with his comment "Compliments to Dr. Jensen and colleagues for an excellent paper. And welcome to a revolution that is well under way" (letter to the editor of JAACAP from Dr. Carey, January 1998).

II

GOODNESS OF FIT: CLINICAL APPLICATIONS

5

CHAPTER

Infancy

Mrs. Phyllis G. called me (A.T.) for an appointment urgently. She had been my patient six years ago, ending with positive resolution of her problems. From her tense and tremulous voice, I could hear that she was under severe stress again.

She was well groomed but agitated and anxious when she came to her appointment on the following day. She sat down and leaned toward me, pleading, "Doctor you helped me six years ago, but now I have new and serious problems. Since I last talked with you, I have married. It is a good marriage, we get along very well, and now we have a six-month old baby, a boy, Eddy. He seems to cry whenever I care for him. He cries when I give him a new food, he cries in the bath, and no matter what I try to make him content, it seems to be worse. All the babies in my family are managed very easily, and I am the only terrible mother. It must be all my fault, you must help me." She was clearly demoralized and began to sob.

☐ Her Past History

As I listened to her, it was a true déjà vu of six years before, when she had exploded with self-beratement with words that were almost identical. At that time she had her first teaching job, with a fourth grade class, and was wailing at her failure as a teacher.

I summarized the first treatment quickly in my mind while she sat crying. Phyllis grew up uneventfully in a stable family, with an older brother and sister. The parents had high academic standards for their children. The older sibs both were highly intelligent, went through school and college with superior grades, and then one had trained in computer work, the other in biochemistry. Both had then immediately moved into good positions. Phyllis, the youngest child, had good intelligence with respectable grades, but not nearly at her older sibs' levels, and decided to become an elementary school teacher. Throughout Phyllis' school career, her parents had scolded her for her mere "average" achievement, pointing to her older sibs' achievements. "Why couldn't you do as well?" was the parental theme. Moreover, when Phyllis decided to become a schoolteacher, the parents were horrified, as if it were a "second hand" career, compared to her brother and sister.

Inevitably, with this denigration and criticism bombarded from childhood onward, Phyllis grew up with low self-esteem and self-confidence, and fearful she would be bound to fail at any decent position she took. She studied hard through college, always passed, but without honors.

After graduation, she obtained a position as a teacher in a suburban fourth grade public school. She started her job with an inner fear, almost convinced that she would fail. She reacted by pouncing at the slightest imperfect behavior on the part of any of the pupils. She threatened them with punishment, the youngsters protested, Phyllis shouted back, and her class was soon out of control. A classical self-fulfilling prediction. After several of these chaotic sessions, Phyllis was sure she was a failure, was afraid she would be fired, and became demoralized and panicky. Fortunately, she had one close friend she had grown up with, and poured out her grief to her, "I am a failure, what can I do?" A good therapist had just helped her friend, and she told Phyllis she must immediately seek professional consultation. The friend gave her my name, Phyllis called, and that was the beginning of the story.

Despite Phyllis' background of self-depreciation, she had answered my questions clearly and in detail. I reassured Phyllis the treatment would work, and gave her a mild sedative and an appointment after two days. She came in, still very tense, but not demoralized. She had no unfortunate confrontations with her class in the previous two days. She was then able to listen to me, as I outlined the reasons why she had become convinced she was a failure. As she grew up—though she had never failed in school, in her social relations, or in living completely by herself—in Phyllis' family myth, lack of superior performance was judged as a failure. "But if any of my pupils misbehave, I will be a failure as a teacher." I told her I did not accept such a judgement. "I suggest you pick out an experienced teacher who appears relaxed and friendly, sit with him/her during lunchtime and ask for advice. I am sure she would be glad to listen. Ask the teacher how she handles all the small disciplinary incidents in her classroom." Phyllis was startled, "I can't do that. If

I do it I will be exposing to everyone that I'm a bad teacher." While she finally agreed to carry this plan out, she was quite shaky and frightened.

She came into her next appointment, two days later, and looked very different. She sat down quietly, not demoralized, but still tense. "I left here two days ago, so frightened, that even if I had promised, I was sure I wouldn't be able to do what you advised. I went right to my friend, and recounted our discussion and your assignment, including that I was too scared to comply. My friend laughed, and said, 'Phyllis, I think you have a sensible doctor. You have to do what he advises you.'

"With your order and my friend's encouragement, I had to do it. But I was still very scared. Yesterday, at lunchtime I looked around, saw one of the older, nice-looking teachers sitting at a small table by himself. I went to him and asked, 'Excuse me, could I sit down and ask you a question?' He smiled, I sat down, hesitantly, but blasted out, 'This is my first job as a teacher, and I do not know how to handle all the small misbehaviors of the class that come out so often.' The teacher smiled, patted my arm, and said 'I had the same worry when I was also in my first job as a teacher. I gritted my teeth, told myself I would not let the problems get me down. If a child had one small misbehavior that did not disturb the class, and otherwise he behaved well, I ignored the single act or maybe twice, and made believe that I did not notice it. If a child had many behavior offenses, that was different. I kept the child after school, talked to him and tried to find out the cause of the behavior. Sometimes I could and was able to help. Sometimes I could not and referred the child to the school psychologist or assistant principal. If there was a major infraction of the school rules, I immediately took it up seriously. Again, I kept the child after school and repeated the same approach. You really have to play by your ear, and as you get more experienced you learn new strategies. Sometimes, a little humor helps to keep the class in control. You will be O.K. If you have a real problem, come to see me. I can probably help you. Good luck."

Phyllis was stunned. This teacher's attitude was so different from her parents' approach. I commented, "You were fortunate in picking the older teacher who advised you sensibly. With that, let me quickly review the reason for your teaching problem, and then give you my judgement and advice. As you grew up, your parents and sibs drummed into your mind that you were an inferior person. Due to this, you lacked self-esteem and feared you would be a failure in any responsible position you achieved. With this deep sense of inadequacy, you developed a defensive goal of obsessive perfectionism. That is, you made sure you corrected even any small mistake or imperfection so then nobody would expose your deep inferiority.

"You did well in school and college and socially with your friends. In those situations, you were able to quickly correct any error you made, were able to achieve your mask of perfectionism, and relaxed. Now, at the beginning of your professional career as a teacher, your pupils have become your identity. Your pupils are eight-year olds. Naturally, they break minor school rules. This threatened you deeply, because if you did not correct all of the pupils' infractions, your façade of perfectionism would be shattered, and everybody would know you to be a failure, and in your mind your career would be ruined. In desperation, your only strategy was to punish all the pupils to make them behave perfectly. This tactic inevitably backfired. If pupils are punished for even a slight indiscretion, they react by all kinds of turmoil to pay back the teacher. And that is exactly what happened, as you have told me. Instead of achieving perfect control of your class, you lost control of it. Your goal of perfectionism is irrational, impossible, and bound to be a disaster for you. Fortunately children forget quickly."

Phyllis listened to me carefully. When I finished talking. She showered me with one question after another. She understood my interpretation, but realized that I was suggesting that she would need to think and behave entirely differently from how she had been doing her whole life.

Changed behavior in the classroom depended upon the success with which Phyllis could achieve a new self-evaluation and enhanced self-esteem. Success with these goals required time, repeated discussion, and repeated inspections of her changed interactions with her pupils. To achieve such profound and fundamental changes was neither easy nor brief. Phyllis was aided in this endeavor by a growing support system consisting of her longstanding friend, her teacher adviser, a growing circle of fellow teachers, and finally her pupils themselves. When she found herself reverting to old behavior, "Perfectionism is out" was a slogan that restored perspective. One incident became a model for her own self-reference.

"One pupil was causing trouble every day. I kept him in after school and talked pleasantly with him. First he mumbled, but finally confessed he could not understand his arithmetic lesson and assignment and he was trying to cover up. I suggested he stay in after school for half an hour and I would go over the lessons with him every day. He agreed eagerly, came after school promptly. Within a week he had mastered the material and all his misbehavior disappeared."

☐ Phyllis G., Now a Mother

After 10 minutes, I finished reading my file of her previous treatment. Then I looked at Phyllis, told her to stop crying, and I obtained the details of her present problem. She answered my questions clearly, injecting the comment, "I'm a failure as a mother," looking at me helplessly and hopefully.

Phyllis' pregnancy and delivery of Eddy were normal. His physical status and growth over the months were also normal.

What were his problems? The mother plunged into a list of caregiving difficulties. He would not take new foods, his nap was very irregular, and he resisted being taken out of the bath. With each item, Phyllis described that Eddy cried loudly and long. "He must be abnormal, and it must be my fault," she kept repeating.

From this list of "symptoms", I suspected that Eddy might be a temperamentally difficult child—irregularity, high withdrawal, non-adaptability, negative and intense mood. I checked on the last item, positive as well as negative mood. "Did he have a favorite toy?" "Yes," she said, "Eddy loves his stuffed teddy bear. And when he plays with it, he shrieks with laughter." Therefore, that seemed to complete the constellation of a difficult child.

How did the mother handle Eddy's behavior? "How did you schedule his daily nap?" "It was an ordeal," she groaned. "I know I should put him to bed for a nap after lunch. When I put him to bed he sat up, shrieked, and cried loudly forever. Finally, I gave up, after a half hour took him out, and he stopped crying and was happy. Finally, maybe an hour, two, or three hours later, he got sleepy, fell asleep, I put him to bed and he had his nap that way."

"What happens when you offer him a new food?" "Impossible," she said. "Except his first food, cereal. He had to take it. At my first effort, he spat it out, I insisted and he kept twisting and crying, until I made him swallow a very small taste. The next time it was easier, and then he took it easily and now eats it eagerly. With the next food, fruit, again he spat it out and cried; I kept insisting he take it. After all, he should have a varied diet. But he made such a commotion, I could not stand it, and I quit. He only has cereal and milk now. That's terrible compared with all the other babies."

"Finally, what was the problem with the bath?" "Eddy now loves it, splashes, plays with his toy boat and laughs. The trouble is that when his bath is finished, and it is time for him to go to bed, he wants to stay playing in the bathtub. I have to take him out, and he cries for at least a half hour when I manage to get him dried and washed. It is another ordeal."

I commented that it was certainly an ordeal to care for a baby who cries so much of the time. "Baby care is so often illustrated by a smiling baby and a smiling competent mother that a new and inexperienced mother often has inaccurate expectations. Since these expectations are a poor fit for the realities of childcare, we can solve this problem by fitting your style of nurturing to Eddy's style of reacting." Because of the prior therapeutic contact, there was already some trust on Phyllis' part. I reminded her that now that she was an experienced teacher, she must be aware of individual behavioral differences amongst her normal pupils. Some moved slowly, some were very active physically, some were very persistent and some were distracted. Phyllis nodded, "Yes, indeed." I then explained that perhaps ten to fifteen normal children have temperament qualities that are harder for the care of parents, and we call it *difficult temperament.* "Eddy's behavior clearly fits into the category of difficult temperament. In addition, if you learn to accommodate your childcare to mesh with his temperamental style, we will have achieved a productive and happy mother–child relationship. Your tendency toward perfectionism makes it more difficult for you. I will provide you with a book for parents about temperament. Read it, and concentrate on the section of the *difficult child.*"

Phyllis found the concept of temperament to provide useful descriptions of her own past pupils. She now set about applying the concept to her child and peppered me with appropriate questions about how temperament manifests itself in infancy and finally asked, "What do we do to help Eddy?" Once launched upon considerations of concrete actions, Phyllis left behind her morbid preoccupation with worthlessness. As a teacher in the past, a new approach, following the directions of her experienced colleague, had freed her to recognize her pupils as children to teach rather than enemies to subdue. Similarly, she now set to work to recognize her son as an infant with an individual style. Once she desisted from trying to make him over into the idealized ever-smiling infant constantly gurgling with happiness, she was able to look about and realized that no such baby existed. The task of accommodating to an infant with difficult temperament in stages mirrored her metamorphosis as a teacher, an accomplishment that provided a useful reference point. Eddy's sleep irregularities could now be recognized as biologic rather than resulting from poor mothering. His loud and persistent protests with each new food, person, or experience could be redefined as her task to give him time to re-experience these events until familiarity was achieved. Now Phyllis could recognize that she could bring about Eddy's expressions of loud and joyful zest if she recognized it to be a task for weeks and not for minutes.

Given the stress of inexperience in motherhood with a difficult child, her perfectionism had recurred. I commented, "That's not unusual, when a patient has been treated successfully for one neurotic problem for it to recur when she is faced with a new stressful demand. That is what has happened to you. Now, you feel you have to be a perfect mother, and pressure Eddy when he behaves differently from many other children. Just life with your pupils as a teacher and your pressure to make Eddy conform to your perfectionism make his reaction worse."

Phyllis nodded slowly, "I understand, but it will help me if you give me some examples."

"For example, his sleep pattern is irregular. When he does not go to sleep after lunch, he is actually not sleepy. When you make the biologically impossible demand that he must go to sleep, he will only cry loudly and long, as you have told me. Instead, if Eddy is not sleepy, take him out, let him play until he gets sleepy, and then put him to bed and he will go to sleep. One day it may take an hour, another day two hours, another only half an hour. His irregular sleep schedule is normal, and just as healthy as for the easy infants who go to sleep on a regular schedule.

"Another example you have given is when Eddy is enjoying his bath. Decide in your own mind that this is playtime. When you take him out, be prepared for loud crying. Start another game with wrapping him in a large towel, drying him, diapering him, and the rest of the bedtime routine. Once he has become familiar with this routine, the crying will become briefer—but it will not stop altogether."

I gave Phyllis several other examples, she nodded, and I completed by emphasizing several points. "Eddy is normal and you and your husband are normal parents. Also, even if you handle him sensibly, Eddy will probably have occasional frustrations, like pulling him away from poking at electric outlets, he will have a tantrum. Later, plug the outlet. Then just wait until his tantrum finishes and then he will be cheerful. As he gets older, I will expect that his tantrums will gradually diminish.

"Finally, a child with difficult temperament has the trait of intensity which will make his pleasurable times happy and cheerful. In addition, with his negative response at first to a new unexpected situation, and his slow adaptation, as an older child he will not be a pushover." By then, Phyllis was nodding vigorously, "I really get the point and my husband will certainly also understand."

I said, "You're on the right track now. Telephone me in six weeks and report how you are doing." She did that, exclaimed that everything was going well, no problems. "I was a good teacher and now I can tell myself that I am a good mother."

Eighteen months later when Eddy was two years old, Phyllis requested a consultation. In contrast to earlier times, she was not disorganized but worried and a little sheepish. Her concern now was Eddy's lack of friendships. She and her husband had recently realized that, while Eddy enjoyed playing with his parents, and was talking well, he had no child companions. They had located an informal playgroup consisting of about a dozen children between 18 months and 3 years of age.

The children played informally while the mothers sat nearby to inter-cede if problems arose. On the first visit, Eddy simply stood on the edge and watched. "I was careful not to push him into the group and after 10 minutes I took him home." The following week they went again. Eddy made no objection but again he remained on the sidelines watching the others until she took him home. It has now been two months of weekly visits. Eddy showed no distress and appeared to be interested in looking, but remained a spectator. Deeply concerned, Phyllis turned to her books on child development.

"I just read a good book on child development. In one chapter, the author described the very serious illness of childhood, called autism. It often starts when the child is about two years, almost Eddy's age, and one of the very important symptoms is that the child can't make a real social relationship with other children, and even adults. Therefore, we are beginning to get worried about Eddy's behavior at the playgroup. Doctor, what is your judgement?"

"Your reading is partially accurate about autism. There are other rea-sons why Eddy is not socializing at two years. I do not believe that Eddy has autism. I suggest that you have a consultation for Eddy with a child psychiatrist, Dr. Stella Chess. I can easily brief her on your history and Eddy's problem. She can examine Eddy and give you a definitive an-swer."

Stella obtained her own history of Eddy's life from his parents, con-ducted a comprehensive clinical evaluation, in a play session. She then told the parents and me that Eddy was normal, showed no evidence of autism, and had a two-year old's socialization capacity. At age two, par-allel play rather than direct interaction is typical. For a two-year old with difficult temperament, his non-adaptive reaction to the completely new and complex environment of an unstructured playgroup is not sur-prising. She supported the parents' intent to enroll Eddy in a nursery school next year, at age three. Stella expected that, if the parents and the school handled Eddy's first month at school properly, Eddy's social-ization issue would be solved. She gave the mother a specific strategy for assisting Eddy's initial adaptation. If the mother had any difficulties with the teacher, Dr. Chess can speak directly to the teacher.

Phyllis called me about 18 months later. She reported that she had followed Dr. Chess' instruction to the letter and the teacher understood the issue at once. In Eddy's first two weeks at nursery school, he had been a watchful sideliner, but he gradually adapted positively, and by now he plays actively with all the children and cooperates easily with all the school rules. At home, he talked with pleasure about his school ac-tivities and friends.

Almost three years later, Phyllis called me. "Could I have an appointment with you for a only a few minutes? I have a lot of good news to tell you." I arranged it, and she came in with a relaxed bright smile. She sat down, and burst out, "I became pregnant two years ago. We now have a second son, Tony. It was amazing. I expected him to have the same difficult temperament as Eddy, gritted my teeth, and kept reminding myself, 'do not be a perfectionist." We could not believe it; Tony turned out to be an easy child. His sleeping and feeding schedule was regular, he took all his new foods easily, rarely cries, and if he does, it is not loud, but just fussing. You know, when you and Dr. Chess gave specific instructions with Eddy's problems, I followed the advice to the T, because we trusted you and it worked. But I always had a little worry in the back of my mind. Maybe Eddy had some special brain problem. The explanation of difficult temperament was clear, but a little too easy. But we have Tony with the opposite temperament and no difficulty at all in his behavior. Now, I am really convinced, it was only temperament and my silly perfectionism."

"How is Eddy doing?" I asked. "Fine. When Tony was born, Eddy did not like it, fussed some about him, but I was patient and did not press him. Now they are good friends, and he proves that he is the older brother. He does very well in school and socially. Occasionally, he has a tantrum, but they are becoming easier and less frequent."

We congratulated each other and said good bye.

☐ Comment

We have described the case history of Eddy and his mother because the issue of difficult temperament and goodness of fit is a prominent but not exclusive issue for the caregivers in the infancy period.

☐ The Capacities of the Infancy Period

In the past, "it was thought that in the early weeks of life a baby . . . seemed a picture of psychological incompetence, of confusion and disorganization . . . all he could do was feed and sleep" (Schaffer, 1977, p. 27). Research studies of the last 30 years have dramatically changed this view of the neonate's functioning. The neonate is capable of a wide range of perceptual recognition, learning by the formation of conditioned reflexes and by imitation, a significant range of integrated behavioral processes, and capable of active social communication—that most basic element of social exchange. (Specific research references are summarized in Chess and Thomas, 1984, pp. 12–14.)

Now in the past few years a new dimension of neural plasticity in infants and adults has been reported by a number of investigators through the use of new neuropsychological research tools (Nelson and Bloom, 1997). ". . . it has been reported that the brain massively overproduces synapses early in life, only to be followed postnatally by selective elimination of these exuberant connections . . . Experience-related neural activity can then select a functionally appropriate subset of abundant synoptic connections" (p. 980).

Moreover, the Nelson and Bloom review also summarized the extensive research findings of neural plasticity in the adult: "there is now strong evidence for critical reorganization following peripheral nervous system injury in the adult human" (p. 982). Following this summary, the authors cite a new report that ". . . suggests that the brain of the adult human can reorganize in response to positive experiences in the environment as well as to negative ones (e.g., injury)" (p. 982).

Thus, as an eminent developmental research psychologist puts it, the newborn "begins life as an extremely competent learning organism, an extremely competent perceiving organism" (Bower, 1977, p. 35). With these functional abilities, coupled with the organism's temperamental individuality, the neonate and young infant enters into an active interactional process with the caregiver. Through this interactional process, the caregiver learns with increasing accuracy what styles of nurturing are most useful, by noting the infant's responses. While mutual accommodations between infant and caregiver occur with differing degrees of smoothness and at different speeds, most parents are desirous and capable of meeting the infant's needs and obtaining a goodness of fit. And if dedicated parents may be confronted by one simple problem or another in satisfying their infant's needs, they usually can find a wise pediatrician, grandparent or friend who will offer appropriate advice in resolving the problem. Through such beginnings of the appropriate routines of feeding, dressing, bathing, and playful interactions, infant and parents become better acquainted, and the child's progressive mastery of the environment begins.

With such a goodness of fit, the infant has a good beginning, and he or she faces, with increasing biological and psychological maturity, year after year, correspondingly complex expectations and demands of the environment. As these interlocking events mount, the child, with successive successful goodness of fit experiences, develops self-awareness, self-esteem begins to emerge, motivations and cognition become clarified, and competencies begin to declare themselves.

☐ The Infants with Poorness of Fit

Most, but not all infants, blossom in their positive development with a secure goodness of fit. Unfortunately, there are a number of unfavorable happenings that may produce a poorness of fit in the individual–environment interactional process in a minority of neonates or infants. Such unhappy factors can include: biological handicaps such as congenital rubella, brain damage created by premature birth, trauma in the delivery process, infections or nutritional deficiencies, severely dysfunctional families, idiosyncratic, pathological behavioral patterns in a parent, an immature, young, single parent with an inadequate support system, or a highly stressful unfavorable environment.

What happens to an unfortunate infant with a poorness of fit? Some cases actually spontaneously change a poorness to a goodness of fit in the early months of life. Dr. Daniel Stern, in a detailed study of the mother–infant interaction, cited an unexpected development in one of his cases. The mother was blatantly intrusive and overstimulating with her young infant, who was reacting by avoiding eye contact with her mother. The situation worsened, and by four months, Stern anticipated he would have to intervene. But then the interchange between mother and child began to improve spontaneously, continued to do so, and the infant went on with a goodness of fit. Stern was never sure why this happened, but emphasized the importance of requiring "much restraint about predicting outcomes and evaluating the need and timing of intervention" (1977).

This spontaneous modification of a parent's unhealthy behavior in giving care to the infant, changing a poorness of fit to a good fit, has been reported to us over the years by mental health professionals and pediatricians, though we cannot estimate the number of such incidents.

6
CHAPTER

The Toddler and Preschool Periods

The greater mobility and social awareness of the toddler and preschool periods, ages two to five, bring new possibilities for the child to explore his or her world, to learn safety limits, both in terms of times and places safe for expression, and those that are prohibited. Most toddlers function during this period with a sense of trust. This can be seen simply by walking along any busy street. Toddlers ride serenely on parents' shoulders, watching their world go past. They walk or run, going ahead, to the side, or behind caregivers. Some tease, catching a mother's gaze, pretending to run away, then run back to complete the game. Even the toddler wailing in a stroller or having a tantrum is demonstrating a trust that his or her message "I want it" is important to the adult. Children are looking around them, and always watching the passing scene. When they see something they find noteworthy, their first action is to bring it to the attention of the caregiver. The good fit here is the caregiver's readiness to respond, to show the value of the child by being attentive to the message.

Sometimes there is also the beginning in this period of profound social lessons out of casual encounters. One day as I (S.C.) crossed the street behind a mother and her four-year old son, I heard the following conversation. Mother: "I will answer your question why the man walked in a funny way, but not now while we are near him." After a pause for distancing, she continued, "It's not polite to point and ask 'Why does that man walk funny,' because it might make him feel bad.

48

Wait till he can't hear you. It is called 'crippled.' Maybe he was born that way, so there is no reason to feel sorry for him. He is just different. That's not good or bad, it is just different." How much did the little boy retain? Probably not much. But the message is most likely to be repeated again and again by this sensitive mother. The ultimate message is the universal one that one should be concerned about the feelings of other people, and variety amongst people is an interesting fact.

This small episode is also an illustration of the fundamental wisdom of toddlers' questions, which go to the heart of the matter. It has been said that children's questions remain fundamental, until they are taught by adults who cannot answer them that the questions are stupid. "Why is the sky blue?" "Why do people hit other people?" "Why do we have to pay money?" "Why does the light go on when we push the wall switch?" "When I grow up will Daddy grow down?" "Why do fish swim so good?" This is the age of fundamental inquiry. The answer, "You are too young to understand," is a put down. "I don't know," is insufficient. Humankind failed to understand basic facts for ages, and many still elude us. A partial answer at the child's level is respectful of the child, and may in fact strain that particular adult's stock of knowledge. "The sunlight goes through the pieces of dust in the air and that makes a blue color," is factual enough and leaves the possibility of pursuit by the child at the moment or years later. But it is a good fit with the parent's appropriate response to the toddler's natural bent for wanting to understand these events that impinge on her growing awareness. To insist on turning a casual inquiry into a formal lesson beyond the toddler's attention span is not a good fit. To brush her off, if she is persistent in her interest, will also not be a good fit. A good fit depends on a number of factors, including intellectual level, motivations, and temperamental qualities. A full discussion need not be immediate, if other needs take priority—it is sufficient to pay respectful attention and then set another time for further discussion. In contrast, for a parent to insist on immediate exploration of the topic with a highly distractible child, who has now lost interest, will be a poor fit, since an expression of casual interest has been turned into a complex, unwanted lesson. The unintended lesson may have been not to ask questions—at least not of this particular adult.

The mingling of four-year old intellectual ability, with its capacities and limitations, and temperamental characteristics is illustrated in the following case.

Four-year old Evan was brought to me (S.C.) by his parents because of fears of a vague but persistent nature. These had begun six months previously when there had been a series of mild tremors in the area, and an earthquake registering 1 to 2 on the Richter Scale. There had been radio warnings and his mother had rushed Evan outdoors as recommended. There had been repeated tremors over the period of a week. Evan had repeatedly asked his mother what made earthquakes happen and had grasped the general idea of fault lines in the earth's crust. He was seemingly reassured by his parents' calmness, but nevertheless continued to have nightmares about the earth splitting and exploding.

Psychiatric workup showed normal pregnancy, delivery, and development. While moderately shy, Evan was attending pre-kindergarten, had gradually adapted, and was now eager to attend, and had friends there. He had always been an inquiring, persistent, and intellectually superior child who grasped explanations at a high level. Because of the persistence and severity of the nightmares, he was seen in therapeutic sessions where I found that his play and discussions did not spontaneously focus on fears. One day Evan brought to the session a favorite book to show me (S.C.). It was a sophisticated, illustrated volume discussing the Big Bang theory of the birth of this universe. Evan went through the volume with considerable enjoyment and no apprehension, reviewing the photographs and explanations with amazing sophistication and understanding. It was difficult to remember that this was only a four-year old with superior intellect. It was necessary to remind myself that he was still subject to age-related emotional responsivity. After we had gone through the book, I asked Evan whether there was any relationship between the Big Bang so long ago and earthquakes. As he pondered, he began to tell how scared he had been when the dishes had begun to rattle on the shelves and some had fallen and broken, how the radio voice had ordered everyone to go outside, and how frightened he and his mother had been. Then he had worried whether his father had also been able to run to safety. He now remembered that he had thought that the Big Bang was happening all over again, and the world might split into pieces. With my limited knowledge of astronomy, I was able at least to state that this disastrous event would not happen now to our solar system. It might happen millions of light years away, a concept that he was able to grasp sufficiently well for the purpose of reassuring him. This opened for consideration a connection between the two events that, in his four-year old intellect and reasoning, had seemed logical, probable, and very frightening. Now, with open discussion and play, both in therapy and at home with his parents, his nightmares gradually subsided.

The poor fit in Evan's situation had been precipitated by a fortuitous event—a mild earthquake that should have merited mild and brief fears. But with Evan's high intelligence, inquiring mind, and a vivid four-year old imagination, the equation of Big Bang and the shaking of the ground became fixed. The achievement of a good fit used his same intelligence, once the realistic explanation had been learned.

☐ Comment

Of what usefulness here is it to utilize the concept of goodness of fit? Would it not have been simple common sense initially to link the child's most recent traumatic event, the earthquake, to his continuing nightmares? Yes . . . but! It might have been, but this linkage in fact did not seem to be accurate. Parents, teachers, playmates all went through a period of worry and gradual relaxation—including Evan. Like his playmates, he had time and reassurance enough to recover from this trauma. However, common sense had failed with its prediction, and a psychiatric consultation was needed. Further compounding the puzzle of his behavior was the fact that the nightmares were Evan's sole symptom. He continued to enjoy school, had no separation problems, enjoyed his play with his friends, continued to explore ideas and events as before. The parent–child relationships continued to be positive and enjoyable. It was even quite possible that some other trauma might be responsible for Evan's nightmares.

With this temperamentally slow-to-adapt child, familiarity permitted trust to grow so that his discussion became more inclusive and free. I heard no evidence that would invoke classical psychoanalytic dynamics such as castration anxiety or oedipal fears. Earthquakes, in Evan's mind, were the reality. They were shelves shaking, dishes rattling, a dash with mother to the outdoors. They were a radio voice giving instructions and information. They were people—adults and children—telling and retelling the tale. But Evan's nightmares continued. Other children of his age had come through the same series of shocks and over time had moved on to other events and left their earthquake reactions behind them.

In his usual fashion, Evan had asked innumerable questions about earthquakes and had added knowledge of tectonic plates to his stock of facts. His nightmares did not bow to factual mastery. He did not recall any details of his nightmares.

It was only when Evan finally had the trust to believe that I would share his big interest that the Big Bang theory came to my notice. It had been a fascination long before the earthquakes, and Evan's continued occupation with the illustrated book was seemingly no different than before. But as the child shared this fascinating find of scientific speculation, it became clear that this might be the missing piece of the puzzle, the one good fit.

It was the "uncommon" and superior cognition of a four-year old inquiring mind that had been alerted to vast elemental processes. The event of an actual mild earthquake, linked cognitively to the Big Bang theory that had been beyond the child's comprehension. The nature of the poor fit, now clarified, pointed toward the steps needed to attain a good fit.

7

School Age and Middle Childhood

By the beginning of school age or middle childhood—ages six to twelve—the child has become well oriented to the cultural standards and ethical values of her community. She may show this by behavior that is consonant with social expectations. If her behavior is dissonant for whatever reason, her awareness of the community's standards may be shown by her selection of actions flouting and opposing the rules. Children's behavior is often quite parsimonious—they do not waste energy opposing those rules about which their caregivers do not care. To the contrary, if a defiant child is deliberately messy, it is likely that her parents value orderliness. If she makes frequent ethnic slurs, it is probably that they decry bigotry. And if parents specially enjoy quietness, the highly persistent, defiant child's tantrums are likely to be expressed with an extra degree of loudness and commotion.

It is also during the middle childhood years that children encounter, in the wider environment, increasingly complex experiences of nuances of relationship, and grow closer to adult patterns of behavior. These youngsters begin to sort out such new interactions, and begin to incorporate into their behavior such concepts as irony, humor, and the differing types of secrets and lies, with growing sophistication and codification. They sort out these meanings against a background of their prior degrees of sophistication and home experience.

☐ **Clinical Vignettes**

A Caricature of Creativity

Eight-year old Derek presented a problem solved through the paradigm of goodness of fit. His parents' first awareness that there was a problem had occurred during third grade. In the fall, his teacher had told his parents that Derek was falling behind in his work for reasons that puzzled her. Although he was quite capable, when she gave class instructions, he did nothing. Later, he would come to her desk and ask what he was supposed to do. When she repeated what she had said to the class, Derek would comply and do the assigned work capably and cheerfully. Yet, on the next occasion he again did not seem to comprehend that he was supposed to act on her instructions to the whole class together. Consequently, he was falling behind. Also, when the children were supposed to group themselves for recreational purposes or group learning, Derek was usually found to be without a partner and not part of any work group. He had simply made no attempt to link with others, and they had totally ignored him. Since Derek was a member of the NYLS, his parents consulted me (S.C.).

With our NYLS data available, from the parental reports, I knew the history of Derek's prior developmental course. This included the parent–child interactions and his relationships with his younger brother and sister. The eldest of three children, Derek's physical and developmental course had been unremarkable. I.Q. testing at ages 3 and 6 in accordance with the NYLS protocol had placed him in the superior range of intelligence. The parental report, verified by the NYLS data, showed him to have had language development in the normal range in both timing and quality of word and sentence usage.

Both parents' occupations were in creative areas—mother was a freelance writer and father was an actor. Both were well established in their fields. These were child-oriented individuals who valued self-expression and spontaneity. This translated for Derek and his siblings at home to a childhood of riddles, dramatized reading, and story telling. The children responded with joy and enthusiastic learning in a wide variety of areas. Prior to this year, Derek seemed to have learned effortlessly both at home and at school. There had been no prior report at difficulty in following directions at home, in school, or when visiting neighbors. He had been part of the neighborhood pack of playmates, meeting on play lawns or in homes.

The report by Derek's teacher of incipient learning problems and beginning social isolation came as a complete surprise. The child's early childhood experiences would have seemed to be ideal for positive emotional and learning progress. In favor of high academic achievement was an excellent school, a class atmosphere conducive toward respect for achievement, interested and well-educated parents, and a home atmosphere that should have predicted high self-esteem and respect for individuality. Derek's parents reported that, during the period of the reported school problem, there had been no change of home behavior. He was a bubbling, cheerful child who continued to participate in family activities. Minor problems had occurred over the years, such as a brief sleeping problem and occasions of more than usual sibling rivalry. Each had been reported to the NYLS and had been solved, after diagnostic study, with parental counseling. They had been judged ordinary exigencies of normal development. In the course of these encounters, the parents had proved to be concerned, flexible, and able to be self-contemplative.

With so much detailed verifiable information, unusual in most clinical child referrals, this diagnostic puzzle was attacked within the framework of the goodness of fit/poorness of fit conceptualization. After obtaining a fresh clinical history as summarized above, I interviewed Derek in my playroom. Our discussion was focused upon his daily activities. When, at home, the parents had asked Derek to tell them about his interchanges with his teacher, he had said, "She tells us what to do and we do it." Then he talked to me about home and school activities, and presented his daily life as enjoyable. He talked of his teacher, Ms. T., with fondness. When he gave me the same description, "The teacher tells everybody what to do and we do it," I explained that I had not been in a classroom for a long time, and every teacher probably taught a little bit differently. Derek obliged cheerfully to describe his day in the classroom step by step: greetings, settling in, roll call, teacher direction. Again, he said, "She tells everybody what to do and we do it." (Everybody together?) "No, first she tells the class, then she tells me what I'm supposed to do." (Is there anyone she tells separately?) "No." (Is there a reason?) "No." (Then, what does she tell you to do?) "She tells me the pages to do, and I start to work. If we have trouble, Ms. T. helps." (Does she tell you to do the same thing as the class?) "I don't know." (Does she give you different work from the class?) "I don't know." (Why is it that you do not know)? "Because I don't listen. I am supposed to get something different to do. Sometimes she forgets, so I don't do anything until she remembers." The child was truly puzzled at my density. Finally, after further patient clarification on Derek's part, I understood his view of school expectations. At home, he explained, everyone did different things. Only occasionally did they all do the same thing at the same time, like dinner or going on an excursion. Otherwise each one was "creative" and did what he or she wanted. If two of them wanted to use the same stuff, they took turns. "That is what is supposed to happen at school." Therefore, if Ms. T. forgot, Derek just waited quietly as he assumed he was supposed to do. The child was simply not aware that his behavior was considered a problem. I now inquired as to the group learning. Derek verified that Ms. T. sometimes asked the children to form groups. As before, Derek waited to be given his personal assignment. Not aware that working alone was inappropriate to the teacher's expectations, he did not feel himself to be a social outsider.

Having once again verified Derek's description of his school actions from Ms. T., I reviewed this material with his parents. In their concern, they had recently been paying closer attention to their children's interactions. Derek, as the oldest, had seemingly arrogated to himself the role of interpreter of proper behavior for his younger sibs. He would often comment that something was "not creative," "it's stupid," or "that's a dumb game—everybody plays that!" "Make up a creative game." They now noted that Derek indeed had fewer friends ringing the doorbell than had been customary. In play with friends, he was free with his assertions that their choice was "stupid" and "not creative" and would refuse to join their activity. Derek's parents were stricken to realize that he had transformed their fostering of creativity and individuality of expression into caricatures of their own functioning.

We were now beginning to clarify the nature of this poorness of fit. First, it was important to identify what was not the problem. Derek did not have deep-seated conflicts that needed to be explored and worked through. There was no failure to be capable of forming affectionate bonds. He did not have a problematic degree of sibling rivalry. There was no organic learning disability. There was no lack of desire on Derek's part to accommodate to his environment—as he perceived it. Yet, his very sensitive classroom teacher had identified a potentially severe set of problems for early therapeutic prevention and intervention. And because of this, Derek's parents had now identified an incipient problem of misinterpretation of family values that was beginning to lead to problems in Derek's relationships and possible social isolation from peers. At home, Derek had no conflict about accepting rules that applied to everyone, such as proper table manners or bedtime routines. He was also happy with the freewheeling and imaginative interchanges. A typical episode which I (S.C.) observed during a routine interview visit was the following: It was the Thanksgiving season. Mother arrived home that afternoon a bit late (I had already arrived a bit early). She said gaily, "I just saw a pumpkin in the sky." The children immediately started guessing the answer to this riddle. Finally one looked out of the window and said, "It's the moon!" And indeed, the moon was an orange ball close to the horizon. From this there followed an interested discussion of how the harvest moon looks brighter and larger when it is close to the horizon and would become yellower and smaller when it became higher in the sky. The formal interview now needed rescheduling because of the time allotted to this genuinely creative and educational interlude in which I had just participated. I had, in fact, enjoyed this interchange as much as had the children, and I had been afforded a most important view of the atmosphere of the household.

The central issue of this behavior disorder was to determine the steps through which Derek had converted this truly creative lifestyle into a poor fit with the expectations and demands of school and social life of an eight-year old. He must have come to his rigid interpretation of "creativity" as part of a gradual process. The second grade teacher had not noted any problem of following directions, of learning, or of social participation in the class during the previous school year. Until the parents' close scrutiny now, they had been unaware of Derek's growing need to be "creative." Wishing to accommodate to the teacher's demands, Derek had solved a real conflict of functioning: He had misperceived the rules in order to bring them into accord with his own perceptions of his teacher's goals. Since he was a cheerful and obliging child, no one had interpreted his behavior, as so often happens, as rebellion, oppositionality, or inattention. Derek's own explanation of his perception of the environmental expectations and demands was the only one that explained all the facts.

The issue was how to help the child make the proper adaptation in school, and with visiting children inside or outside his home. At age eight, this was not a great problem. Since there was a legacy of good relationships with the children with whom he had played as a toddler, a restoration of the old relationships within school was not hard. It was necessary to give Derek actual instruction of what school behavior was supposed to be. While adaptive, Derek had not been temperamentally sensitive enough to the behaviors going on around him—he needed specific directions. Given permission by his parents to conform to a group instead of having to be "creative" under all circumstances, Derek now began to cooperate with the group. Each time the teacher introduced a new procedure, she was now alerted to making certain that Derek was aware that these expectations included him. So were some of his classmates, who became self-appointed monitors. Derek was in fact a good companion and often contributed ideas to work groups, so that his contributions were valued. Thus he learned two manners of functioning: home functioning in which individuality was prized, and school and peer functioning in which individuality was to serve as part of a co-operative style.

Special Interests

Another problem was brought to me (S.C.) by parents who were worried over the implications of their son's behavior. The boy, Neil, nine years old, was passionately interested in nature in many ways, but not in athletics. He took out nature books very frequently from the public library and read them avidly. He had a rock collection and a pet rabbit. He had no involvement in the suburban baseball Little League, one of the highpoints of many of the families of the community. He did socialize actively with his peer group in the neighborhood, enjoyed playing with them the casual kind of games of that age group, but left plenty of time for his reading.

The history revealed no abnormal factors in his prenatal course, birth, or development. Neil was an easy child temperamentally, did well in school, was reliable and responsible, and there were no complaints about his home behavior. He got along reasonably well with his seven-year old brother.

What was the problem? The father was emphatic in his concern, "Neil won't play ball, refuses to join the Little League, no matter how many times I have urged him. He reads so much, but it is only on nature. I do not mind his interest in these oddball subjects if only he also had normal interests. But when I bought him a few books on baseball, he did not touch them. He's a sissy, and I'm afraid he will grow up as a homosexual."

The father was a successful businessman, educated, with a relatively mild and pleasant manner, and by no means a "macho" physique or attitude. He grew up always interested in athletics, and had kept up with sports news as an adult. The mother, on the other hand, respected Neil's interests, and did not think he had a problem. She felt that she and her husband had a congenial marriage and that he was a good father, except for his increasing worry, "Will Neil become a homosexual?" He was scornful of Neil's rock collection and haunted by the boy's refusal to join the Little League. She was concerned that with her husband's attitude, Neil was becoming less and less spontaneous in the family's conversations at home, and was becoming secretive and ashamed of his interests.

I decided that it was worthwhile to have a series of weekly sessions with Neil for several months to ascertain his functioning, so that I could make a definite judgment and recommendations.

The parents agreed, and Neil was willing to come, but reluctantly so. At his first session, he appeared reserved and wary, and I noticed he had a book tucked in his coat pocket. I asked him about the book; he explained reluctantly that he had just taken it from the library. It was a book on exotic and unusual species of fish. A chapter caught my attention as being particularly interesting. It was about a blind school of fish living in a cave pool in total darkness. When I finished reading, I looked at him with spontaneous interest. "That was fascinating. Are there any other unusual fish like that?" Immediately, Neil brightened and launched into an exciting story about a number of other exotic species. His account was no means by rote, but thoughtful and dramatic. I thanked him for this interesting story, and invited him to pick any one of the games in the room. He chose a rather complex jigsaw puzzle that he finished and the session ended.

At the next session he came in eagerly, with a tale of a special new book on dinosaurs, began to show it to me, and was surprised and pleased that I knew about dinosaurs. After that conversation, I steered the discussion to his feelings about his family. Neil began with an unhappy look. "My mother is great, and I get along well with my brother. But my father bothers me all the time. He just always thinks something is wrong with me because I do not like to play baseball. I just cannot get up any interest in that, and I am too busy with all my nature projects to join the Little League. He keeps calling me a "sissy" and by now I think maybe that something is wrong with me. Do you think I'm a sissy?" I answered promptly, "Of course not. So far, all I can see is that you are a perfectly normal boy. Whether you play baseball or not, has nothing to do with being a sissy." "Great," he said. "Can you convince my father?" "I'll get to that with your father, after I've known you even better, then I'll talk to him." At this time my goal became the restoration of Neil's self-esteem and self-respect.

We continued our weekly sessions, with his stories of his activities, and his various games with me. As I watched, I found no evidence of any problem with his neuromuscular dexterity, or any perceptional or neurological difficulties. He was also an intelligent and thoughtful youngster. At the beginning of the third month, Neil told me that a new family had moved into the neighborhood. One of the boys of the family was about his age. It turned out he was also a nature fan, and they had become good friends, with all kinds of nature projects like exploring caves, comparing rock collections, and so on. "And believe it or not, he also likes baseball and is joining the Little League. I told him about my father's worry about me and he laughed, 'That is stupid. If you do not like baseball, so what. There's no law that says people have to play baseball.' I was so relieved."

After the next weeks, when Neil and his friend were firmly established in their friendship, I arranged a parental meeting to give an overview of Neil's status. The father's first question was, as before, "Is

Neil a queer?" I responded, "Queer in what way? Are you asking whether something is wrong with his personality or whether he is a homosexual?" "Both," the father said. I gave him an emphatic answer. "I have played and talked with Neil, and watched him, and have found no evidence that he has any personality problem. He has manual dexterity and is well coordinated. His interests are quite appropriate for his age and sex. I find him entirely normal psychologically. It is not 'queer' for a boy or girl to be attracted to some special activity so passionately that he or she just ignores one or another of the routine social or athletic activities of the community. You know this boy who has moved into the neighborhood has now become a good friend of Neil because they have mutual interests in nature. He happens also to like baseball, so now you have the evidence that a boy can be a nature bug, and you can't call him 'queer' because your separate standard links maleness with baseball." I went on further to describe many youngsters I have known with special interests or talents who have moved on to develop these special interests. "The problem is that, with your assumption that these interests are 'queer,' Neil has himself begun to doubt these healthy, constructive, special interests. The danger is of damaging Neil's self-esteem and self-confidence because you have hammered at him that he is a 'queer.' Fortunately, now Neil has a good friend who is a nature fan who is respected and encouraged by his parents. It is not necessary for both of you to become interested in nature yourself, but it is essential that you show respect for Neil, that he finds that you consider him to be a normal boy in every way, and that you approve of his special interest, which he is pursuing in a serious, constructive, and stimulating manner. As to whether Neil is a homosexual that is another question. He has no signs of being effeminate, and you know that yourself. However, no psychiatrist or I can predict whether a normal nine-year old boy will show up as a homosexual when he is in adolescence or early adult life. There is no test available to predict that. The chances are statistically that Neil, like the majority of middle childhood youngsters, will blossom sexually in adolescence as a heterosexual. A minority becomes homosexual. You just have to wait until Neil grows up. There are star athletes who are homosexual—this even is no predictor."

The mother listened with no comment but nodded to show her agreement. The father was taken aback. He now involved himself in a serious confrontation of his stereotyped concept of masculinity, although it was clear that he questioned my statement that male athletes could be homosexual. He now understood that, in his preoccupation about homosexuality, he had been overlooking his son's many positive qualities. He was genuinely interested in regaining a positive relationship with his son. The father sat silently for a few minutes, shook his head and said, "I can't argue, you make sense. The clincher is seeing Neil's new friend as also being a nature bug, and he certainly is not queer. I didn't realize I was harming Neil. It's the last thing I ever wanted to do."

In my last session with Neil, I explained that I had told his father that he was not a "sissy." "He really cares for you, and understands that he just made a mistake about this baseball business. He is a good father. You can now both begin to respect and love each other." Neil then discussed very insightfully the issue of stereotyping expectations.

As usual, I arranged a follow-up session with the family a year later. Neil's spontaneity had blossomed, he was very busy with his and his friend's nature activities, was doing well at school, and the father expressed, "Now, I am proud of Neil."

☐ The Myth of "The Latency Period"

Clinical psychiatrists and psychologists frequently label the developmental period of the 6 to 12-year old child as the "latency period." This term had its origin in psychoanalytic theory, based on Freud's concept that at 6 years the Oedipal period has passed, and in the "latent" years until 12, the beginning of adolescence, "infantile and incestuous longings are repressed, and a widening array of adaptive defenses, including intellectualization, humor, identification, obsessional interests, are utilized" (Marans & Cohen, 1991, p. 137). "The central theme to the latency-age child is the re-emergence or breakthrough of the original sexual and aggressive fantasies of the oedipal phase, particularly when associated with the impulse to masturbate. Sleeping difficulties, nightmares, worries about burglers, bodily injury and death; . . . may be some of the behavioral phenomena" (Marans & Cohen, 1991, p. 137).

This concept of latency in the classical Freudian theory has led a number of psychiatrists to question its usefulness. Thus, Lidz stated that "psychoanalytic psychology has increasingly little to offer concerning the critical aspects of the period" (1968). This criticism of latency was echoed by another authority, who stated that it is an "unfortunate term since it suggests that nothing really important is happening and that the child is simply waiting for puberty to begin" (Shaw, 1966). Also, a host of developmental psychiatrists and psychologists have spelled out the wide variety of psychologically healthy new levels of activities, talents, and emotional and cognitive functioning in the middle childhood years without any indication of sexual inhibition. (The specific references to the comments by Piaget, Sullivan, and others are to be found in Thomas and Chess, 1972, pp. 332–333.) Beyond that, the data from our NYLS emphasize that school age and middle childhood youngsters encounter and cope with more and more complex experiences with increasing maturation of development as they meet a wider environment.

In conclusion, "we suggest that this term [latency period] be abandoned and that simple descriptions, such as middle childhood and elementary school age, be used in its place" (Thomas & Chess, 1972, p. 339). It has taken three decades of powerful critiques of the term "latency period" for there to be an increasing trend toward its disappearance in the professional literature and discussions.

8

CHAPTER

Adolescence

The clinical usefulness of the concept of goodness of fit is particularly evident during adolescence. During this developmental period, there are significant alterations on both the sides of the equation of individual–environmental interaction that may potentiate the presence of either a good or a poor fit. The rapid changes in body proportions and sexual maturation demand from the youngster a constant re-evaluation of individuality and body image. The changes are very different for boys and girls; and the peak ages of change are earlier for girls. However, constant comparison of self-appearance with that of age mates are essential elements of life for most adolescents. Similarly, fashions of banter, the rapidly changing buzzwords, degree of respect for intellectual functioning, as well as idealization of physique vary from environment to environment. Any group of eighth graders shows how great is the variation in physical appearance and social behavior. Adolescent self-esteem depends heavily upon conformity to the group and acceptance by it.

Adolescence is also the second important developmental period of increasing independence. While the adult world almost universally applauds the infant's rapid acquisition of skills of locomotion, language, and decision-making, and sees self-assertion as a welcome sign of maturity, the same is not always true of the adult view of the adolescent period. Aware of the dangers of some types of experimentation, caregivers worry that some unfortunate consequences can even be irreversible. Many parents, recalling their own adolescent brinkmanship, try to protect by undue restriction. On the other hand, the new capacities and responsibilities of the adolescent period can often present a new opportunity to alter a previously poor fit with the environment. A shy and retiring girl, attempting to gain acceptance by the group, may turn to a more outgoing friend who will teach her effective social maneuvers. A stormy and belligerent boy, whose bullying had heretofore been accepted, may no longer be bigger and stronger than everyone of his group; faced with shifts within the group cohesion, he can now accept the necessity for learning how to play a less dominant role. An arrogant teenager, no longer the smartest person around and newly within a class whose members are equally swift in intelligence, may learn for the first time the need for study habits.

Another hallmark of adolescence is the pressure to conform to the behavior and standards of a peer group. Since its exact activities are highly colored by cultural factors, there is a wide diversity in many of the overtly expressed attitudes, behaviors, and mannerisms from group to group. Choice of hairstyle, speech pattern, clothing, stated enthusiasms, and codes of loyalty are expressions of group cohesion. The youngster whose individual personal development leaves him or her out of step with the peer group often becomes an outsider.

To illustrate the complexities of the interactions of the adolescent with his or her parents, peer group, and social environment, as well as the adaptation of the adolescent to rapid extensive physical change and self-image, four clinical vignettes are presented. The four cases highlight different patterns of difficulties in coping with special environmental expectations, resulting in manifestations of deviant behavior and its consequences.

☐ Clinical Vignettes

Case 1: Group Pressure on Sexual Behavior

Grace came to me (S.C.) for consultation at age eighteen, in the spring of the year. She had just dropped out of her freshman class at college. She was depressed and unable to concentrate. The precipitating incident was a date during which she had been coerced into acquiescing in sex. Before giving details, I feel it important to indicate Grace's background functioning.

At age twelve, puberty had already begun. Grace's menses had commenced at age eleven and she had beginning breast development. Despite her physical development, she was socially unsophisticated. Grace was still a young girl, with interests to fit. She was shy, but had gradually accumulated a group of compatible friends. All were adequate students, liked to learn, joined in athletics with average skill, and had little interest in boys. With the move to high school, Grace and her friends found changes in the school atmosphere. In class, she was called on less and less by her teachers, and gradually she had given up even volunteering answers or joining in discussion. It was the boys who were called on in Math and Social Studies. She tried to join the chess club, but found herself often without a partner despite the fact that she won half the time. Her wins were clearly considered unimportant or even accidental by the group. Bored, Grace quit without making a fuss.

College life was at a large university campus at which social activities and athletics were prominent. Having many of her old friends there, Grace settled into a comfortable set of habits. She found that she was able to take a more active part in class because some of the other girls asserted their right to speak and many of the instructors sought full class participation. It began to appear as if Grace had moved from her tenuous fit at high school to a good fit here. Then her friends took on the issue of introducing Grace to the social scene. Till this time, she had had no dates, and her relatedness with male students was limited to friendly daytime conversations about studies. This situation presented no problem to Grace, but her friends urged her to at least try dating. There was one very popular upper classman who had often asked Grace for a date. Although there was no actual relationship—they had met occasionally at mixers but she had not had much to say to him, and Grace was not adept at small talk—under pressure from her friends, Grace finally acquiesced.

The date at first seemed passable. They went to dinner and a movie. The young man, Jack, had a line of chatter, but essentially Grace found him self-absorbed and of little interest. On the way back, Jack began to pressure Grace for sex. His pitch was that this was a new era of sexual freedom, and it was her obligation to herself to explore her sexual feelings. Since she was a virgin, he could assure her that he would be gentle. Bewildered, naive, and a bit drunk, Grace agreed. The experience was distasteful—in the back seat of a car, undignified, devoid of emotional meaning, and with a vague sense that she was not being true to herself. Soon after, her friends became aware that Jack had been boasting that he had added a virgin to his list of sexual accomplishments.

The experience was devastating to Grace, and nothing that her friends said out of their own guilt for pressuring her could take away her feelings of having been soiled. She did not feel "ruined"—but she did feel defiled. She had been so easily persuaded to behave in a manner contrary to her own identity, and she was unable to stop ruminating. She could not concentrate on studies, was unable to return to her social life with her friends, and so ran home. There she found solace, no recriminations and no loss of her parents' love, respect, and support. But that was not sufficient, and I arranged a series of discussions with her.

In the therapeutic sessions, several themes were explored. Grace was now clear that the protection she had given herself in early adolescence from the sexuality of her group, although appropriate at the time, failed to provide her with the experience she needed in a more sophisticated environment. This was a serious poorness of fit for her. But, out of this event, Grace found other unsettling questions: Am I incapable of mature sexual emotion? Am I frigid? Am I a lesbian and do not know it? Am I a misfit?

Despite high motivation and earnest searching, we were not able to find any evidence of previous maladaptive functioning—unless one held a belief that all children should have a history of sexual exploration, which here was absent. There was clear evidence that friendships had been close, and in no way was Grace an emotionless individual. As summer came close, Grace felt that she must have a change of scene, and through friends she learned of an Indian guru who held a summer residential seminar on self-examination. Inquiry by Grace's family and me showed that this teacher had a reputation as a serious philosopher. There were anecdotes of his refusing admission to young, family-supported people whose purpose in applying for the course was to "find myself." He had advised them to work for a year and, when they had enough money to pay the tuition themselves, to reapply. Grace's application, with a note from me, gave her acceptance.

Grace returned from this experience much changed. The seminar group had been a surprise—its members ranged from very affluent business people to artists and blue color workers, with some students. All were serious. The seminar was essentially a study of a range of philosophies in which all opinions were given courteous attention. Affairs were not part of the agenda, and Grace had felt respected, safe, and valued. Her depression had lifted and she was ready to take up life, but at a different college.

Now, Grace was determined to establish a goodness of fit in life, and her seminar experience gave her the desire to learn how to develop as a truly mature, independent person. She came back to therapy with me with this resolution. Our discussions focused on the exploration of the meaning of freedom. The false note that had led to disaster was her having accepted the belief of her adolescent peer group that freedom necessitated sexual exploration.

In therapy, Grace learned the concept of genuine choice—the freedom to say either "yes" or "no", to decide which pathways were important and which were unimportant or premature. Most useful to her realization was the fact that she had no need to apologize if she differed from the majority in ideas and behavior, even if her preferences put her in a "conservative" stance. During this new college year she achieved a genuine self-respect, moved at a self-selected social pace, and discovered that others respected her for her quiet dignity. Grace was still a rather average individual with average abilities. But she had now achieved a good fit, free of turmoil, and free of pressure from undesirable conformity to her peers' attitudes and values of the moment.

Case 2: Sociopathic Behavior with No Basic Psychiatric Disorder

Bernice S., one of our NYLS subjects, had severe problems at age 15. Her recently widowed mother, an advertising executive, had made a series of catastrophic discoveries. She had phoned the dance class that Bernice attended to give her a routine message, only to learn that Bernice was not there, and was not on their rolls. She had not shown up since the day she had signed up in her mother's presence months previously. Other equally disastrous information quickly turned up. Bernice had been cutting school all term and had kept the notices from her parents. Her private school had already determined to expel her and three classmates, all of whom cut school and were failing in their studies. From other sources, it also became clear that Bernice was known by her former friends to be experimenting with sexual promiscuity. This news explained why the classmates from her previous years no longer invited her to their homes after school or for birthday parties—she was on their parents' proscribed lists.

In order to understand what had happened, Mrs. S. and the both of us studied all the longitudinal material in Bernice's NYLS file. In her infancy and young childhood, the most outstanding temperamental characteristics had been high approachability, swiftness of adaptation, moderate intensity, and positive mood. On occasion, Bernice could also show high intensity, with tantrums over occasional issues—not considered by her parents to be unusual or any great problem. She was moderately impulsive—again, no great problem at that developmental period. The real contrast came from her nursery school records. When Bernice was age four, her teacher had called her "the most mature child I have ever had in my class." This opinion was derived from behavior that was also present at home. Bernice was alert to the slightest expressed need. If an adult mentioned a need—for a book, an intent to set the table, to bring out the next set of toys—Bernice usually anticipated and waited proudly for her praise. She even comforted other children when they banged themselves or gave help with a difficult puzzle. At home, paradoxically, this quickness to accommodate had a down side. Bernice was so speedy that her slower-moving older sister had begun to complain that she never had a chance to help, and her little brother complained that she was always doing things for him when he wanted to do them for himself. These had been very minor issues, easily dealt with, and Bernice had accommodated. In our ratings at that time, we had considered Bernice to have a good fit at school and at home.

When Bernice had moved into school age, in the elementary school years, she had experienced the usual interactions. She and her classmates experimented with pushing limits, evading rules, being rude, and picking on other children who were easy targets. With hindsight it could now be seen that Bernice had more than a tendency to go with the flow. Being bright intellectually, she was one of those children whose hand was up almost before the teacher had finished explaining, and her answers were usually correct. She was part of the most popular class group. And she rarely repeated a behavior for which she had been admonished. But in re-examining events, it seemed that her parents had sought advice from us about Bernice more often than they had about their two other children, who were also members of the NYLS. The sibs, it appeared, seemed to have incorporated family mores into their behavior to a greater extent than had Bernice—and they also seemed less demanding of constant praise and recognition for simple every day actions of courtesy. Nevertheless, in general, during middle childhood, Bernice's interactions seemed to demonstrate a good fit with the demands and expectations of her environment. She was learning well, had a group of friends, was happy, and seemed to have positive self-esteem. At the time, this was developmentally appropriate and the positive aspects of her high adaptability were on the ascendance.

It was at adolescence that Bernice's temperamental qualities began to demonstrate their negative potential. What had been such an asset in learning social behavior, her high adaptability now began to take on chameleon-like characteristics. Intrigued by a small group of girls at her private school who had begun to skip class, Bernice joined them. The initiation of this set of circumstances had been at age thirteen. At first, this did not reflect upon her grades because of her high intelligence. The group would show up in the morning to be recorded as present, then often spend the day wandering about the city. Exactly what they did, the school was never certain. In order to cover up, they became increasingly more ingenious. Bernice seemingly did not have her own yardstick of appropriate behavior. The most worrisome part of this period was that she had not been troubled in her conscience. The approval of these companions was enough for her adolescent adaptive needs. To the best of our ability to recapitulate the events, there had been no desire to get back at parents for being strict, Bernice did not dislike learning itself, and there seemed to be no deep motivation for turning against family and school values. The only discernible pattern was accidental, chance-determined opportunities and the fact that Bernice had been able to

cover over successfully, and hence had not been called to account before the behavior had escalated toward serious consequences. The timing of events was a particular tragedy. The first spate of truancy at age
thirteen had occurred prior to Bernice's father's death and seemed, at
that time, to have been contrary to the full pattern of her behavior. It
had been dealt with by discussion and a period of grounding, and had
been judged by the parents as part of growing up—equivalent to events
they recalled from memories of their own pasts. After all, she was only
thirteen. Whether Bernice would have been more restrained now at age
fifteen, were her father still alive, cannot be known.

Faced with her own grief and the economic needs of the family, the
mother was unable to bring about change. Mrs. S. appealed to me
(A.T.), and I arranged for regular sessions of psychotherapy with her.
My treatment was basically supportive. I also gave her a number of suggestions that might change Bernice's behaviors. She accepted my ideas
and tried them, but all failed. Bernice's response to all attempted intervention was either stonewalling or hysterical shouting that no one ever
believed her. One dramatic night, when her mother, awakened by a
noise, found a naked young man going to the bathroom, Bernice
shouted her mantra, "You never believe me!" Recalling that she had,
several times, found the door off the latch in the morning, Mrs. S. realized now that Bernice had been bringing her sexual adventures into the
house itself.

An evaluation was now planned with a view toward arranging psychotherapy for Bernice. She had previously recalled meetings with in-
terviewers throughout her childhood and these had always been
pleasant. But in this tempestuous situation, she came to my psychiatric
interview with great suspicion. Requests to learn her own point of view
were unavailing. She sat stone-faced. Her only comment was, "You are
on her side." There was "no problem." Everything was "lies." The school
was against her, her mother was against her. It had taken several years
for the situation to escalate from her thirteen-year old school cutting to
her serious 16-year old indiscretions. On two separate occasions when
Bernice had insisted that no one at home was sympathetic, the mother
had initiated treatment with psychotherapists who were specialists in
treating teenagers. In both attempts it soon became clear that Bernice
was not interested. Either she failed to keep appointments, or she used
them to list grievances, but avoided any discussion of her own feelings
or motives. Now there were frequent screaming matches at home. The
older sister was about to go off to college. The younger brother begged
to go to boarding school so as to have some serenity and be able to see
his friends without worrying that he would be embarrassed by his sister's combativeness. Mrs. S. now was concerned for the well-being of

these children. It seemed that no intervention would change Bernice's functioning.

The focus now changed to the needs of the family members. The mother now realized that the two other children were being sacrificed to Bernice's behavior without this helping Bernice herself. Mother's own emotional state was also at risk. She was torn at her children's distress, she was exhausted, and was having difficulty maintaining her work status; she was depressed. With each of Bernice's new misdeeds, mother tried to keep calm. She could neither tolerate Bernice's behavior as acceptable nor could she ignore it.

After the basically unsatisfactory therapeutic sessions with Bernice, I decided to pose mother with the one possible solution. "Mrs. S., when Bernice reaches the age of 18, legally you can end your responsibility for her. Tell her this, and give her a choice. If she changes her behavior by the time she is 18, you will be happy to have her continue to live at home as a pleasant member of the family. If she doesn't change, when she is 18, she will have to leave home, find her own living place, and get a job to earn enough to be independent financially."

The mother gasped at me, "How can you suggest that? Bernice is not trained for anything, and also, on her own, God knows what terrible things she would do." I nodded, "I won't call it brutal, but it is a gamble. There is the risk, as you just mentioned, that she might not be able to cope with such a sudden, severe demand, and her leaving might lead to some disastrous outcome. However, nothing else has helped, and, if she stays at home after 18, unchanged, you and your other children's lives at home will continue to be perpetually disrupted. You only have to wait two years, and if Bernice is away and on her own, you can achieve a degree of patience and hopefulness."

Mrs. S. thought quietly, then nodded, "It is brutal, but, as you said, there is no alternative. Let's see what happens."

At the next session, the following week, Mrs. S. walked in a little more bravely. She reported, "When I left your office, I decided that if we did that plan, I would start it now. That evening, I talked to Bernice about my legal responsibility ending in two years, and if she didn't change she would have to leave here and make her way in life on her own. I thought she would shriek at me but, to my amazement, she was silent, and left for her own room. Nothing has changed since, except now I have had only a few confrontations with her, saying to myself, 'I only have two years.'"

In the succeeding two years, no basic change happened. The mother entangled less with Bernice, but her behavior didn't change and she never referred to this ultimatum. At the fateful 18th birthday, her mother told Bernice she had to leave, she packed, gave her mother, sister, and brother a cold good-bye and left.

Bernice found an apartment and job as soon as she left. She wrote a note to her mother with her address and telephone number.

Mrs. S. reported the situation very regularly. Bernice was indeed surviving on her own, and the mother and children began to experience a peaceful, pleasant life together without Bernice. The son and daughter began their careers, Mrs. S. quickly began to lose her demoralized and burdened feelings, worked and socialized actively, and after some years, married happily.

As to Bernice, our next comprehensive NYLS follow-up was scheduled and I contacted her when she was 22 and, *mirabile dictu,* she immediately and pleasantly consented to have an interview. We set up an appointment quickly. She gave a cheery greeting with a bright smile and made a charming appearance. She responded to each question with animated, relevant replies. As to her adolescent antisocial behavior she said, "I was the one who would run out of the house at 4:00 a.m., steal from my mother's purse, I cut classes. I did a lot of bad things, then, but I was ready to blame others. Now I take all the responsibility on myself." She was now self-supporting, self-reliant, and through her own initiative was launched on training toward a career which absorbed her. Her social relationships were active and positive. Her relationship with her mother, sister, and brother however was distant, though superficially friendly. Her mother in a separate interview confirmed all this.

I asked Bernice how she explained this dramatic positive change from adolescence. When her mother made her leave home when she was 18, "It was brutal but it worked. I went down a little, floundered for two years, worked in a bar." Then she mobilized herself, drew on her interest and talents in photography, applied for professional training to a top institute, and went through her training successfully. With luck and the help of a friend of her father's, she obtained her first job with a prestigious photographic studio. She had been doing well and was just promoted. At this time, there was a good fit of her talents, motivations, training, temperamental qualities, and environmental opportunities.

But Bernice was by no means entirely out of her psychological woods. Her self-image was quite ambivalent, her heterosexual relationships did not involve any clear intimate feelings, and she was very vague as to the basic factors in her own characteristics that had produced her prior, admittedly horrendous, antisocial behavior. She refused to consider seeking psychotherapeutic help for current psychological problems. Her self-image was quite ambivalent. She spoke positively of her talents, of "feeling on top of everything," when working. On the other hand, she emphasized her "insecurity," and still "disliked" herself at times. She had a number of heterosexual experiences, without any sexual problems as such, but without any sense of emotional closeness. She felt on guard, "didn't want to be out of control, didn't want the heartaches of a relationship." It was my impression that Bernice's further maturity was a toss-up. If her career were to blossom and she was lucky to meet the right man who stimulated her positive feelings, fine. But if she were to go along on the same level, adapted but precarious, her further outcome might go downhill.

I contacted Mrs. S. about six years later for our next scheduled NYLS follow-up, since I could not reach Bernice. Her mother's account was discouraging. About four years before, when Bernice was 24, she had begun an affair with a glamorous athletic star with a reputation as a womanizer. With that affair, Bernice spent a great deal of her time hanging around him, and quit her photographic career. Sadly, but predictably, the athlete treated her shabbily and contemptuously, maintaining this affair up to date, along with several others. Bernice drifted along with odd jobs, kept herself very distant, from her family, and discouraged her sibs' several attempts to try to establish a real relationship with her. Occasional word from Mrs. S. indicated that Bernice continued to be self-sufficient, distant, and uninterested in the lives of her sibs and mother. Once again, Bernice had adapted uncritically to the mores of the immediate environment, apparently ready to interpret absence of censure as if it were acceptance.

Case 3: Normal Boy and Parents with Tragic Outcome

Howard was born in an exceptional and fortunate family. The father was a famous writer with a number of best sellers, the mother had a successful career as an interior designer. The older son had a brilliant academic record in high school, was talented in mathematics and computing, and was accepted to an elite college where he intended to train toward a computer career.

The family was closely-knit and harmonious with high moral and ethical standards. Despite their busy careers, both parents were resolved to making it a high priority to give their sons their affection, attention, interest, and support.

As to Howard, he developed happily and profitably in this atmosphere and achieved a goodness of fit. As he grew through childhood and early adolescence it gradually appeared that his intellectual ability or any specific talents were average compared to his parents and brother. Howard was a "nice boy" but became more and more unhappy at the widening gap of accomplishment compared to the rest of his family. The parents recognized this problem and devoted themselves to giving Howard every encouragement and support they could. But the facts were invariable, and all of the parents' efforts failed. Howard plodded along through school with an average grade and no talents, followed all the rules of the family's routine, living mechanically, and became more and more despondent. Howard was truly the "ugly duckling" of the family. The parents watched his self-denigrating feelings grow and decided that treatment by a good psychiatrist would be his best and last chance. One of their good friends recommended me (A.T.) and the appointment was arranged. Howard's reported comment was "If my parents want me to see the doctor I'll come, but it won't help me."

When he came to his first appointment, Howard presented himself as a tall, well groomed 16-year old boy, well dressed, with a pleasant appearance, but with clearly expressed depression in his face, voice, and body. He willingly gave his point of view: "I am the only failure in my family. They have tried to help me, they are wonderful people, but it's no use. What future can I have? I have no talents, and I'm not smart enough to achieve a real career." "How about athletics?" I asked. He laughed bitterly. "It's the same story. I like sports, my parents encourage me, have arranged all kinds of lessons, but I'm still average, and I'll never become a real athlete."

I wanted to start Howard with an appropriate anti-depressant drug, but he refused. "It won't help, and the one good thing, I'm determined to never become a drug addict."

I treated Howard's depression for a year for two sessions a week. He always came on time, answered questions politely, but the sessions were a complete failure. In our discussions, Howard's reference point was his family's standards and ambitions and his failure to have the capacity to meet these. He was unable to identify his own desires. He was aware that his parents would back him in any endeavor directed toward his own goal. But Howard's self-awareness of his averageness predominated. In conferences with his parents it was clear that, despite their desire to give Howard support, there was an assumption that superior functioning was their standard. Tragically, six months later, Howard was driving his car on an icy highway, skidded, and crashed on a post, fatally. An accident or suicide, we never knew.

I often think of Howard ironically. He was born into a special family, with apparent great fortune, but it turned into a disastrous poorness of fit. If he had been born into a stable, lower middle-class family, with a father with a routine civil service job, a mother also of average talents, and with sibs who were average academically, Howard could have lived happily and successfully in that kind of family, with goodness of fit, and with a modest but satisfactory life course.

Case 4: Girl with Social Problem and Favorable Outcome

One November, Mr. and Mrs. R. requested an urgent consultation about an adolescent daughter. She had been accused by her school of several serious offenses, including setting a fire while smoking in the lavatory. She had also been cutting school, and receiving failing grades. With the family's four children enrolled in our study, and all of them now in or past adolescence, I (S.C.) had considerable awareness of the family atmosphere and the children's development. The girl, Laura, who was the subject of this consultation, had not previously needed any clinical attention, nor had her sibs. Minor needs for advice had occurred, and these had been solved in a cooperative fashion. The parents were astounded at these recent offenses, and could not believe Laura to be capable of such actions. Mrs. R. reacted with outraged indignation, ready to attack the school for lying, while her husband, equally supportive of his daughter, had been clear that these uncharacteristic actions had actually occurred.

Laura was new in this school, since the family had recently moved from Paris. They had timed the move so that all the children would start their new schools in the fall term. Laura had previously been a good scholar, had had a group of friends at the American School in Paris, and had seemed to participate in the family move without distress. They had not been aware of any difficulties prior to this cataclysmic event.

The R. family was closely knit, particularly so because of the many family moves. Mr. R., a businessman, worked for a multinational company as a trouble-shooter who was sent to subsidiary units whenever they had problems. Periodically, this resulted in his spending several years in a European country, and the entire family was relocated. The children attended the American schools, and previously they had adapted. The teaching seemed to have continuity, and making friends had not been a problem. Laura, now fifteen, had two older sisters, an older brother, and a younger sister. The children had minor squabbles but basically got along well and served as a social base for each other. However, now the family had moved to Connecticut. The other siblings had transitioned smoothly into school and made friends as before. Laura had had slight misgivings. She had remarked that, in Europe, many of her classmates were also new, having similar mobile families, but here the members of the class seemed to have been friends from kindergarten. However, after a week, Laura had apparently made some friends and had said everything was OK. Her mother, a housewife, heard Laura talking on the phone often with friends and assumed that all her children were now adapted to life in their current locale.

The fire incident had been dramatic. Suddenly, the building was filled with acrid smoke; it was evacuated and the fire department tracked the fire to the school bathroom where a vinyl toilet seat had caught on fire. The investigation was a serious one, and the school had concluded that Laura and Laura alone was the culprit. The school's report was that Laura had started the year as a good student, then had begun to cut classes in company with two other girls, often wandering around town together, and that her work assignments were often not handed in. On the day of the fire, the three girls had been in the lavatory smoking when they heard a teacher coming. The cigarettes had been tossed into the toilets, but a paper towel had caught on fire and ignited a toilet seat. In the interrogation that followed, Laura had owned up to her actions, but the other two girls stated their total innocence and blamed the incident entirely on Laura. The school authorities accepted this as the official account. The school psychologist had then tested Laura, both with an intelligence test and with projective tests. Her IQ was well above average. The projective tests were interpreted by the psychologist as abnormal, and psychiatric treatment was recommended. Later, I learned in my talks with Laura that she had taken the tests still thinking the situation to be a tempest that would blow over. On the advice of her "friends," she had given some responses intended to be funny, which were the basis of the pathological conclusion.

I now interviewed Laura who, by this time, was thoroughly frightened. She was aware that her family—not only her parents but her sibs as well—was on her side, and felt that she had been made a victim. All agreed that her actions had been wrong.

Because Laura saw me as a friend of the family and had been aware of the NYLS interviews as benign events, it was not difficult to establish rapport with her. As discussions proceeded, it turned out that Laura had not coped with the family's previous moves as well as had her sibs. Always shy, she had taken a long time with each change to feel comfortable. Different from her gregarious sibs, she tried to hide her discomfort from her parents. However, as she had moved toward adolescence, she had found each family dislocation harder to tolerate. She had tried to keep in touch with her former friends by letter but had soon realized that her life was no longer important to them. Finally, in an effort to protect herself, she stayed away from the girls she saw as potential friends in her Connecticut school in order to protect herself from the next family move. It had not occurred to her to discuss these feelings with her parents in any depth, since when she had brought up her timidity in the past, she had been met by exhortations to change her own behavior. Laura had concluded that she was abnormal in her shyness.

Reviewing Laura's NYLS records, I found that she had been slow to warm up, but sociable. In her early school grades and in early family moves, her parents and her older sibs had been aware of her need for more time to familiarize herself than the other children, and this need had been heeded. But with so many family moves completed, all assumed that each family member, including Laura, was now accomplished at the techniques needed to integrate themselves into each new social situation. Out of synchronization with the rest, Laura hid her unhappiness. It had never occurred to her that periodic family upheavals could be stopped. In this final move, Laura had avoided those to whom she might become attached and let herself be caught up into activity with girls she did not like much. The agenda of activities had been theirs. Unused to their values, she had no self-protection; she trusted them as she trusted her family. She was naïve. She adapted to their standards, but with private dismay.

It now was appropriate to review my diagnosis with Laura's parents. Laura gave me her permission to reveal her personal feelings to her parents. She correctly anticipated that her mother would be hurt by Laura's failure to confide in her. I reviewed with Mr. and Mrs. R. the discussion as it has been given above. Both parents concurred that Laura's behavior had been neither intentional nor malicious. There was suspicion that the school had allowed the student outsider to take blame that also should have been given to the other two. But Laura was our concern. Mr. R was particularly focused on his new awareness that, as an adolescent, Laura's shyness and depth of relationships had a greater impact than in earlier childhood. While Mrs. R., a highly outspoken woman, struggled with this changed concept of her daughter's inner life, Mr. R. had immediate empathy. He could easily understand her reactions and immediately turned his mind toward a solution. After brief thought, Mr. R. declared, "At this point, I have the position in the company to make decisions as to how I could be deployed. In any case, the needs of my family have priority." Turning to his wife, he asked whether she agreed with him on that score. With her enthusiastic assent, the first action toward social and environmental goodness of fit with Laura's needs had been taken. Laura could now be assured that any friendships she formed would not be abruptly terminated by family upheaval. This was also a parental statement to Laura that they considered her personality and preferences to be normal. The setting for her personal self-awareness, her own self-approval and self-esteem, and the task of re-establishing her in her adolescent community could be begun.

Mr. R. now addressed himself to a fuller comprehension of the genesis of Laura's crisis of behavior. Why, he wondered, were the other children able to accommodate to and even thrive on the nomadic life-style and not Laura? The temperamental features involved were that Laura was prone to withdraw from new situations and to accommodate and adapt slowly. When she did form attachments, they had always been intense. While she was not a screamer, it was well known to family and friends that her loyalties were intense, her dislikes were deep, and her promises were unbreakable. These were the qualities that had led to her suffering, and these were the qualities that had led to her silence about this suffering. Continuing psychotherapy with me was arranged.

Then I suggested to Mr. and Mrs. R. another possible problem for Laura that we needed to anticipate. "Depending on the kind of school, a good teacher and principal will accept my report and recommendations, and welcome Laura back to school with pleasure. Given time, the other students will recognize her good qualities. I am sure that she will gradually make new good friendships, and there should be smooth sailing. But if the teacher and principal reinstate Laura reluctantly and suspiciously, and do not really accept my findings fully, they may subtly communicate a negative judgment of Laura to the other students, and she might easily become a scapegoat. Unfortunately, I have seen that happen at some schools. You and I have to promise Laura that if the staff or the students are beginning to treat her unfairly, both of us will pitch in to defend her. I know from my contacts with you that you can be a very determined person." Mr. R. laughed, "Thank you, Dr. Chess, for bringing up that possible problem. If it happens, I know my wife, and she will tear that school apart."

I had a last appointment with Laura several weeks later. She came in glowing, "My father has arranged his work so he doesn't have to travel again. My principal and psychologist got your report, and reinstated me at once. I am now determined to get to the top of the class with my school grades. I am avoiding those nasty girls like the plague, and I already have met a very nice girl with the same interests who is a good student. Everything is fine, but if something does go wrong, though I'm sure nothing will, I will tell my mother." In the three follow-up appointments at monthly intervals, Laura and her mother reported a continued positive course.

We did a routine follow-up of the NYLS subjects after eight years. Laura had had no further problem in high school. She was now teaching at a good nursing school, married, and expecting her baby in two months.

☐ Comments

There are many factors responsible for serious behavioral problems in adolescence: the childhood development of severely traumatized dysfunctional families; child abuse and incest; severely impoverished families; communities and schools; temptations for delinquency; alcohol and illegal drug abuse and trade; unemployment and racism, and so on. The studies of any one of these issues could fill books, and have.

However, we have chosen four cases without risk factors, with similar positive background and childhood lives, but with a wide diversity in behavioral disturbances and outcomes. In these cases, we have been able to illustrate the variety of environmental expectations and stresses in the adolescent age-period. Grace, Bernice, Howard, and Laura all grew up within stable middle-class families, had supportive parents, similar goals for their academic and social success, and an absence of any specific substantial traumatic childhood or pre-adolescent experiences.

Yet, the four adolescents were all unable to cope with specific, age-appropriate, unhealthy environmental influences, resulting in idiosyncratic unhealthy behavioral patterns. Of those that had psychotherapy, one was successful (Grace), and two were failures (Bernice and Howard). One (Laura) required minimal therapy along with parental counseling.

Grace and Laura had successful outcomes in their adult lives. Bernice dramatically improved after her mother's drastic action at 18, but her lifestyle was highly unstable in her twenties and thirties (we have no information on her life beyond her thirties). Howard's problems became the focus of parental mobilization. Keeping the inner drama of his struggle to accept his own awareness to himself, Howard made a point of honor to struggle alone with his depression. Was his tragic outcome accident or suicide?

To conclude, we have presented a diversity of behavioral difficulties and levels of ability to cope with environmental stresses. These four adolescent children are illustrations of a range of problems of fit with the demands of the environment.

☐ Adolescent Turmoil

Bernice and Laura could have been characterized by the traditional term "adolescent turmoil." Depression in adolescence (an example is Howard), can also be considered as a symptomatic expression of turmoil.

Traditionally, both in popular and professional writings, adolescence has been viewed as a period of marked emotional upheaval and turmoil arising from rapid physical changes, the onset of adult sexuality, and the expectation for increased responsibility within the family combined with beginning autonomy in functioning. This view was stated vividly by G. Stanley Hall in his classic volume on adolescence in 1904: "The teens are emotionally unstable and pathic. It is a natural impulse to experience hot and perfervid psychic states, and it is characterized by emotionalism" (1904, p. 74). This concept was further developed in the psychoanalytic literature, in which adolescence has been viewed as a period of emotional lability and instability, in which the upholding of a steady equilibrium would in itself be abnormal (Blos, 1979; Eissler, 1958; A. Freud, 1960). The psychoanalytic formulations have been summarized by the Offers: "Psychoanalytic theory describes adolescence as a time of psychological imbalance, when the functioning of ego and superego are severely strained. Instinctual impulses disrupt the homeostatic arrangements achieved during latency, and inner turmoil results, manifesting itself by rebellious or deviant behavior, mood swings, or affective lability. Unresolved preoedipal or oedipal conflicts are revived; the repression characteristic of latency is no longer sufficient to restore a psychological equilibrium . . . The physical, muscular, and hormonal growth of the adolescent endows the rearoused drives with a potency denied to the former child and frightening to the developing adolescent" (Offer & Offer, 1975, p. 161). The psychoanalytic view of adolescence as a period of turmoil was further extended by Erikson's influential concept of the "identity crises" of adolescence (Erikson, 1959, p. 116).

These psychoanalytic formulations have been derived primarily from data obtained from adolescent or adult patients suffering from one or another psychopathological syndrome. Thus, the Offers point out that "Erikson does not present examples of healthy and adaptive adolescence. Surely, examples of true 'normative' crises ought to come from others than patients, exceptional individuals, and fictional or biographical profiles. These are the adolescents with whom Erikson has had contact, and they then circularly support the theory that he has spun based on his experience with them" (Offer & Offer, 1975, p. 163).

Indeed, the studies of unselected groups of adolescents do provide a different picture of this developmental stage. Rutter's comprehensive and systematic review of the pertinent literature came to a clear judgment: "It is also evident that normal adolescence is *not* characterized by storm, stress, and disturbance. Most young people go through their teenage years without significant emotional or behavioral problems. It is true that there are challenges to be met, adaptations to be made, and stresses to be coped with. However, these do not all arise at the same time and most adolescents deal with these issues without undue disturbance" (Rutter, 1979, p. 86). Similarly, the Offers (1975), in a study of 73 middle-class, Midwestern adolescent males, found that 23 percent were characterized by smooth, continuous progression and 35 percent by alternating periods of spurts and leveling-off in their development, though functioning as adaptively as the continuous growth group. Only 21 percent of the group could be characterized as tumultuous, with substantial internal turmoil that manifested itself in overt behavioral conflicts at home and in school.

In addition, most of the NYLS subjects confounded the stereotype of adolescent turmoil. The new demands of adolescence, whether social, sexual, academic, or work-related, were mastered constructively with expansion of their horizons, interests, and activities. Stress and tension may have accompanied their responses to these new challenges, but not excessive stress requiring evasions, retreats, or other defensive maneuvers. Symptoms of behavior disturbance were conspicuous by their absence. The changes in the youngsters' self-image and self-expectations, stimulated by physical maturation and the knowledge that they were entering a transition period between childhood and adulthood, were both exciting, but not threatening. By and large, these were the youngsters who had sailed through childhood in the same constructive fashion. On entering adolescence, they had a firm foundation of self-esteem, healthy behavioral patterns, positive relationships to family and peers, and effective coping mechanisms, which they then brought to bear on the challenges and demands of this new and more complex developmental stage.

☐ Overview

Many adolescents succeed in coping with the new demands and pressures of that age period. Some cannot. The histories of Grace, Bernice, Howard, and Laura emphasize anew the fallacy of applying any unidimentional theoretical or treatment model to this or any life-span period.

Adulthood

The discussions of goodness of fit in the previous chapters have indicated straightforward developmental age-periods. Infancy, the toddler period, middle childhood, and adolescence have in common a clearly identified progression of developmental evolution in regard to biological maturation, increasingly complex environmental demands and opportunities, and crystallizing motives and goals.

Adulthood, that age-period stretching from the twenties to the eighties or nineties, presents a host of differences and complexities in the person–environment interactions in individuals' experiences and abilities to adapt. Some of the adulthood issues are discussed in the two following chapters on Personality Development and Biopsychosocial Model.

The discussions and clinical case examples in these chapters still only illustrate a fraction of the many issues with which adults cope during their life course: work and career, aging, lifestyle, tragedies with family and close friends, community and political activities, financial contingencies, power struggles, and more. All of these may be pertinent to the application of the goodness of fit concept.

In this chapter, we have decided to focus on work and career. Work is a central expectation of many, if not most, adults. The three cases in this chapter indicate some aspects of the complexity of work concerns of adults.

☐ Case 1: Transitions

In late 1946, I (A.T.) was referred a young adult, Mr. Robert D., with symptoms of severe anxiety. Age twenty-seven, he was of medium height and athletic build, was neatly dressed, well groomed, with a pleasant face which was distorted by visibly tight muscles. His voice was clear and soft with a slight tremble. As he sat, his posture was rigid and his fingers were clenched. He clearly was suffering from severe anxiety.

Bob answered all questions promptly, appropriately, and objectively. I was able quickly to obtain a comprehensive chronological story of his life's history.

His father was a skilled worker, both parents were affectionate and responsible in caring for their three children, of whom Bob was the oldest. The family was stable, economically modest, and without any financial or other crises as Bob grew up. He did well in public school and had an active social group of congenial friends in his community. His parents encouraged his educational efforts and, because of his family's financial limitations, Bob went to the free New York City College. He picked history as his major, but had no clear goal for his work career. His college grades were good but not spectacular, and he always worked part-time in simple office jobs to contribute to his family's finances.

He joined the ROTC college unit voluntarily and enrolled each subsequent year. He explained that in the mid- and late thirties the political future of Europe was ominous, and posed a possible threat to war even for our country, and he was certainly right. The war exploded on December 7, 1941, when he was expecting to satisfy his last courses in the spring term and graduate. With the army services mobilizing, as a reserve lieutenant he was called into active service in March. With that, he was assigned by random selection to a huge quartermaster army base. Bob was highly motivated to do his patriotic duty to the country, and plunged into his duties and assignments at the base. He learned quickly, demonstrated high reliability and responsibility, was promoted to captain, and given increasingly demanding duties at which he was invariably successful.

His next stop in his military career was his transfer to the American quartermaster unit based in England, preparing for the final D-Day invasion into France. The American quartermaster base was commanded by a General Roger M., who had been highly successful in civilian life building an extensive, powerful corporate system, and also had friendships among many political and military officials in the government. Mr. M. offered his services out of his own burning desire to win the war. His government friends eagerly accepted his offer; there were not many army officers with Mr. M.'s abilities, and he was appointed as chief of the quartermaster service, with the rank of General.

Bob was chosen for his transfer to England as part of the effort to build up the expanding American base with a cadre of talented and experienced officers. With his superior's high recommendation, Bob found himself a member of General M.'s staff. With this opportunity, Bob worked strenuously and capably and soon came to the General's attention. Bob was given increasingly important tasks, always successfully accomplished, and General M. was impressed by his abilities. The war went on, with Bob's successes and General M.'s confidence in him escalating, until the Axis powers were vanquished in August 1945. In a few weeks the General called Bob in. The army was now beginning to demobilize. Within several weeks, General M. planned to return to civilian life and take charge of his companies. Looking at Bob he asked, "You are scheduled to return to civilian life in a month or two. What are your plans?" Bob was taken aback, and blurted out, "I was too busy to think about my future. My one goal is to get my college degree." General M. smiled, "I can tell you, I have watched your work and I am impressed by your intelligence, how you learn quickly, and your great reliability and administrative ability. You are just the right kind of young person who could become a real asset as a staff member of one of my companies. I suggest that when you come back to New York, as a civilian, that you make an appointment at my New York office, and I will set you up for a promising position."

As Bob told me, "I was stunned. I was given a precious opportunity to break in the right way into the business world. I thanked the General, and said I'd come up to his office as soon as possible."

As soon as Bob was discharged, he arranged a meeting. Mr. M. introduced Bob to William K., a senior executive, "This is Bob, whom I found to be such a great asset for the company. Bill, I'll turn Bob over to you. Find a good promising spot for him, and get him started." Bill smiled and said "Mr. M. never gave such a great recommendation before, and I'm expecting to find you valuable for the company. Let's get started." Bill took me on a quick tour of the eight floors, introduced me to many of the managers in different areas, and then said, "It occurs to me that we just have a vacancy in the supply department, I know you are experienced from your quartermaster service, and you can start there." The supply chief, David I., was introduced to Bob. Bill explained Mr. M's recommendation and suggested that Bob start to work, which he did.

Bob worked industriously, became familiar with the company's routines, and also enrolled in evening college to complete his courses for graduation. "For almost three months everything was fine, and suddenly, there came what I can only call disaster. I was called to Bill's office, and met with him and David. Bill started immediately, "Bob, I can't believe it, but David has just reported that you made a serious, careless error in your accounts." I was stunned, "I've never made such an error before, I can't believe it." Bill shook his head, "David showed me the error, and both of us agreed that if you were more careful your work would be OK."

"I was shocked, I did all my work, checked and triple checked, and after a few weeks I relaxed. But after two weeks, I was hit again with the same disaster. Bill called me in; David sat there, and charged me with a similar mistake. Bill warned me that this was my last chance, and if it happened again he would have to report to Mr. M. and recommend that I be discharged.

"I was devastated. Something must be wrong with me; I'm terrified that I will make another mistake, and here I am." I did a standard mental status check, and a neurological examination. All the findings were negative.

I said to him that there were three possible explanations for his two serious mistakes at work:

"The first possibility is that you have contracted some medical or neurological disease that is affecting your mental functioning. Bob, in my observations of your speech and behavior, and my careful mental status examination, I have found no evidence of any disturbance of your mental functioning. To check further, you have been attending your college courses. Have you had any problems with them?" Bob shook his head violently, "My courses are a breeze, I'm getting all A's with them so far."

"The second possibility is that you may have found difficulty with learning the company's procedures and rules, and have just not learned enough yet to prevent such mistakes." He burst out, "That's not possible. The supply system was really simple. I learned it within a few weeks, and I have doubled and even tripled my procedures. I had to learn the complicated army quartermaster rules in the army—some were tough, but I learned them quickly and never made a mistake."

"Then, if we rule out the first two possibilities, there is another answer. You have made no mistakes, but Bill and David have ganged up on you deliberately for some reason." Bob was shocked. "How could that be possible? Both of them always acted to me in a friendly way and praised my conscientious work. Why would they undermine and threaten me now?" I commented, "You have never had any previous personal experience in the business world. It's a cliché, but true, that the business world can sometimes be a real jungle."

I asked Bob whether he had any real friends among the company staff. "Then pick one or two potential friends, go to lunch or dinner with each one, tell your story, and ask what kind of people Bill and David are. That's your assignment."

Bob was startled, "I still can't believe it, but I'll do what you tell me to do. Actually I can already pick two reliable and honest friends."

Bob came back for his next appointment the following week. When he walked in, his anxious appearance had disappeared, but he was shocked and angry. As soon as he sat down, he burst out with a nasty story. "I spoke to Kenneth, who had worked in that office for 15 years, had a busy and relaxed appearance, and was always ready to talk in brief casual and friendly chitchats. He had never been drafted in the army because of some mild physical handicap, and felt a little guilty compared to my service record.

"I talked to Kenneth, told him I had a problem in the office, asked if he could advise me, maybe go to dinner and discuss it. He said 'Sure,' and we arranged for dinner that evening. Once we sat down in the restaurant, I told Kenneth the story of my mistakes with Bill and David, and their threat. That kind of thing had never happened to me before. What's happened to me?

"Kenneth listened carefully, sat back, thought for a moment and then burst out, 'Bill and David are sons of bitches, real monsters. You are the fair-headed Mr. M.'s protégé, you're clearly smart and a highly reliable worker, and you are a threat to them. Bill and David are competent, but are no great shakers, and in five years you could very well be promoted over the two of them. There was another case like yours, about 6 to 7 years ago. Mr. M. had a nephew, a bright, attractive young man, whom he set up with a beginning career in a job in the supply department. Just as with you, Bill and David concocted 'evidence' of the poor nephew's 'serious mistakes,' and threatened to report this to his uncle. The young man was crushed, told his uncle he could not get interested in the business world, and resigned. As I remember, the nephew went into some academic field."

"What about you, Kenneth, how have you survived so well?" I asked him. Kenneth laughed, told me that a kind, elderly man, who was retiring, warned him to watch out for Bill and David. 'I watched their maneuvers and got solid evidence that the two of them were conniving and stealing money from the company. So, when they called me in to charge me with incompetence, I interrupted them, told them I had investigated them, and had collected a whole series of records proving that both of them were stealing. 'I'll give you a choice,' I told them. 'Either you stop harassing me, give me good reports to the boss, and give me my regular salary increases and bonuses, and I will just leave the records in my safe deposit box. Otherwise, if you try to discredit me, I will bring my records to Mr. M.' They have never bothered me, and I now work in peace."

Bob looked to me, "I got furious when I found out the truth, but I couldn't follow Kenneth's example. I'd have to live in such a corrupt and dirty atmosphere and live with the Bills and Davids of the world."

I nodded, "Bob, knowing you, I'm not surprised at your decision." He called in Bill and David, told them he had discovered their thievery, that he was resigning, and that he would not fight with them about their thievery if they gave him a good recommendation. He would just thank Mr. M. and tell him that he had decided to change to a different kind of career. He gave two weeks' notice, said good-bye, and walked out of their office. "And that was that."

We then explored the kinds of careers Bob could enjoy. With the GI Bill of Rights, he could get tuition and financial support, especially with his service record. Determined not to make a hasty decision, Bob reviewed his army functioning. He realized that during the war when he was an officer working with large numbers of enlisted men and women, many would come to him for help or advice with some personal problem. He always listened sympathetically, and found the answer for most of them and helped them. "I felt good during the war; I was useful, not only to my country, but also to the individual soldiers whom I helped. In the business world, I might become rich, but not at the cost of living in a jungle, as you put it.

"I've decided to become a social worker. I will finish my credits at college in a month, get my degree, and apply for social work training at one of the good schools. My parents and friends approve of my choice."

Five years later, I received an important gift, a visit from Bob. The door opened, there was Bob, with a shining face, walking in together with an attractive young woman. "I have to introduce Mary, we've been married for a year, and she's a great graduate student." I hugged both of them. "I came in to tell you I have a good position at an excellent community center, and I'm enjoying every day." And Mary chimed in, telling Bob, "And everybody respects you, and you have been promoted already."

As in the case of Frank, which follows later in this chapter, Bob's anxiety had been focused initially on his work situation but had gradually spread until he found himself full of self-doubt about his functioning in general. This was in contrast to his previous experiences. He had gotten into a free college on merit and simultaneously managed to work part-time to help the finances of his working class family. Drafted into the army a brief while before graduation, Bob had turned his random assignment into a successful work situation. This in turn had led to a civilian job in business which he undertook at an unexpectedly high level. But now, seeming incompetence bedeviled him. He could neither dispute the charges of accounting errors leveled by his friendly superiors, nor could he find and eliminate the cause of his seeming malfunctioning. Where action had heretofore always assured success, now the path to remedial action was impenetrable. Hence, his massive anxiety, demoralization, and call for help.

Clearly there was some area of poor fit. At the onset of this psychiatric investigation, there were no pointers; the symptoms were global in nature. The psychiatric investigation at this point was akin to a patient coming to an internist and reporting general malaise and dizziness.

The nature of the poor fit, given these summary facts, was obscure. It had been necessary to review Bob's entire life in order to identify the probable area of poor fit.

☐ Comment

This vignette sounds like a soap opera, but it was all true. I picked this case to illustrate how the goodness or poorness of fit can result from unexpected patterns and transformations which can occur in the life course of an individual's differing involvement in work.

☐ Some Examples of the Significance of Work for a Good or Poor Fit

Most young adults face having to decide on a career choice for the future. Some individuals are fortunate in having their interests and talents clearly decided. They can cope effectively with the environmental demands and opportunities to succeed in launching a career of their preferred choice. Their motivations and talents are compatible with the demands and opportunities provided by the environment.

Several examples will highlight the diversity of the character or change of the nature of the fit.

☐ Clinical Vignettes

Case 2: Change in Career Choice

Jeffrey K, one of our NYLS subjects, matured from infancy to adult life with positive personal characteristics, successful in family, school, and social life, and never showed any evidence of behavior disorder. In early adolescence he became interested in music, selected the clarinet as his instrument, pursued his musical training consistently as one major subject of his college undergraduate courses, and then was accepted as a graduate clarinet student at one of the leading musical institutes. When I came to do our routine early adult follow-up, Jeffrey was 27 years old. He was an attractive young man, cheerful, relaxed, and friendly. He told me in a clear, succinct fashion that he had changed his career. As he went through his graduate training, he enjoyed his mastery of his instrument, yet when he compared himself to his fellow students, he realized that his talent as a clarinet player was good but not on a superior level. He thought about it and estimated his chances as a clarinetist in the musical world. He decided he could not reach the level of a soloist with a lucrative career. His ability was only great enough to enable him to become a member of one or another orchestra, with a salary and income at a relatively modest level. The most he would achieve would be a limited standard of living, supporting a family with children, and he would be unlikely also to be able to support any special interests he or his family would desire. Fortunately, he also had a talent for mathematics, and had a superior record in all his math courses. The field of computers was booming and Jeffrey took the chance of shifting his career to computers. He enrolled in a good computer institute and his ability in that field blossomed. After two years of training he obtained a position at a top-notch expanding computer company and has been promoted with a salary increase plus bonuses, and has an interesting and affluent life ahead. He expects never to give up his clarinet and intends to maintain his skill as an enjoyable hobby. I gave him my congratulations, impressed by his thoughtful and precise judgments. He smiled, "You will never hear me as a famous clarinetist, but my decision was a good one."

To summarize, Jeffrey, as a clarinetist, was faced with the likelihood that the standards and demands of the environment would leave him with a poorness of fit for his desirable standard of living. His healthy psychological development from childhood onward had developed in him the high self-esteem and confidence that enabled him to take the chance to change his career, and ensure that he could achieve his goal with a goodness of fit.

Case 3: Another Example

Mr. Francis K. was referred to me because of symptoms of mild and chronic depression. He was in his late thirties, well groomed, with a dull voice, and a mildly depressed appearance.

He was the only child in a stable suburban middle-class family, with his father pursuing his occupation as a real estate broker, a career that was moderately successful and comfortable, although not affluent. The community respected the parents.

Frank had developed through childhood and adolescence without any significant problems, and easily adjusted in his social and academic life but without any special flair or interests. He graduated from college without any specific career goals. His father was a dominant but not authoritarian figure in the family, and urged Frank to join his small real estate firm when he completed college. He had no enthusiasm for this choice, but had no other strong interests, and so took the easiest course by joining his father's firm.

Over the years, Frank attained basic competence as a realtor, and worked conscientiously with his father. He married in his late twenties, had two children, and his family lived a sedate and relatively modest life. His father died four years ago, and Frank automatically took over the family real estate firm.

As to Frank's depression, this began when his father died, and has persisted with slight increase. His symptoms had not had any significant biological features, or major recurrent episodes. His findings appeared most likely to have been a dysthymic disorder, in which "the symptoms cause clinically significant distress or impairment in a social, occupational, or other important areas of functioning" (DSM-IV, 1994).

While there might have been a biological basis, I focused on the possibility of a chronic poorness of fit in his life course. Outside of his work, Frank expressed no interests and pursued no avocation but went along in a routine manner with a depressed mood. I got the first clue when I probed strongly into the nature of his past academic choices and completion of major assignments. He said reluctantly that he had taken a number of English literature courses, and this had been his major interest. But his parents, especially his father, belittled this choice. "You don't have a brilliant academic talent, you won't become a professor of English. Stick to our real estate business. That's real, it will be a safe life if you stick to our firm." Frank let himself be persuaded.

"Were you really interested in that field?" "Not really, I have been competent, but real estate work is dull and not interesting. But I stuck to it, it gave me a decent living, and what else could I do?"

"How about all your years since college? How much have you read, how much have you been interested in the good books you have read?" A flash of life transformed his depressed appearance and voice for a moment. "Reading is my refuge. I read a great deal, it stimulates me. But what would that reading get me?"

"You might not be a great writer, but maybe you could teach literature. Would that have interested you?" He shrugged, "I did mention it to my father, but he discouraged me. He did not think I would be a good teacher, I rebelled for a time, but gave up the idea. I didn't feel my father would be wrong."

I thought for a moment and looked at Frank's frustrated appearance. This was the time to challenge him. "Frank, suppose you took the credits for an English teacher, you could get them while you were rearranging your real estate business, and could be appointed as an English teacher, not as a professor, but in one of the high schools of your community. You would probably make less money than in real estate, but your salary would be enough for a modest lifestyle for your family." His face lit up, he took a deep breath, then shook his head. "It would be wonderful, but it's a fantasy. My wife and mother wouldn't let me."

This comment illuminated Frank's life course. He had always been a "good boy," never challenged his assertive family. He had friends, but if one of them came up with a good idea of what they should do, he always went along. "Tell me, do you select your clothes, or the menu at a restaurant?" He sheepishly shook his head.

We then discussed his passive approach to life. For some people like himself, going along with someone else's initiative is easier and more comfortable. But he had paid the price of giving up his own right to become a literature teacher, a choice that would have been vital for him. But to avoid a stressful and contentious time with his family, he had given up what he had really wanted.

"But my wife would blow up. Our income would be less, and our social position in the community would drop from that of a business man to that of a school teacher."

"True, but your wife would live, your children would too, and most important, you would have a chance to live your life in the kind of career you wanted. If you were to do so there is a high possibility that your depression would disappear. That is your choice—either drag along in life frustrated and depressed, or come alive for the first time in your life, and gain your self-respect by making your own important choices."

Frank was shocked. "I heard you. I will think about it, and see you at next week's appointment."

I waited for the appointment, keeping my fingers crossed. He might be crushed by my direct challenge to him.

Frank came in, and he was literally transformed. He came in standing erect, walking in briskly, and with a determined face. "I've done it." First he went to the Board of Education and found out the requirements to qualify as a high school teacher. It only required a few special courses, and he could take them at the local community college. He had checked the college schedule and found that he could carry the course load while continuing to supervise his real estate business with the help of a very good secretary.

"Then, I announced my decision and plans to my wife and mother. This meant that when I obtained the teaching position, I would sell our real estate firm, though I'm sure it wouldn't be worth much. As you can imagine, both my wife and mother exploded. They said I was crazy, threatened to take legal action (thcy couldn't do anything, I was the sole owner), and my wife said she would divorce me. After the storm subsided, they kept hammering at me, but when I carried through with my plan, had the college registration, and revised my real estate schedule, they subsided into a cold peace. You know, this was the first time in my life I ever stuck to my guns, and now, when I did it, it was really easy.

"I have one request of you," Frank added. "I realize that my passivity undermined my whole life, and left me with no self-respect. I very much want to have a series of discussions with you to help me to understand how I became passive and how I can change it."

His psychotherapeutic sessions required a year, and by then, his unhealthy passive structure was resolved and he terminated his treatment with a successful conclusion. During this year he took his required courses, passed them easily and enjoyed them. Fortunately, a vacancy in the English department of the community high school became free when he finished his courses; he had an excellent recommendation from his teachers, and was appointed to the position. He was apprehensive when he started, but quickly became an effective and stimulating teacher in the school and reveled in his enjoyment of teaching.

His depression disappeared, and his control of his passive tendencies earned him another unexpected bonus. His wife sulked and complained when Frank started his new activities and became more assertive in his personal functioning. But, as the months went by, his wife actually changed. She began to respect him, bursting out one evening, "For the first time, you are a real man." They felt closer together, and their sexual life improved markedly. She took a part-time office job to enhance their family income, and discovered that it gave her satisfaction.

☐ Comment

Frank had accepted his psychopathological passivity, always functioning with a poorness of fit. The results of his poorness of fit finally led his unhappy frustrated life to a chronic depression. These symptoms precipitated him to obtain professional help. That clarified his basic problem of a chronic poorness of fit. The dynamic analysis of this passivity led to a successful adaptation to a positive life style.

☐ **Discussion**

In the area of work, the environmental demands and opportunities un-equivocally have to mesh with the individual's talents, motivations, and temperament. If he or she can cope successfully with the environmental demands this leads to a goodness of fit and a successful life course. If the individual cannot cope adequately with the environmental demands this leads to a poorness of fit with an unhealthy, frustrated lifestyle. Beyond the resolution of a simple poorness of fit issue, a therapist often also has to deal with other significant and even crucial psychodymamic problems in order to effectively change a poorness of fit to a basic goodness of fit life course.

10

CHAPTER

Personality Development: Continuity and Change

"Every limit is a beginning as well as an ending. Who can quit young lives after being in company with them, and not desire to know what befall them in their after-years? For the fragment of a life, however typical, is not the sample of an even web. Promises may not be kept, and an ardent outcome may be followed by declension, latent powers may find their long-awaited opportunity; a past error may urge a grand retrieval" (George Eliot, *Middlemarch*).

Now that we have traced the individual's developmental age-stage periods from infancy through the several childhood periods, adolescence, and adulthood (Chapters 5–9), we can examine the concept of *personality development*. We cannot attempt to summarize the voluminous literature with its cornucopia of differing research findings, clinical data, and theoretical concepts of personality. Rather, we will limit our discussions to the various formulations of personality development gleaned from the summaries of the pertinent material on infancy to adult development in the previous chapters.

The term *personality* has long been used in psychiatry and psychology. Despite the difficulty in formulating objective criteria for its categorization, it has proven a useful concept, especially for practical clinical activities. Over the many decades, however, innumerable definitions of personality have been offered. "There are nearly as many definitions as are authors who have dealt with the problem," (Rioch, 1972, p. 576). A voluminous literature of personality keeps growing with each year. But

Rioch's judgment in 1972 as to the lack of any consensus of the definition of personality is as true today. We suggest an imprecise definition.
Personality can be considered to be the composite of those enduring
psychological attributes which constitute the specific individuality of
the person, and which are expressed in diverse behaviors in different
life situations, both concurrently and over time.

☐ Maturation of Personality Over Age Sequences Through Childhood and Adolescence

The development of personality can be considered as starting in the
newborn. At birth, the infant is equipped with various biopsychological
attributes that begin to interact with those of the caregivers in an organized fashion characterized by either goodness or poorness of fit. With
this biopsychosocial process, the rudimentary aspects of the child's personality begin to appear—cheerfulness (an easy child), feistiness (a difficult child), the embryo of shyness (a slow-to-warm-up child). As the
months pass, other behavioral characteristics and environmental influences emerge that also begin to shape other beginnings of personality,
such as level of persistence, sensory threshold, and adaptability. With the
appearance of important new capacities in the toddler and the preschool
child, such as language, motoric expertness, and the beginning of motivational interests, the enhanced interaction with the caregivers and
other environmental influences crystallizes specific personality characteristics. In middle childhood, with further maturation of new abilities
and motivations, and through interactions with greater environmental
expectations and opportunities, his or her personality qualities are consolidated and deepened.

Adolescence constitutes an age-period in which rapid biological
change is coupled with qualitatively new environmental demands, expectations, and opportunities. For the youngster with a healthy childhood developmental course, adolescence can be an expansive and
stimulating period of personality growth. For others, who have suffered
from a behavior disorder in childhood, new coping potentials created by
the rapid maturational process and the changed environmental opportunities of adolescence may lead to a mastery over their personality
problems. For still others, however, the new demands of adolescence
may prove excessively stressful, with the crystallization of a personality
problem or the exacerbation of a previously existing problem.

As the adolescent goes through this rapidly changing age-period, he
or she then reaches the threshold of independent adult life. Many or

most healthy adolescents arrive at adulthood blossoming into independent persons through the assets of their solidified and positive personality attributes. For those with pathological personality attributes,
problems may be ahead. (See clinical vignettes in Chapter 8.)

A few developmental psychologists who have studied the significance
of temperament have tended to equate temperament with personality
in the child and adult (Buss & Plomin, 1975; Eysenck, 1967).

Temperament is an important variable in shaping the origin or development of specific personality patterns, but it should never be
considered as an all-important single variable. The temperamental constellation of slow-to-warm-up may appear to be the single variable of
the personality characteristic of shyness, and a difficult temperament
may seem to define the feisty personality. However, as we have indicated in several earlier chapters, if parental handling promotes a goodness of fit with both constellations, the negative sides of the shyness or
feistiness will be minimized in the child's personality development. On
the other hand, if parental or other environmental influences promote a
poorness of fit, the negative sides of shyness or feistiness will be intensified and become significant personality factors over time. The single
temperament factors by themselves do not produce significant personality characteristics, however the combination of their interactional process with environmental influences do.

☐ Self-Esteem, Motivations, and Defense Mechanisms

The comments on self-esteem, motivations, and defense mechanisms in
previous chapters indicate the significant, but by no means exclusive,
importance of goodness or poorness of fit in the development of these
variables and their crystallization into various healthy or pathological
personality characteristics. Also, while self-esteem, motivations, and defense mechanisms constitute specific independent variables in the development of personality, they nevertheless influence each other. Thus,
a child or adolescent may develop one or more defense mechanisms
in trying to cope with the excessive demands of the environment. The
mechanism may increase or diminish the level of self-esteem or influence specific motivations. For example, the teacher at school may give
to one of the students a special assignment that the youngster fears,
from his or her previous experience, will be especially difficult, uninteresting, or confusing. Let us say that the student contrives a rationalization of one sort or another, asks the teacher for a different assignment,

and the teacher accepts the excuse and offers a substitute that is just as difficult but different, and a topic of interest. The youngster carries through that task splendidly and achieves an increased self-esteem. Should the teacher have refused to accept the rationalization, the youngster would have struggled with the initial assignment, producing a mediocre achievement, and his or her self-esteem will not have been enhanced.

☐ Adulthood: Continuity, Change and Predictability in Personality

In Chapter 3, we have criticized the developmental concept of infantile determinism, namely, that the young child's psychological characteristics are shaped for life by his/her experiences and conflicts. In addition, our case histories, at all subsequent age-periods (Chapters 5–9) have illustrated how different individuals often face unpredictable, new biological and/or environmental influences in shaping their personality into adulthood.

Edward Zigler, Professor of Psychology at Yale has put it well, "I, for one, am tired of the past decade's scramble to discover some magical period during which intervention will have particularly great pay-offs. Some experts emphasize the nine months in utero, Pines and White, the period between eight and 18 months, others, the entire preschool period, and yet others emphasize adolescence. My own predilection is that we cease this pointless search for magical periods and adopt instead the view that the developmental process is a continuous one, in which every segment of the life cycle from conception through maturity is of crucial importance and requires certain environmental nutrients" (1975).

☐ Clinical Vignettes

To elaborate on Zigler's polemic, we will describe three cases: Barbara, with a continuously positive personality development from childhood to adult life; Nancy, with a dramatic change of direction from her middle childhood personality to her subsequent life course; and Norman, starting in middle childhood with a drastic poorness of fit with his child–paternal interaction, and who demonstrated a remorseless, pathogenic life-course development.

Case 1: Barbara

Barbara had an easy and persistent temperament from infancy onward. Her parents were divorced when she was two years old. The prediction from longitudinal research is that, for many children, parental divorce had a long-standing traumatic influence (Wallerstein 1985). But, for Barbara the divorce was far from traumatic. (Rutter 1972/1981 has emphasized the deleterious effect parental discord has on the child, as contrasted to actual separation or divorce.) Her parents' separation was not acrimonious. Both subsequently remarried; Barbara lived with her mother and stepfather, though she also maintained a continuous and friendly relationship with her father and stepmother. She had clearly been able to use four parents, instead of two, as sources of strength and support, and to identify and compare differing styles of coping in the two households, taking what was best from each.

This positive experience for Barbara stands in contrast to the all-too-frequent tragic situations in which two parents are divorced, continue fighting against each other, and exploit their child to become a weapon against the other, with disastrous effects on the child. Barbara, fortunately, had two reasonable parents, both committed to her welfare, and she responded positively to both stepparents. It was clear that Barbara easily charmed the four parents with her cheerful and easily adaptable temperament and high intelligence (her I.Q. score, tested at three years, was 164).

Barbara's teachers were entranced by her personality, with enthusiastic reports starting from nursery school. As an example, at age seven, her teacher described Barbara as having "good attention span, works quickly. With adults is warm, natural, and spontaneous. She is a leader, other children ask her for help, which she gives. Interested in both things and people. An outstanding, superior type, no flaws in her personality."

With this spectacular beginning in childhood, and faced with neither unfavorable demands nor opportunities as she grew up, Barbara matured and functioned highly positively both socially and academically. From her interview in adolescence, we gave her the highest adjustment rating on our scale. The same story was reinforced in her college and professional years, and she graduated medical school at 23 years of age. One of us (S.C.) visited her for a follow-up interview when she was 27. Barbara was married to another physician. The marriage was clearly a very congenial one. When I had called her to arrange the interview, Barbara was delighted to meet me. She explained that she had the position of chief resident of pediatrics in the hospital, but was on a short period of leave, because she had just delivered her first child, a healthy baby, and was in the process of moving to a larger house. I commented that I should not impose on her time now, and wait later for the appointment. She exclaimed, "No, no. You are busy too, I'm sure if we set a specific time for the interview (which we did) I can arrange to be free for several hours for you." She picked me up at the airport, greeted me with a bright smile, and on the way home chatted about her wonderful baby, delighted with their new house, absorbed in her professional and social life, and how lucky she was to meet and fall in love with just the right man. Her four parents were thrilled at being grandparents and were planning to visit the following week.

Barbara was charming, well groomed, responded quickly and thoughtfully to my questions, and clearly presented herself as a mature, sensitive, efficient, responsible, and charming person. She commented that, "I was lucky to have good parents, teachers, and friends." I answered, "It wasn't only luck. With your cheerful and easily adaptable temperament, and also with your high intelligence, curiosity, and quick enjoyment of learning, everyone in contact with you, as child, adolescent, or adult, would find it a pleasure for you to be a daughter, student, friend, colleague and wife. As your baby grows up I'm sure you will also be a good mother." She laughed, "I guess you're right. It was a pleasure to see you," and drove me to the airport with a warm farewell.

We describe Barbara almost as a fairy story. It is true, she was almost "perfect" but very real. One of the great enjoyments we have experienced in pursuing the demanding task of collecting the data of the NYLS has been to find how many of our subjects have blossomed and developed into mature and healthy young adults. Some of them have lived a relatively easy life course, with a good fit of their individuality–environment interactions. Some others have had stressful challenges with difficult temperament and/or difficult parents, or one or another special traumatic event, but still struggled to cope successfully with their stressful demands and came through into successful, healthy, social and occupational lives.

Case 2: Nancy

Next, there is the dramatic story of Nancy. She was a very difficult child temperamentally from early infancy onward. The parents responded to her intensity of reactions, biological irregularity, negative mood, and slow adaptability in a way that produced extreme stress and disturbed development. The father was highly critical of her behavior, rigid in his expectations for quick adaptation, and punitive when she did not respond to his demands. The mother was intimidated by both husband

and daughter, and vacillated in her handling of her child. Truly, Nancy suffered from a severe poorness of fit. I (S.C.) had a number of sessions with the parents trying to help Nancy by applying parent guidance (see Chapter 7). All my efforts to help the parents to understand that Nancy's temperament was normal, despite its inconvenience to them, failed. They persisted in trying, unsuccessfully, to change her difficult behavior pattern. I was totally unsuccessful. The father kept repeating, "She's just a rotten kid," and adamantly refused to consider any change in his attitude and behavior toward Nancy. And, the mother remained helpless and confused about the girl.

By the age of six, Nancy had developed multiple symptoms of behavior problems: explosive anger outbursts, fear of the dark, thumb sucking, and hair pulling, and had alienated her peer group. Ominously, she began to take coins from her parents' pockets with which she would buy candy and offer it to her age-mates in the hope of being accepted into her peer group. This "stealing" was the first sign of the formation of an unhealthy defensive system. If her disturbed functioning continued, as seemed inevitable, she would develop a pathological personality structure.

The father, himself a clinical psychologist, saw his daughter's symptoms as being all her fault, repeating the mantra, "She's a rotten kid," and arranged psychotherapy for her which resulted in very modest improvement.

However, unexpectedly, a change occurred when in the fourth and fifth grades Nancy showed evidence of musical and dramatic talent. This brought to the parents increasingly favorable praise of Nancy from teachers and other parents. Fortunately for Nancy, these talents ranked high in her parents' own hierarchy of desirable attributes. Her father now began to interpret his daughter's intense expressiveness as "artistic temperament"—not as a sign of "a rotten child," his previous label, but as evidence of a budding artist. She was now a child he could be proud of, and he made allowances for "my Maria Callas." With this view of Nancy, the mother was also able to relax and relate to her positively. In the next few years, Nancy's symptoms literally melted away. When seen in the routinely scheduled adolescent interview at age 17, she was bright, alert, and lively. She was involved in a number of activities that interested her, reported an active social life, good school functioning, and a pleasant relationship with her parents. Her early disastrous poorness of fit was now transformed into a happy goodness of fit. There was no evidence of pathological symptoms. She described herself as "hotheaded," which was confirmed in a separate interview with her parents, but neither she nor they considered this as a problem. Her promising artistic interests as a child did not blossom into a substantial talent, but remained as an enjoyable hobby. Her serious goal was rather to be trained for a professional career.

When seen again at age 22, Nancy's adolescent report of positive functioning was reaffirmed. She was a senior in a prestigious college and had demonstrated talent in her chosen field. She felt some tension in her first college year, but adapted successfully and thereafter enjoyed her academic work. Her heterosexual relationships also tended to have tempestuous beginnings, but then settled down positively.

Two years later, she asked to see me in a consultation. As before, she was poised, relaxed, and self-assuring. She had started a professional career, but was concerned at its limited future. She was unhappy about her social life. She had a number of friends, but was not satisfied with the depth or permanence of her heterosexual relationships. She expressed a wish for professional counseling for these problems of living. I agreed with her assessment, and referred her to an experienced psychotherapist. I kept in touch with the therapist, who was impressed by Nancy's positive characteristics, and found no evidence of any significant psychopathology. Her treatment lasted two years, resolved her professional choice, and she was launched on the career of her choice. Her personal relationships with men were stormy to begin with but she learned to cope with this issue, and had started a stable and very promising relationship with a young man. With that, her treatment terminated.

Case 3: Norman

Then there is Norman, whose history has truly been an inexorably tragic life course. He had been temperamentally distractible, with a short attention span from infancy to adulthood. Otherwise, he had an easy temperament. There was no history of organic dysfunction in either his prenatal development and delivery, or his early childhood history. Intelligent and pleasant, he started his schooling with good mastery. Though his attention span was short, he concentrated well, learned easily and quickly, even in short spurts. Teacher reports in his early school years were uniformly positive with regard to academic progress and social behavior, and there was no evidence of any learning problem.

However, his parents, especially the father, were impatient and critical of him because at home he showed quick shifts of attention, dawdling at bedtime, and apparent "forgetfulness." The parents asked for a consultation when Norman was approaching five years of age and I (S.C.) did a thorough clinical evaluation.

Norman was a cheerful, friendly youngster, and cooperated immediately and easily with all of my suggestions. However, when he started one or another task with interest in the playroom, he was dexterous but quickly dropped one activity after another. Peripheral stimuli engaged his attention; for example, when the telephone rang in the adjoining room, he stopped his play with the darts and wanted to know who was calling.

In my informing interview with the parents, I gave my judgment that Norman was a completely normal boy, despite the behaviors of which they were complaining. I explained the concept of normal individual differences, or temperament. In Norman's case, his important temperament traits of risk were distractibility, and inability to concentrate on any task with persistent undivided attention for any long period. But, with his other attributes, he could learn well in short spurts, as the teachers had reported. I gave the parents the various simple suggestions and rules that could minimize the annoyances of his distractible and short attention span. He was a highly cooperative child, and was capable of following a simple set of rules—two attributes with which he could function well both at school and home.

The parents differed in their opinions. The mother nodded, but hesitantly, and said, "I guess you are right, and we will try to follow your instructions." The father exploded, "Nothing doing! You cannot convince me that Norman has a normal character. What you call distractibility and short attention is temperament, according to your language. What I call his behavior is irresponsibility and a lack of character and will power. I cannot accept your suggestions. He has to shape up and that is that." The mother was intimidated, did not argue with her husband, and the discussion ended in a complete impasse.

Both of us kept in touch with Norman and his parents over the years. All we could do was watch, feeling helpless and disheartened. Year by year, Norman's symptoms grew worse, and his academic standard slipped. His father, a hard driving, very persistent and successful professional man, became increasingly hypercritical and derogatory of Norman. The mother was completely overwhelmed at her husband's adamant judgment, as he repeatedly charged the boy with terms such as, "lack of willpower and character," and "laziness," and made it clear that he disliked his son. He was convinced that Norman had an irresponsible character and was headed for future failure—indeed these provided the seeds of a self-fulfilling prophecy.

There were several times when the boy tried to comply with his father's standards and made himself sit still with his homework for long periods. This only resulted in generalized tension and multiple tics, and he could not sustain this effort so dissonant with his temperament—another proof to himself and his father of his failure. During Norman's middle childhood years, I made several efforts to alter the father's destructive behavior with the boy. The father would come in readily at my request, and when I started to talk about Norman he would interrupt with, "I know exactly what you will say," repeat my judgment and recommendations with my exact words, end with, "thank you for your concern, but you are entirely wrong," and say good-bye pleasantly.

When seen at 17, Norman had already dropped out of two colleges in one year. He was dejected, extraordinarily self-derogatory, said he could not finish anything he started, that he was lazy, and did not know what he wanted to do. "My father loves me, after all he has to. I am his son but he does not respect me. Why should he?"

At age 18, he asked his parents for psychiatric help, and they arranged it with a very competent psychiatrist. But the treatment was a complete failure. At a later interview, Norman explained that he became annoyed because the psychiatrist "expected me to work my ass off." He ended by "bullshitting him" to get him off his neck.

At age 22, I (A.T.) interviewed Norman at home, where he was still living with his parents. He was not depressed but essentially nonfunctional. He slept most of the day away, and held an occasional brief simple job. He explained that he would work long enough to gain enough money for his expenses, then maneuvered to be fired after some argument with his boss. Then he would collect unemployment insurance and supplement his modest income by "borrowing" from friends, parents, an uncle and aunt. He was not self-depreciating himself, as when he was younger, but a denial defense mechanism was very noticeable. He asserted repeatedly that he was fine and getting along well with his parents, and that he knew his career as a musician and song composer would blossom in the near future. It was clearly useless to challenge his grandiose fantasy, so I wished him luck and told him I was always available and he could call me if he wanted my help or advice. His diagnosis was narcissistic personality disorder, severe.

Three years later, Norman did call me, asking to have psychotherapy. I suspect he had come because of his parents' pressure. I arranged a schedule of weekly sessions for him. His lethargic and parasitic lifestyle with occasional brief jobs and exploitation of family and friends had continued as before. He reported to me in detail at each session his exciting plan for some vague grandiose project in the suburbs, and was busy negotiating with various unnamed officials. He was always on the verge of making the "deal," but each time some "problem" came up, but he would solve it "the next week." I seized this last opportunity to try to explore with him the reasons for his school and job problems and his difficulties with his father. I also tried to interest him in the concept of temperament and the nature of our research program, and why and how he became a subject of the study. If I could have succeeded in getting his attention, then I might have had an opening to discuss his own temperamental characteristics, why his father reacted, etc. But all my clinical strategies failed completely. He stonewalled (his defense mechanism), either looked blankly, lethargically didn't listen, but went back to his negotiations and problems with his grandiose plans. He kept his appointments for our sessions, but was always late. He would rush in with the same explanation, that he was on his way to my office, but was delayed or distracted by some "unexpected" situation.

After six months, the discussions were completely fruitless, and he himself suggested that we terminate them because he was "too busy." I agreed, told him I would be available again if he needed me, we said good-bye, and as he left, I stared sadly after him. Of all the varied life-courses of our NYLS subjects, Norman's story was the most disastrous. His prognosis was indeed grim. Periodically, Norman phoned or came for a discussion. His own stated purpose for the most recent such meeting was to be able to boast to his friends that he was part of the New York Longitudinal Study they had seen mentioned on the Internet.

It was after several decades of immersion in the NYLS that I happened to re-read Middlemarch. We had started our study with no intention to make it longitudinal—merely to investigate our hypothesis that behavioral differences in children did make independent and unique contributions to the environment–organism interaction.

But time extended and we could not "quit young lives after being in company with them, and not desire to know what befell them in their after years?"

The case vignettes given in this chapter, as well as those throughout the book, illustrate George Eliot's comment that ". . . the fragment of a life, however typical, is not the sample of an even web. Promises may not be kept, and an ardent outcome may be followed by declension, latent powers may find their long-awaited opportunity; a past error may urge a grand retrieval."

☐ Comment

Our NYLS case vignettes indicated that in the course of personality development, whether healthy or pathological, a basic, but by no means exclusive, influence was shaped by goodness or poorness of fit. Striking consistency in temperament over time was evident in some individuals, marked inconsistency in others, and various combinations of consistency together with inconsistency in still others. The three cases described above were typical examples: Barbara with her splendid goodness of fit throughout, Nancy with her pathogenic poorness of fit in her first decade of life, then a transformation to a goodness of fit by a totally unpredictable individual–environment interaction, and Norman with his remorselessly disastrous poorness of fit. We have detailed the many reasons for the marked consistency and changes in our subjects, (Chess & Thomas, 1984). The marked variability in life-course of our NYLS subjects confirms the fact of the inability to predict successfully what the characteristics of the development of personality will be. This is confirmed by George Vaillant's findings in his extensive Harvard Grant study of almost 100 Harvard students, gathered with extensive data from the childhood years, and followed into middle age. Vaillant observed that "the life cycle is more than an invariant sequence of stages with simple predictable outcomes. The man's life is full of surprises, and the Grant Study provides no prediction table" (1977, p. 373).

III

THE IMPORTANCE OF THE BIOPSYCHOSOCIAL MODEL

CHAPTER

Intertwining Goodness of Fit and the Biopsychosocial Model: Challenges to the Biopsychosocial Model

In 1977, Dr. George Engel, Professor of both Medicine and Psychiatry at the University of Rochester, published a seminal article in the prestigious journal, *Science*, entitled, "The Need For a New Medical Model: A Challenge for Biomedicine."

In his paper, Engel contended that "all medicine is in crisis and, further, that medicine's crisis derives from the same basic cause as psychiatry's, namely, adherence to a model of disease that is no longer adequate for the scientific tasks and social responsibilities of either medicine or psychiatry." After spelling out his thesis, Engel then challenged the psychiatrist and internist. "The physician's basic professional knowledge and skills must span the social, psychological, and biological, for his decisions and actions on the patient's behalf on all three" (p. 133).

Then, in 1986, Dr. Leon Eisenberg, Professor of Psychiatry and Professor and Chairman of the Department of Social Medicine and Health Policy, both at Harvard, gave a lecture with the intriguing title, "Mindlessness and Brainlessness in Psychiatry." In the early 1960s he recounted the evidence of the ascendancy of psychoanalysis, and doubted the value of the credibility of the presumed research tool of psychoanalysis for the investigation of the personality. This "basic science" of psychoanalysis with the presumed unimportance of the brain, Eisenberg labeled as the period of *brainlessness*.

He then turned to the late 1960s with the discovery of effective psychoactive drugs, as a stimulus that "provided the research in neurobiology. The scientific yield has been extraordinary" and Dr. Eisenberg summaried the dramatic discoveries of one find after another of the neurochemical functions for the brain (p. 500). He then posed a crucial warning, with this exhilarating effect of psychiatric research, "We may trade the one-sidedness of the 'brainless' psychiatry of the past for that of a 'mindless' psychiatry of the future" (p. 500).

In his conclusion, Eisenberg echoed Engel's challenge to psychiatry and medicine: "biomedical knowledge is necessary but not sufficient; the doctor's transactions with the patient must be informed by the social sciences" (p. 505).

In the psychological field, Dr. Richard Lerner, a researcher, theorist, and teacher in developmental psychology, has also formulated a concise theory of the biopsychosocial formulation. He cited an approach from the data of several researchers, including his own work, that "provide solid biological and psychosocial evidence for the centrality of these relations in structured and functional developments across life . . . They are the core of what human development is all about" (1991, p. 31).

☐ Goodness of Fit and the Biopsychosocial Model

To recall, in 1956 we began systematically to study the characteristics and significance of temperament (see Appendix). From the beginning, we were careful to avoid over-emphasizing the importance of temperament. By 1968, when our data collection had been analyzed substantially, we declared that "As in the case when a significant influencing variable is identified, there is an understandable temptation to make temperament the heart and body of a general theory. To do so would be to repeat a frequent approach in psychiatry which, over the years, has been beset by general theories of behavior based upon fragments rather than the totality of influencing mechanisms. A one-sided emphasis on temperament would merely repeat and perpetuate such a tendency and would be antithetical to our viewpoint, which insists that we recognize temperament as only one attribute of the organism . . . Existing theories emphasize motives and drive states, tactics of adaptation, environmental patterns of influences, and primary organic determinants . . . We recognize that the same motive, the same adaptive tactic, or the same structure of objective environment will have different functional meaning in accordance with the temperamental style of the given child" (pp. 182–183).

Beyond our concern for the biopsychosocial model in the study of temperament, we had this same consideration in our elaboration of the concept of goodness of fit (see Chapter 1). In our refined definition, we have included as a final sentence "Goodness of fit is never an abstraction, but is always goodness of fit in terms of the values and demands of a given culture or socioeconomic group" (Chapter 1, p. 2).

To implement the elaboration of the interrelationship between goodness of fit and the biopsychosocial, model, beyond the NYLS, we initiated three additional longitudinal studies with special populations with varied environmental, cross-cultural, biological, and psychological circumstances (See Chapter 1). The findings from these studies, from the NYLS, from our other clinical activities, and from the reports of other researchers, have supported the applicability of the goodness of fit model in its close interrelationships with the biopsychosocial model posed by Engel, Eisenberg, and Lerner.

In succeeding chapters, we describe a number of specific clinical vignettes which demonstrate a variety of biopsychosocial characteristics and their interrelations with the goodness of fit concept.

12
CHAPTER

Socio–Cultural Issues

☐ The Masai Tribe Story

In 1984, Marten deVries, an American medical student with strong interests in anthropology, took a year's leave, with a fellowship, to do a series of field studies on several East African tribes. One of his projects involved the collection of temperament data on children of the Masai tribe in Kenya, living in the sub-Sahara region. deVries obtained temperament ratings on 47 infants, aged 2–4 months, using a translation of a standard temperament questionnaire, at a time when a severe drought was just beginning. With these ratings, he identified the ten infants with the easiest temperament, and the ten with the most difficult temperament. He returned to the tribal area five months later, by which time the drought had killed off 97 percent of the cattle herd.

At that period, the basic food supply was milk and blood, both derived from the tribe's cattle. The loss of the herd meant the threat of starvation and the need to make life and death decisions in the allocation of food.

deVries was able to locate the families of seven of the easy babies and six of the difficult ones. The families of the other infants had moved in an attempt to escape the drought. Of the seven "easy" babies, five had died, whereas all of the "difficult" infants had survived! Clearly, the parents of the Masai tribe had a selective level of care of the easy vs. the difficult babies in this catastrophic environment.

With inadequate food available in the drought period, we can assume that the difficult infants, with high negative mood temperament, cried

110

loudly and frequently, while the easy ones, with low negative mood temperament, cried less loudly and less often. With these responses, the parents gave more food to the difficult babies, either to stop their extreme crying, or possibly to choose for survival these lusty expressive babies who had more desirable characteristics according to the tribe's cultural standards.

By contrast to the Masai's highly stressful tribal living circumstances, is the very different environment of our NYLS sample. In their early childhood years, the temperamentally difficult NYLS youngsters comprised 23 percent (ten cases) of the behavior problem group, but only four percent (four cases) of the nonclinical sample, (Thomas, Chess & Birch, 1968, p. 78). In our society, a difficult child places special demands on parents and acts as a stress factor, hence our labeling of the children with those temperament characteristics as "difficult" (See Appendix).

☐ Working-class Puerto Rican (WCPR) Story

Our 131 NYLS subjects have come almost exclusively from middle-class native-born families. We judged that it would be desirable to compare the temperamental and goodness of fit NYLS findings with another population of different class and ethnic background. With that in mind, we initiated a longitudinal study in 1961 of 95 children of semi-skilled and unskilled working-class Puerto Rican (WCPR) parents (see Chapter 1). The families were mostly intact, stable, and committed to the care of their children; 86 percent lived in low-income public housing projects in Spanish Harlem in Manhattan. The staff interviewer, a Puerto Rican psychologist, was trained to do the parents' interviews with the same protocol as with the NYLS. The children of these families were followed from early infancy to middle childhood, and the interview data were scored and rated for temperament by the same raters as for the NYLS sample. Any of the children who developed behavior difficulties were referred to me (S.C.) with the same clinical schedule as for the NYLS. The Puerto Rican interviewer acted as interpreter when necessary.

The temperament ratings of the NYLS and WCPR samples were compared in the infancy period. The differences between the two groups were significant for rhythmicity and intensity, were of borderline significance for activity level, mood, and threshold, and were not significant for the other four categories. Overall, the differences were not dramatic (Thomas & Chess, 1977, p. 147).

On the other hand, the difference between the two groups regarding the incidence of a specific type of behavioral disturbance in the preschool and middle childhood periods was striking. In half of the WCPR clinical cases under nine years of age, the complaints were of excessive and uncontrollable motoric activity, whereas only one NYLS youngster displayed this symptom (and this was a brain-damaged child). These marked differences in incidence clearly appeared related to environmental circumstances. The WCPR families usually had more children than did the NYLS families. They also lived in small apartments with little extra space available for constructive activity required by the basically normal, temperamentally highly active youngster. Furthermore, these highly active young children were even more likely to be kept cooped up at home for fear that if they ran around in the streets unsupervised they would be in special danger of accidents. This was a realistic fear in the Harlem area in which these families lived. Beyond this special issue, safe playgrounds and recreational areas were not as available as they were to the NYLS highly active youngsters, who often lived in spacious apartments or private homes with backyards, and did not develop excessive motor activity. One of the WCPR children who had been described by his teachers as "uncontrollably active" and by his parents as a "whirling dervish" became much more manageable when the parents were able to move to a private house with a small yard (Chess & Thomas, 1984, p. 223).

☐ Comment

The data gathered by Martin deVries on the dramatic events endangering this Masai tribe highlighted an important cultural dilemma in behavioral research. In our initial study, the identification and labeling of the nine temperament qualities and the three clusters were accomplished within the framework of a middle class, urban, educationally oriented group of parents. Hence, they were oriented to this specific cultural group. The titles of the temperamental clusters—easy, difficult, slow-to-warm-up—were arrived at during the infancy of the study children. Hence, these labels pertained to the children's responsivity to childcare practices and values. In retrospect, it would have been better to use a term such as "feisty" instead of "difficult" which can too easily be equated with the value judgement of a "bad temperament."

When the PRWC was initiated eight years later, there was no difficulty in translating the identical interview protocol into Spanish and in having scoring done in an identical manner. In so doing, cultural differences in childcare practices were revealed along with differing interpretations of which child temperaments were difficult or inconvenient.

In obtaining temperament assessments of the Masai babies with a translated NYLS interview, descriptions of infant behavior and of care-giving practices were not difficult to obtain. Such areas as feeding, cleansing, and sleeping occur in all cultures. The sameness of the questions highlighted the differences. One cannot learn 'how an infant behaves when left alone' in an environment of multiple care givers in which a baby is never left alone. The initial temperament interviews and classifications were accomplished in a non-stressful period. The drought, with its life threatening consequences to all the members of the tribe, brought out the question, "how do we explain the protective nature of the 'difficult' cluster?" The two most prominent answers that were offered by deVries were that these babies called more vigorous attention to their needs, and that such vigorous behavior may have been culturally more valued; two reasons for priority in breast-feeding.

The data from these two cultural groups, the Masai and WCPR groups, illustrate clearly the interrelations of goodness of fit and the biopsychosocial models.

The Masai tribe, suffering extreme food privation, coped successfully with the survival needs of their temperamentally "difficult" infants whose vigorous behavior was in fact culturally valued. By contrast, the mildly protesting infants were both easier to ignore and not equally valued. The scarce food went more to the vigorously protesting infants who survived. In addition, and simultaneously, the life-course experiences were shaped by biological (temperament), psychological (the parents value judgement of easy vs. difficult children) and social (the disastrous environment due to the drought) factors.

A similar analysis of the WCPR children confirms the interrelationships of the goodness of fit concept and the biopsychosocial model. The interaction of highly active children cooped up in small apartments, and unsafe streets, created a poorness of fit and behavior problems. With the low activity youngsters, their restraint of activity did not produce excessive tension and a poorness of fit or a behavior problem.

The two reports above suggest the importance of the significant cultural or socio-economic factors in a society or community in influencing the goodness or poorness of fit in an individual's development or function. The social psychologists Charles Super and Sara Harkness have put it well, "The 'development niche'. . . consists of the physical and social setting children are found in, the culturally regulated customs for child care, socialization, and behavior management, and the psychology of the caretakers, including beliefs and values about the nature of development. Each of these three dimensions of the developmental niche has its own set of ties to other cultural features, such as physical ecology, methods of economic production, marriage patterns, political organization, and ethics" (1986, p. 133).

☐ The Significance of Stress and Conflict

The concept of goodness of fit does not imply that an optimal developmental environment is a restricted one, making no "upsetting" demands on the individual, nor does goodness of fit mean a static condition of minimal demands for functioning. Rather, it suggests that a "good fit" is one in which reorganizations of functioning resulting from environmental requirements proceed in an orderly and progressive manner, and "poor fit" is one in which there is disturbed or retrogressive direction of development.

Furthermore, the concept of progress is always a social value, which, in most cultures, includes the anticipation that with increases in age the child will achieve expanded environmental mastery and productive social involvement. Thus, goodness of fit is never an abstraction, but is always goodness of fit for certain end results. For example, behavioral distress resulting from the introduction of a slow-to-warm-up child to a new social situation should not be a signal to the parent to withdraw the child in the interests of the youngster's immediate comfort. Rather, with the initial distress, if the child can cope with the new demands, the parental efforts should be encouraged and, if necessary, assisted. If, however, an evaluation indicates that mastery cannot be readily achieved at the given time, other more effective tactics may have to be elaborated for the development of the youngster's expanded social competencies (see Chapter 17, "Prevention and Early Intervention of Childhood Behavioral Problems," and Chapter 19, "Guidelines for Psychotherapy").

Behavioral distress or stress can be distinguished from an easily accomplished demand or difficult mastery of a new activity or task. The demand, even, if difficult, can be consonant with many of the child's characteristics and capacities. In this case, expanded environmental mastery and developmental progress will occur, and the demand will have constituted a healthy stimulus for the child. If, however, the demand is so dissonant with the child's capacities that mastery is not possible, its persistence will not contribute to a healthy outcome. In this situation, the poorness of fit will produce excessive stress and if continued, may lead to a clinical behavioral development.

Cross-cultural research is very vulnerable to the possibility that data may be culture bound either in the manner in which it is obtained or in its interpretation or both. This has been highlighted in the controversies about intelligence. Tests constructed in one culture have been given to children in the original language, in a manner not conducive to thoughtful answers, not dealing with areas familiar to the test taker, and more. Language-free tests have been employed in an effort to make them "culture free." However, tests, interviews, and observations cannot be constructed to be culture free. Even the drawing of a person is influenced by the dominant and traditional art forms. The strength of cross-cultural studies is to seek out the cultural bias so that it can be an instrument of obtaining and interpreting the data.

13

Educational Issues

☐ Clinical Vignettes

Case 1: Developmental Dyslexia: Difficulty in Word Finding

Mr. and Mrs. K. were referred to me (S.C.) with a problem of their six-year old boy, Carl. The teacher had informed the parents that Carl showed peculiar behavior in class and needed psychological help.

The teacher's description was that Carl's odd behavior occurred mainly when called on to answer questions. At times he answered correctly, and his stock of knowledge seemed excellent for a first grader. However, at other times when called on, he started to answer, then he would run around the room flapping his arms and making unintelligible noises. The other children laughed and had begun to egg him on, so that his behavior had become quite frequent. When routines were going on, such as lining up, he did not give difficulty. Yet, no such behavior occurred at home.

Carl had a normal birth and his developmental history showed normal milestones except for language. He had spoken his first word at age 2, and had been slow in adding words to his vocabulary. Nevertheless, Carl was interested in ideas and in watching the public television programs on science, such as astronomy and animal behavior. His language history was puzzling. While language accomplishment had been slow, the school's psychologist clinically assessed Carl as being of high intelligence. Although he often had trouble finding the correct word, he persisted in asking questions. Since he frequently used incorrect words in the same category as the ones he meant, the psychologist had learned to understand him and at no time had she observed bizarre behavior during testing itself.

The clinical interview was conducted in the playroom. My (S.C.) effort to establish rapport with Carl through friendly discussion was unsuccessful; he answered in a low voice. He did not pursue answers to my questions about what activities he liked best or other such positive topics. However, when he looked over the toys at my suggestion, he gradually became involved and more at ease. Using the rubber-tipped darts, he was clearly well coordinated; he became more at ease when I joined him in a dart contest, particularly when his throws were superior to mine. He then began to use the doll house representational toys. As he was out of my vision, I asked what toy he was using. He looked upset, scanned the toys and said, "oven." I moved to see, and noted that he had just put down the toy refrigerator. Hastily, he took some toy celery and shoved it into the toy refrigerator, which he had just declared to be an oven. Now, suspicious of a possible anomia, I probed, "Do you cook celery in an oven?" Immediately Carl began to look distressed, ran about the room in a disorganized manner on his tiptoes, making high-pitched nonsense sounds. I waited, but there was no indication that Carl would spontaneously cease this behavior. It appeared to be the behavior described by the classroom teacher. Wanting to learn how tenacious these actions were, I moved to an activity which he had enjoyed, and threw a dart at the board, then handed him one. He threw it, achieved a bull's eye, and all the bizarre behavior abruptly ceased while he devoted himself to the darts.

The remainder of the interview was now devoted to an exploration of this language difficulty. During this portion of the diagnostic interview, his actions were organized and cooperative. I read to him from an easy child's book until he grew interested. I then asked him to find a word he knew—he pointed to *the*. However, when Carl wrote this word, he produced *eth*, a typical dyslexic problem with letter sequence. Further diagnostic probing confirmed this diagnosis. But when my questions became too revealing of Carl's difficulties, his typical response was disorganized vocal and motor activity, which did indeed look bizarre.

Carl's parents had no difficulty comprehending my diagnosis of a language, not a thought, disorder. Being psychologically sophisticated, they were aware that "thought disorder" could be childhood schizophrenia and asked for a discussion of this diagnosis. Review of his recent language usage seemed to indicate acceleration in Carl's receptive language and a lesser speeding up of his usage of expressive language. Reading was also improving, but writing continued to be a significant problem. At this point, I included Carl in our discussion of recommendations.

I recommended a capable remedial teacher, with whom Carl was scheduled once weekly. The teacher would also orient Carl's mother to the problem, so that she could help him with his homework by correcting his word mistakes. As I talked to his parents, Carl listened carefully. When I finished, he blurted out, "Will I ever be able to learn to read?" I smiled, "Of course, and do you want to learn to read?" Carl then poured out his embarrassment at school when called on to read and his desire to be able to read so that he could learn by himself. His cooperation was assured. I predicted that Carl's dyslexia would gradually diminish so that it would not be a problem. His odd behavior, which was due to anxiety, could become a real problem if it persisted.

One of my recommendations, therefore, was that Carl take on the goal of eliminating these behaviors. We would confer with his teacher to make sure she only called on him when he raised his hand.

These recommendations were implemented. Fortunately, Carl was in a stage of accelerated development. With his inquiring mind, his goal of reading independently was quietly on the way so that he felt assured of final success. Losing his mannerisms was not as easy and for this endeavor we set up a series of discussions. Carl learned to abort his reactions and, with his increasing ability to find words, and the teacher's sensitivity to his problem, his classmates found they could no longer turn on this spectacle. The teacher, who had clearly doubted the accuracy of the diagnosis of dyslexia, could now recognize that the flamboyance of Carl's attempt to turn attention from his shaming public disgrace had in fact camouflaged his very real learning problem. While spelling difficulty remained prominent, he recognized this as a common, hard to eradicate, component of dyslexia and made sure that this did not now become an issue.

The concept of goodness of fit was a crucial instrument in diagnosing Carl's behavior. The use of the descriptive word "bizarre" had in itself diagnostic implications toward childhood schizophrenia. Bizarre behavior is a reflection of disordered thinking. But, on the other hand there were indications of orderly behavior most of the time. At home, Carl's parents described age appropriate demeanor that was well adapted to the daily routine. He continued to have neighborhood friends and his relationships with them were unremarkable. In school, routines were not a problem. It appeared that the bizarre behavior had started as a response to being requested to answer questions before the class. Now a major aspect of his actions at school, it was initially triggered only occasionally. When his classmates began baiting him, the proportion and peculiar actions increased. There were also discrepancies in the report of the school psychologist. During testing, Carl's language usage was often incorrect; yet, he indicated the correct concept through his overall replies so often, that an intellectual estimate had been possible. Also, there had not been bizarre behavior during this testing, which had taken place without outside distractions and without adverse comment.

This poorness of fit of Carl's peculiar actions in contrast to class decorum could not be explained as disordered thoughts. Childhood schizophrenia as a diagnosis did not fit with the total description. It was necessary to find a pattern—to isolate whatever stimulus triggered Carl's disordered behavior. The possibility must also be considered that this might be the uneven pattern of an emerging but not yet fixed thought disorder. Or was there a basic goodness of fit with a discrete area of environmental expectation that constituted a poorness of fit? Since the school environment had academic and social expectations organized to fit children's developing skills, the general expectations for mastery should have been within Carl's grasp. Yet his neighborhood social skills were a good fit and his intellectual curiosity should have made a learning situation just right. The identification of a developmental delay crucial to the mastery of reading supplied the core of the poorness of fit, and with that, the available facts seemed to fall into place. Diagnostic testing for dyslexia confirmed this diagnosis and Carl's opening of his tortured feelings was further confirmation.

It is only fair to recall that, in the 1960s when Carl's care came to my attention, awareness of dyslexia was not high, although it had been well studied by Samuel Orton. Also, this was in a period when awareness of childhood schizophrenia was high.

Five years later, I did a final follow-up on Carl. Carl was happy to show how well he functioned. He had progressed normally, both academically and socially. Now 11 years old, he still read or wrote an incorrect word now and then, but not often. The residual problem didn't bother him and he was willing to discuss it openly.

Case 2: A Difficult School Adaptation and Its Treatment

When 13-year old Janet was referred to me (S.C.) for psychiatric evaluation, her problems were considerable. She had many assets. She was of very superior intelligence, was well coordinated, had a wide range of interests and, with high persistence, became easily proficient at any skill that caught her fancy. Yet she had made no lasting friendships, was constantly fighting with her two younger sisters, her parents, her teachers, and schoolmates as well. The parents' relationships with 11-year old Susan and 9-year old Vera were good.

Dr. and Mrs. Stone, were themselves very intelligent and competent. Dr. Stone, a research chemist, was in charge of a large division of a pharmaceutical concern. Mrs. Stone had been a teacher before the birth of her children. In place of formal employment, she now devoted a great deal of time to parents' associations and volunteer church and community work. Janet had been a wanted child, healthy, and her development had been normal and advanced.

Complaints about Janet were reported to have started with the beginning of nursery school. Prior to that, although Janet had been a colicky baby, and as a toddler had had mammoth temper tantrums, both parents had dealt with these without considering them unusual parenting issues. Janet had always had a difficult time adapting to new events, but this too had been handled appropriately by her parents, who introduced their advancing developmental expectations gradually and respected her style of slow accommodation.

In school, however, Janet's social behavior was increasingly problematic. As she grew older, her tantrums continued. With increasing size and sophisticated vocabulary, she alienated both teachers and classmates. At home, increasingly she violated the family tone of reasonable discussions. Her parents had initially questioned the competence of her school, but after two school changes had concluded that the fault lay in Janet's own behavior.

As I reviewed her history from the parents, it became increasingly clear that Janet's style of behavior since infancy had fit the temperamental cluster that we have called "the difficult child" (see Appendix). She had been biologically irregular from infancy on, withdrew from new situations and people, adapted very slowly, was more often in a negative than a positive mood and showed her feelings with high intensity. To this cluster were added the temperamental traits of high persistence and high activity level. Although each of these qualities was entirely normal, in combination they were formidable. On those occasions when her desires coincided with those of her parents, teachers, or classmates, she was a great asset and her zest was enjoyable. But when she grew older she had increasing numbers of disagreements, and these became louder and more emphatic in expression. With her persistence and high intelligence, the quality of her arguments was very burdensome. In school, such episodes brought classroom teaching to a halt, and other children, after one or two miserable adventures with her tongue-lashings, preferred to keep her at a distance. Once each episode was ended, Janet would forget it and could not understand why other people held such unreasonable grudges against her. Hence, she would not realize that she had contributed to this growing, distressing situation when "everybody was picking on me." The good fit that her parents had managed to maintain through Janet's toddler and pre-school period was fast eroding.

While it was clear that Janet's temperamental qualities had been prominent in the creation and maintenance of her behavior disorder, it was equally clear that the constantly accelerating vicious cycle would not be able to be reversed simply by clarifying her temperamental component. The Stones had come with the assumption that psychotherapy was essential, and proved to be capable, objective, and intelligent colleagues in a therapeutic process, which, we all agreed, would not show immediate success. The ultimate aim of psychotherapy would be for Janet to gain self-knowledge and learn how to use this to be in control of her own behavior. During this process, it was also our aim to restore her own self-esteem, which had been fast dwindling, and to help her to develop a social intelligence in terms of gaining awareness and respect for the behavioral styles of other individuals. Most particularly, Janet needed to learn the differing social expectations against which to judge the appropriateness of her own spontaneous reactions. Literally, up to then she seemed unaware that reducing a friend to tears was an unfriendly act, or that calling a teacher ignorant, even if true, was not appropriate in a classroom.

Most important, Janet was highly motivated to change her life. True, she saw herself as the victim, the guardian of truth in a world of hypocrites, but basically she was deeply attached to her family, was capable of generous actions, and genuinely believed her parents to be a refuge when the world crashed down on her in so bewildering a manner. Therapeutic advance was an irregular process. My meetings with the Stones enabled me, through their amazingly objective descriptions of noteworthy episodes, to extend Janet's limited perceptions to obtain realistic pictures of interactions. Gradually, it became possible to enlarge her own awareness by my own persistence in asking for her own literal blow-by-blow accounts. Even in her social blindness and lack of empathy, Janet was amazingly accurate in reporting her own stinging words. Finally, with these, it became possible to take her own accounts as a basis for examining the effect of her actions on the needs and feelings of others. With that, my focus shifted to helping Janet to learn to be effective in expressing her ideas rather than antagonizing others. The first four times, when I suggested a modification of her contentious manner of presenting an idea at school, she blew up at me and treated me to typical samples of her contentious behavior. I listened quietly until the smoke cleared. Then I told her I was impressed by the thoughtfulness of her opinions, and that if others agreed, modified, or criticized her idea, that did not mean that they were her enemies; quite the contrary, such responses indicated that her idea had stimulated meaningful thought. This might result in agreement, in modification, or in disagreement. Another might even expand the essence of her idea. "So, when you just made that interesting comment to me, I respected your thinking. But if you want your classmates to listen to you, you must learn how to join a discussion and to respect their opinions. Only if you respect and really listen to what they say, will they be ready to do the same for you." Finally, on the fourth such occasion, in place of denouncing me, she really began to listen to my comments and began to ask me to explain what I meant.

The real breakthrough occurred when Janet phoned me one day before her next appointment. She said she was all steamed up about an injustice in school that had occurred to a classmate and she knew she would create a humungous commotion in which she would lose any possibility of being listened to. I suggested that my judgment would be more helpful if she obtained a larger picture of the situation from her parents. She did, and it turned out that she was right about the current injustice. However, the class, in an atmosphere of their rightful annoyance, had ignored her due to other recent campaigns she had waged over rather insignificant slights. I arranged to have a discussion with Janet and her parents early the next morning before school. In this atmosphere in which three adults were willing to re-arrange their schedules because they found her needs so important, Janet was able to make her first giant step toward self-knowledge. She carefully rehearsed the presentation she planned to make in the class, with her parents suggesting useful touches. She was also fortunate that, overnight, the school authorities had also realized that, although crying "wolf" very often, this time Janet had identified a genuine grievance that they considered important. She was surprised at the school's attitude, they were surprised at her ability to state her position in a reasonable manner, and a new and positive dynamic of behavior was now initiated.

Let me not give the impression that the course of further therapy was a smooth, benign cycle. Janet continued to adapt slowly, saw the negative aspects of a new situation or person automatically, and familiarity was a necessary precursor for positive interactions. She continued to be highly intense, highly persistent and in need of a great deal of physical activity. But, more and more, these temperamental qualities were applied productively and there were more expressions of zestful enjoyment than of explosive, destructive episodes. And, as she approached young adulthood, she used her home support system increasingly often to clarify issues before acting. At her own desire and with her parents' approval, for a period of several years, Janet would arrange appointments with me during college vacations during which she would review events, both positive and negative, to gain more objectivity. More often than not, she had found her own solutions. Yearly Christmas cards brought up to date the picture of a successful career in the areas of her own choosing. By then her predominant positive intensity showed her bubbling, spirited expressions in her periods of absorbed and pleasurable involvement in her interest, with a productive goodness of fit with school, friends, and family.

☐ Comment

Janet's course illustrates the formulation of goodness of fit and individual strands obscuring by sound and fury. Essential in this process was the unusual combination in Janet's parents of intelligence, sensitive perception, and dedication to their daughter's real needs. They had been able throughout her earlier childhood to distinguish between the obnoxious tumults Janet created and her reasonable intentions. But, after the parents had suspected that several schools were overly regimented and too unaccommodating toward children's individual differences, it had become clear to them that Janet's school problems were in fact due to Janet's own behavior. If Janet was to be helped to become a happy and competent person, her problems must be tackled. This was a formidable support system indeed. This degree of positive liaison between parents and me was rare in my experience. It permitted the use of an effective goodness of fit analysis as a basis for successful therapeutic action.

Janet's case history, detailed above, is a paradigm for the development of a goodness or poorness of fit of academic and social functioning, taking into account a student's individual characteristics in interaction with the school's demands, expectations, and opportunities. This model can be applied to the many specific characteristics of the student, and the school—both changing at successive age-periods, from nursery school to graduate school.

A number of students with marked difficult temperament patterns are at high risk in school, but children with a slow-to-warm-up temperament may also be vulnerable to a poorness of fit. For both of these groups, expectations of being able to cope with the content and methods of academic and social functioning may be difficult to meet. The symptoms of excessive stress on children with difficult temperament are generally highly intrusive. The slow-to-warm up group, in contrast, displays an initial social shyness and may not be able to learn new academic material until it has been presented repeatedly enough to become familiar.

The persistent student will usually gain approval of his or her ability to concentrate, which the teacher will see as the mark of a good student. If the persistence is extreme, the student's absorption may be so great, that in any specific activity he or she may become frustrated and unable to obey a teacher's demand for a quick change in the topic or schedule.

In contrast, the student with distractibility and low attention span may have problems ignoring a demand or new stimulus, which may divert her from the task at hand. She may therefore learn slowly and the teacher may misjudge the student as "misbehaving" or label her as of low intelligence or suffering with Attention Deficit Disorder.

The very highly motorically active student will find it difficult to sit quietly for long periods, and soon becomes a problem to the teacher because of his restlessness and fidgeting. The student at the opposite pole with a low level of activity may be labeled by the teacher as retarded, and/or may become his classmates' victim of teasing because of slowness of movement that delays the class.

The model for the teacher for the intervention and change of the poorness of fit to a goodness of fit is similar to the parents' responsibility outlined in Chapter 16.

☐ The Interrelation of Goodness of Fit and Biopsychosocial Models

The data from these two youngsters, Carl and Janet, with severe educational adaptive problems, again illustrate clearly the interrelationships of goodness of fit and the biopsychosocial model.

Carl had such an extreme poorness of fit in the classroom that his episodes of bizarre behavior gave rise to a suspicion of childhood schizophrenia. The interaction of the elements that produced his poorness of fit were: the biological, his developmental dyslexia; the psychological, his determination to hide his difficulty in reading by his defensive, avoidant, bizarre behavior; and the social, his teacher's expectation that he demonstrate publicly his ability to read, something that he could not do.

In the case of Janet, with her disruptive and destructive behavior at school, the elements that produced her serious poorness of fit were: the biological, her temperament; the psychological, her defensive paranoid pattern ("everybody is picking on me"); and the social, the expectations of both Janet and the teacher for her to adapt to the expected social rules and values of her community.

14
CHAPTER

Sexual Issues

☐ Clinical Vignettes

Case 1: Poorness of Fit With Homosexuality

In the 1980s Mr. Bruce S., an eminent musician, was referred to me (A.T.) by his business manager. His manager reported that Bruce's actions had become increasingly bizarre over the past few months, including one arrest for disorderly behavior. His friends and colleagues were convinced that Bruce was becoming more and more addicted to drugs and alcoholism. He refused to go to a psychiatrist, but a close friend, whom I had previously treated, persuaded him to talk to me.

In order to assure his compliance, no matter how reluctant, I arranged a special appointment for that evening. I recognized Bruce from having attended several of his concerts. He was about 45, with a striking broad build, a handsome face and a sensuous voice. He spoke in a charming and friendly manner and was truly a charismatic figure. I asked Bruce to tell me something about his past, and he rewarded me by a long dissertation about his childhood and adult life, jumping from one incident to another. He then lectured to me about his new special musical programs for a new, spectacular, but rather vague venture.

I listened for two hours, picking out his life story in bits and pieces from his discourse. It became clear that he was suffering from a manic episode, but not a drug addiction. His mood was expansive and infectious, his speech was distractible and under pressure, and he mentioned one grand idea after another. After the two hours, he was exhausted, and promised to see me again the following evening. I called Bruce's manager the next morning, and insisted that he meet me with Bruce and a few of his close associates the same evening. They came, Bruce gave me a hearty greeting, and started to tell me about another idea he had. I managed to quiet him, and I concisely gave him the diagnosis of a manic episode and explained what this meant. Fortunately, the drug Lithium had just recently been established as an effective remedy, though not a cure, for a manic illness. Bruce initially refused to take any pills, but his friends insisted. I prescribed the lithium for several regular times a day, and made his associates responsible for his taking the medication.

Bruce came back in ten days, transformed, and now asked for help with another problem. He was a homosexual and felt himself to be an inferior person. He could not respect his actions and had tried to hide his sexual orientation.

Briefly, Bruce, an African American, was born into a poverty-stricken sharecropper family in a small village in Mississippi. In the area, racism was rampant, and the white community treated him and his family with contempt and humiliation. As he grew up, his poverty and race were drilled into his brain through his childhood as shameful. His mother had noticed that Bruce had evidence of interest in music, and maybe even talent. She saved money by scrimping from the family income earned as a washerwoman, made sure that he graduated from the segregated school, and found him a scholarship to attend a good college in Southern California with an excellent music department.

At first Bruce resisted going. He expected to be treated to the same outrageous racism by his teachers and schoolmates. And he had another problem that he kept secret. When he became sixteen, he realized that his sexual impulses attracted him to men and not women. No doubt, he was a homosexual, and this became clearer with every year. And, in those years, to the uncivilized community he lived in, a homosexual would be isolated, condemned, and mocked by everyone, white or black.

So Bruce came to college, feeling deeply inferior—black, poor, unsophisticated, and worst of all, a homosexual. Nevertheless, responsive to his mother's values, he made a serious commitment to education. To his surprise, although he suffered from his poor self-image, he enjoyed learning at a good college. And beyond that he found a few congenial classmates in his music department. He selected the horn as his instrument as a performer, learned about the theory and practice of musical composition, and flourished. He was clearly talented.

In his last two years in college, Bruce obtained part-time jobs with a local jazz band, and one of his teachers recognized his great talent, taught him extensively, encouraged him, and got him a position in a promising new band that was just forming. Bruce's talents flourished, he was welcomed into this new band, and within a few years, he became a leading member of the group. Beyond that, he began to write jazz compositions himself. Within the following few years, the music critics and his audience in Los Angeles hailed his work, and the band moved to New York. Again, he was enthusiastically praised, especially for his compositions, and soon he was a celebrity.

But in spite of the great success Bruce achieved by himself, starting as a deprived, poor farm boy, and his now being respected and admired by educated people and in cultured circles, he remained frustrated. He couldn't help feeling inferior because he was a homosexual. In New York, he met one after another attractive homosexual, especially now that the gay movement was beginning to demand acceptance of gays as normal and equal to everyone else. Bruce knew this, made advances to mature men he respected and who attracted him 'intellectually,' and acquired a few real friends, but was unable to have sexual feelings toward them. He had only been attracted to dissolute young male homosexuals who hang around the street corners in notorious spots in Manhattan. His sexual life had consisted of picking up one of these disreputable individuals, taking him home, where they spent the night together sexually, paying him, and sending him off. For Bruce, this routine was a continuous, vicious cycle. He felt deeply that homosexuality was a fixed attribute of his personality, and felt inferior to a mature respected homosexual adult with whom his sexual impulses were completely inhibited. By contrast, he had no trouble with a sexual drive and consummation in a sordid one-night stand. He felt himself corrupted. This further inhibited his sexual impulses toward any mature partner. He felt unable to break out of this demeaning sexual cycle.

It did not take him long to expose this sexual pattern, he understood its reinforcement for his poor self-esteem. He agreed that his deep sense of inferiority as a homosexual was completely irrational, but telling himself that, or my telling him, failed to help. We explored possible psychodynamic formulations and special environmental influences in an attempt to expose the possible reasons and mitigation for his deep sense of inferiority as a homosexual, but they all came to dead ends. All the respect and acclaim he received for his outstanding artistic accomplishments pleased him, but never made the slightest dent to the malignant core of his deep sense of inferiority. At the same time, his social and professional relationships and activities were charming, imaginative, and sophisticated.

I failed in my intensive psychotherapeutic efforts to change his disastrous pattern of one-night stands with unsavory young men he picked from the street.

When the AIDS epidemic developed, that struck so destructively in the homosexual population, the possibility arose that Bruce might face the deadly consequence of his dangerous sexual pattern. He recognized the threat, struggled with himself, but just couldn't change his risky, sordid sexual life. His final remorseless tragedy was played out. After two years, he was stricken with AIDS, and he succumbed to his symptoms, which killed him in a year's time.

☐ Comment

This case history has been offered here because of its complexity. It is an opportunity to explore the usefulness and limitations of the goodness of fit conceptualization. All pathology, of course, represents a poorness of fit inasmuch as the individual's productive functioning is impaired. After any lengthy and expansive interview, a set of priorities needed to be set. First and foremost, the diagnosis of manic-depressive illness had to be treated so that Bruce's mood disorder could be controlled and his artistic functioning could be restored. Then, the nature and degree of his alcohol and drug use could be evaluated and treated. Finally, the character of his sexual functioning was self-declared to be undermining his fragile self-esteem.

The concept of goodness of fit is not a Procrustean bed. It is an orienting concept which provides clarification and direction. In the case of Bruce, once the clinical diagnosis was clear, it was possible to make his associates responsible for monitoring that he took his medication properly. Once stabilized as to mood, Bruce was able to examine his own functioning, using his intelligence and personal values. In the absence of the dysphoria, it had become clear that there was only minor alcohol or drug use. His distress was focused now on his pattern of expressing his sexuality. While Bruce was aware that his homosexuality was a biologic fact and knew intellectually that it had not been a choice under his control, this sexual orientation, when it had first emerged, would have been, if known, one more element in the overwhelming contempt his rural Mississippi environment had for his black, poor, sharecropper family. Despite his family's closeness and private values, this overwhelmingly racist social attitude was ever present as he grew up.

One of the puzzling features of Bruce's own self-image was the dichotomy between his respect for his intellect, his musical talent, and his ability to achieve decent friendships on the one hand, and his sexual self appraisal on the other. He was able to overcome to a major extent the effects of racism in all other areas as he found his place as one of the more outstanding in a group of competent and worthy people. The goodness of fit he achieved from his college years provided a benign cycle fueling his positive persona. Interestingly, he was a shy and modest man socially. In the circles which Bruce now inhabited, homosexuality was respected and not often closeted. Yet, although he achieved close friendships with mature and respected gay men, sexual feeling with them was never aroused. His sexual drive could only be aroused in the casual one-night stand encounters with callous youngsters, which he despised. It is easy to be aware of the malign nature of such a cycle: self-disgust intensifying feelings of unworthiness, in turn perpetuating the activities that brought his own disrespect for himself. Bruce himself could comprehend intellectually that it was irrational to despise himself for being homosexual while respecting those amongst his associates who were also homosexual. His insight into this particular area of poorness of fit failed to give him any success in controlling his compulsive, self-destructive pattern.

The vast numbers of professional studies of the cause of homosexuality have investigated various possible environmental factors, especially some malignant influence of the parents in the offspring's childhood, but none of the theories have held up in replicating studies. A comprehensive study of homosexuality done with careful attention to its methodology has come from the Kinsey Institute (Bell, Weinberg, & Hammersmith, 1981). The Kinsey Institute researchers have leaned cautiously and tentatively toward the concept of a deep-seated biological pre-disposition. Our own findings from the NYLS have been similar. Of the subjects, one male and three females all became fixed homosexuals by early adult life. Our detailed information on the parents and on these four subjects from early childhood onward have not revealed any consistent patterns in the parents, their relationships to each other, or their other relationships to the child. In none of the cases could we find evidence that if the parents had functioned in some specific special way that the youngsters would have had different sexual preference outcomes. One of us (S.C.) in the course of her consultative practice has treated several children with behavior disorder in early childhood who became aware of their homosexuality in adolescence. In reviewing their records, she found that in no case could she have predicted the sexual preference outcome.

Case 2: A Heterosexual Issue

Mr. and Mrs. H. were referred to me (S.C.) because of the serious behavioral problem of their 14-year old son, Mark. The boy's behavior appeared to them to be oppositional. He automatically refused to accept any request, chore, or rule, even to protect against danger. The initial and outstanding example had occurred at age 8 when Mark asked for a bicycle as his birthday present. Since Mark had mild epilepsy, he was told he could have a bike if he would promise to wear a safety helmet each time he used the bicycle. Mark agreed immediately, the parents bought the bike and helmet, he learned to ride quickly, but then refused to use the helmet because it embarrassed him. The convulsive disorder had been given a full diagnostic workup but no definite etiology could be found. He was otherwise in good health. An appropriate schedule of anti-convulsive medication was prescribed. Because of a medication side effect of drowsiness, the dose was small. Since beginning the drug, the seizures had been rare, but did occur and could be a danger.

The parents were terrified, but felt that they could not take away his bicycle since he would simply borrow one from a neighbor. This was the most extreme of the increasingly frequent parent–child confrontations.

I reviewed Mark's developmental history and the parent–child inter-actions over the years to try to find some clue to the formation of this dangerous oppositional behavior pattern. They summed up with rueful smiles, "Dr. Chess, we are not incompetent or indifferent parents. We have raised two other children who are delightful youngsters, with no important problems. And our attitude with Mark in his early years was no different."

When I had completed a full history, I told the parents I would now talk to Mark by himself. They laughed sadly, "We can make him come with us, but he has already stated that he wouldn't talk to you or any psychiatrist."

On the appointed visit, when I invited Mark to enter my office he came in without fuss. I sat down and asked him to sit down on the chair at the opposite end of the desk facing me. He did so and promptly put his feet up on my desk. My only view of him was the soles of his feet. I said, "I do like to see the face of the person I am talking to. Would you please move your feet?" Mark then moved his feet at an angle, forming a V-shape so I actually could see his face within the V. He announced, "I said I wouldn't talk to you and I won't." This was said blandly—no belliger-ence in tone or body language. All my efforts to obtain his own views were a complete failure. All he did was nod or smile, but he refused to say a word. I told Mark then that his desire for privacy was his privilege and not mine to try to invade. Should he ever change his mind, then I could try to help. We parted without anger—whether it was amiable was hard to know.

In my informing interview with Mr. and Mrs. H. I had little to offer. "You have tried everything, now I have also failed. We can hope that as Mark matures, some event or healthy motivation will unexpectedly make him aware that this oppositional behavior is really detrimental to him, and he may himself then look for help. I have seen this occur before, but there is no way of predicting how and when this could happen. All you can do is stay on the sidelines, give him the opportunities he really wants, but don't try to make deals with him or bribe or lecture him. I really do believe some dramatic change may occur, since he is an intelligent boy and has grown up in a healthy family."

Mark's convulsive disorder, though mild with widely spaced seizures, was potentially dangerous. The safety limitations his family tried unsuccessfully to impose had become confrontations, which had extended to most parental requests no matter how innocuous. This poorness of fit then extended to academic matters. Despite a general family atmosphere of respect for learning, Mark would study only in a cursory manner. His father, at first helping with homework, had gradually increased his input until he was doing some of Mark's reports in great part. The boy now increasingly had declared himself incapable of learning. In these evidences of poorness of fit, the confrontations were not loud and angry. Mark had the temperamental cluster of the easy child, with quick adaptability, and mild intensity. He refused by ignoring and mostly he was amiable with rare displays of anger.

Five years later, when Mark was 19 years old, I unexpectedly received a telephone call from him, "Dr. Chess, you must remember me, Mark H. When I saw you five years ago, I gave you a hard time. Now I have a real problem, I need help. Will you let me talk to you now?"

When he walked in, Mark was an impressive young man. He was tall, had an athletic build, was neat, well groomed, and handsome. He greeted me graciously, but did appear depressed. Before listening to Mark's presenting problems, I wanted to make certain that he was really motivated for help. "Why," I asked, "did you come to me now when you had previously not wanted to talk to me at all?" His reasons were convincing. First, he had problems that he himself felt an imperative to solve. Second, since I had not tried to talk him into therapy before, he now felt assured that I would not try to coerce him into long-term therapy against his desire. I clarified that I was not going to solve his problems for him, but my role was to provide the technical tools for him to work out his difficulties. His seizures had ceased and the neurologist had taken him off anti-convulsive medication.

First and foremost, he had found himself sexually impotent—this was really the driving problem. As we reviewed Mark's functioning, there was a general sense of helplessness and inferior functioning. He was also impotent in his ability to study or to carry through satisfactory personal relationships. He had finally realized that throughout his life his first reaction to any new demand was to assume that it was beyond his ability. He had gotten through high school with his father virtually writing his assignments.

In his first year in college, he lived in a dormitory. He had written his own essay for the first time and found to his surprise that it was worthy of a positive comment from the teacher. Then he pulled a stunt that jolted even him. The college had announced a crackdown on drugs and given a date when a room search would take place. Not a drug user himself, Mark procured some marijuana and deliberately placed it so that it could be found. To his shock, the authorities stood firm and he had to leave college. He realized, to his surprise, that he did want an education.

It was this combination of disasters and dim awareness that revealed to Mark that he had some positive potential and brought him for help. Most probably, the sexual impotence was the essential motivator.

After a period of several years during which he had engaged in a useful community program as a volunteer, Mark had on his own initiative applied successfully to another college. His convulsive disorder was no longer present. He presented his impotence to me as an isolated area of dysfunction. He had several times moved into friendly intimacy with one of the girls in a group with whom he socialized. Sexual intimacy soon followed. After sexual arousal with an erection, he lost the erection as soon as he attempted penetration. He never had successful sex. Humiliated and angry, he would exact from the girl a promise of secrecy. Increasingly he was avoiding socialization to protect himself from still another sexual disaster.

I suggested that we review Mark's childhood problems to learn if they were relevant. That brief study at age fourteen held much information. Despite his previous overt rudeness (feet on my desk at age 14), he had otherwise been calm and polite. He verified that his oppositionality was targeted toward his relationship with his parents. Examining the unfolding dynamics from a goodness of fit perspective was revealing. Temperamentally, Mark had been reported to be an easy child, and early relationships, socialization skills, and safety education had been learned in a positive atmosphere. Parent–child interaction had been a good fit. The poor fit began in the child's responses to the special safety measures needed for his first bicycle. Because his convulsive disorder had been handled without fanfare, Mark had given it little prior thought. He reacted to what he perceived to be public humiliation in the wearing of a protective helmet, with denial of danger, noncompliance, and recklessness. In terms of his mild intensity, previously a good fit, he quietly endangered his life. There has already been recounted the parental effort to bring obedience and the widening areas in which he expressed his defiance. The poor fit extended Mark's growing incompetence and dependence. This was played out particularly in the educational arena. In a school, peer, and family atmosphere in which education and work accomplishments were important measures of success, Mark was increasingly impotent to function independently. When I brought up this possible link, Mark thought that it might be relevant. Despite his current adequate functioning outside of sex, he thought of himself as stupid, educationally incompetent, and not worth much as an individual. He elected to pursue this analysis.

Our first task was to define what would be the purpose and method of psychotherapy. Mark's expectation was that he would present each problem of functioning and I, as therapist, would furnish the solution. His theme, in his own repeated words, was "You have to do something about . . ." The dots to be filled in might be as diverse as motivating him to study for an impending examination, helping him to manage a date with a girl so as not to be embarrassed sexually, or helping him figure out a way to get his father to fulfill some refused request.

He was a reacting entity and not an initiator of plans. Ideas for action came from the outside world. Mark might well have accepted the rest of his defective functioning out of sheer inertia had it not been for his vital goal to function in the sexual area.

Upon my insistence that we could not tackle the sexual area successfully as a first step, Mark agreed that we examine his early development and try to learn how he had arrived at a status which was, admittedly, unsatisfactory (his pre-adolescent history has been given above). I proposed a theme for our examination, namely to leave behind "See what they did to me" and replace it with "Now that I understand, I intend to be in charge of my life." An essential element for Mark to make this change possible, an absolute necessity, was our initial agreement that Mark could end treatment whenever he wanted. Without this open door, he would have felt coerced. His agreeing to this new theme as a goal was illusory at this time. It sounded good, but under his current functioning, feeling that he was in charge went no further than knowing that he could depart at will. Yet, as we continued, this goal to be in charge of his life finally became real. With each new accomplishment, such as learning useful study habits, the positive results did bring about a developing sense of mastery. An interaction was occurring that was a good fit. The expectations and demands of his environment increasingly were becoming identical with the demands and expectations of Mark himself.

With an emerging desire for self-exploration, he now understood his childhood interactions with his parents. They had a correct concern for his safety. He realized that he had interpreted the parental order to wear a protective helmet as a harassment and reacted with rebellion. This was the start of his oppositional behavior. Now he understood that the parents were right and were not harassing him.

With this insight, in a similar way, Mark reinterpreted his oppositional behaviors with parents, peers, school, and the wider world. Mark now began genuinely to master his life. He now took the lead in introducing areas to explore and attitudes to question. With the concomitant improvement in functioning, he began to realize that the people of his surroundings took his good functioning for granted; that he was indeed respected.

With his established new persona, Mark had moved on his sexual problem on his own. He told me that he had found himself in a growing relationship with a fellow student that had become truly important. He had decided to divulge to her his sexual problem. Far from being amused or repelled, she had in turn told him of her former frigidity, which she felt that she would now overcome. In this atmosphere of mutual support, he had achieved sexual fulfillment.

☐ Comment

The simple three-letter word, sex, connotes an extraordinarily broad set of issues and factors that influence the personal lives of individuals, groups, and even of communities, of culture, of history, science, and art.

In this volume, we can only indicate the importance of sex within the framework of the theory and practice of the goodness or poorness of fit in the context of the biopsychosocial model regarding the psychological development and functioning of the child, adolescent, and adult.

☐ The Sexual Dynamics in Psychological Development

The enormous variability of the sexual factors in an individual or group's life course in civilization have been given testimony in stories of playwrights, authors, poets, historians, sociologists, psychologists, and psychiatrists. Sigmund Freud, with a few colleagues, was emboldened a hundred years ago to develop a systematic, comprehensive, complex, sexual, and presumably scientific course of a life's style and history from infancy through childhood, adolescence, and adult life. One needs hardly mention the tremendous influence that Freud's concepts of sexual structure have had on so many cultural and scientific students during the first 50 years of the twentieth century. But Freud's unitary, systematic structure, so intriguing and persuasive and embraced by so many, has by now been very seriously challenged and fragmented (see Chapter 2). It is clear that sexuality is so complex that the biological, psychological, and sociocultural sexual influences are variable and interrelated in different individuals. It would be impossible to construct a comprehensive structure of sexuality that could explain all the many differences in healthy or pathological sex. As an example, the development of Mark's sexual impotence as a young adult. This symptom cannot be explained by the psychoanalytic theory or a pathogenic sexual influence by his parents, or even by some accidental, sexual, traumatic experience in his childhood or adolescence. The onset of his convulsive disorder and the side effect of the necessary medication had no direct influence on his infantile sexuality. Neither was there any pathogenic sexual influence by one or both parents. His development of a serious oppositional disorder then led to his sexual impotence.

The goodness of fit concept may be useful in helping us to understand the specific dynamic factors in the shaping of some individuals' sexual life. But in many other persons, the goodness of fit may play only an insignificant part, and other specific factors determine the development of their sexual lives.

15
CHAPTER

Marital Problems

☐ Unusual Case of Marital Therapy

Professor Stephen D. was referred to me (A.T.) with a specific marital problem. He stated his concern clearly and concisely. His wife, Evelyn, was frequently angry and dissatisfied with his behavior and their relationship. At these times, he pressed her to voice her criticisms and annoyances, so that he could face them and try to work out the problems together. But she could only express vague generalizations: "It's your general attitude and that's the only way I can say it." This left Stephen in the dark, he said. He was sure that they loved each other, but he was afraid that with continuing years of friction, the future of their marriage was in great danger. He emphasized that he would be happy to identify his faults or defects. He wasn't trying to just blame his wife's behavior, but the mystery of their unhealthy relationship must be clarified. "That's why I'm here, I need your help."

Stephen was born in a stable lower middle-class family with an uneventful childhood. With very superior intelligence he had zoomed through school quickly, and by the age of 23 had received his Ph.D. in theoretical physics. He was then appointed at a major university in New England, taught both physics and philosophy, and now, at 33 years of age, was a tenured full professor. He had a rather short and stocky stature, sat relaxed with a pleasant smile and twinkling eyes. He asserted quietly that he is an excellent teacher, and easily makes friends with colleagues.

His wife, Evelyn, had a similar childhood background. She became interested in fine arts, graduated from college with her major in that field.

She teaches high school art in the same community. She dabbles at painting (her own term), enjoys the activity, but knows her talent is limited. Very intelligent, she has a sensitive perception of patterns in colors and in the design of landscapes and fabrics. Both Stephen and Evelyn are sociable, but she is more lively and expressive than he.

They met together in the sixties, ten years before my work with them, in a local anti-Vietnam war campaign. They were quickly attracted to each other, and had many similar moral, social and political values and interests. They were married after two years. They had no sexual problems. He stated that he has not been interested in another woman since their marriage, and is sure his wife has had no serious interest in another man. They have a five-year old daughter, consider themselves to be good parents, and basically agree in their childcare practices and activities. And, finally, they have no substantial differences in their value system, nor any financial issues. They enjoy many activities together and respect each other with regard both to his academic interests and her artistic ones.

After this review, Stephen said with a wry smile, "Our life sounds idyllic, but there is some snake in our Eden. How can we find it?" He came to the next session with a description of a typical interactional disaster. "Four evenings ago, Evelyn and I, and a good friend, also in the philosophy department, began to discuss a serious problem with racism in our department. Henry and I outlined a strategy for dealing with the problem. We looked at Evelyn, because she was shaking her head. 'You are all wrong,' she said, 'Professor M. is an important and influential person in your committee, and he will violently oppose your proposal, and you have to figure some way around him.' Henry and I were flabbergasted, and argued with her. But we know Professor M. and he considers himself to be without prejudice, and we have never noticed any racist attitudes or behavior over the years. Evelyn, what reasons do you have for your judgment? She just said stubbornly, 'I know. I don't have to give you logical reasons.' Henry and I persisted, Evelyn blew up, and was angry at me for the whole evening and the next day."

Stephen stared at me with bewilderment. "I can't understand," he said. "Henry and I were even begging her to explain, and we respect her judgment, but the discussion was a disaster, and I just can't understand it."

I felt that this incident might be a key to their marital problem, but that his report was incomplete. I asked whether, at the meeting, his strategy had succeeded.

Stephen reported, "Evelyn's prediction was accurate and our strategy was a complete failure."

"Have there been other instances, similar to this one four evenings ago, when you and Evelyn disagreed sharply on some issue, and Evelyn couldn't offer a logical reason, but she, in fact, was right?"

Stephen thought for a minute or two, then nodded his head, "Yes, that has happened on some occasions over the years."

"A final question. Can *you* explain those occasions when you were wrong, and Evelyn was right?"

He shrugged and spoke hesitantly, "I don't know. Maybe it's just a fluke. Maybe she has this stereotypic term, 'feminine intuition,' which is sexist, and I couldn't accept it."

I then proposed a different concept. "There are a number of cognitive styles that the cognitive psychologists have classified. To simplify, I propose that the answer is that you, as a scientist and philosopher, have been trained automatically to think deductively. Deduction reasons from the general to the specific, from a premise to a logical conclusion. Your wife, as an artist with a talent for identifying subtle, specific situations like patterns of color, probably also the expressions and movements of people, undoubtedly thinks *inductively*. Induction, again to quote the dictionary, gathers separate facts or incidents to prove a general statement. In other words, deduction reasons from the general to the specific, induction from particular facts to the general conclusion. I am sure you are clearly aware of this difference in cognitive style. Scientific work frequently uses inductive as well as deductive thinking. The philosopher concentrates primarily on deductive ideas and theories. To repeat, an artist, like Evelyn, thinks inductively, or even intuitively. In some instances, you and your wife are disagreeing, probably not on the facts, but in the different ways you think.

"The basic premise is that you have to *respect* each others' cognitive styles—deduction versus induction. Each of your cognitive styles is not infallible. In view of the frequency with which Evelyn has been on target you should be seeking her opinion rather than arguing. It is clear to her that you don't respect her thinking when you disagree, and she, understandingly, blows up and gets angry at this."

Stephen thought carefully for a few minutes, then said, "What you have just explained is begining to make sense. Let me summarize your thesis, to be sure I get the point."

His summary was concise and accurate. He even added, "Now that I think this over, I realize then, even though I am a good parent, Evelyn sometimes understands immediately why our child is suddenly fussing or crying, and I have missed the reason. So, she thinks inductively, and her caretaking style is better than mine."

Stephen had another puzzle. When he had challenged Evelyn's judgment as unreasonable, why had she not described her way of thinking.

I reviewed several possible explanations. Many bright girls have been warned by their parents and friends not to show openly that they might be as smart or smarter than a boy or they won't be popular. Hopefully, your daughter is growing up with less of that terrible sexist formula than Evelyn encountered twenty-five years ago as she grew up. In addition, in an academic community, logical deductive reasoning is prized, and your wife may be intimidated by the brilliance of logical thinking. But let me correct something. Deductive versus inductive thinking by no means correlates with sex. Some men think inductively, some women think deductively. And there are also some men and/or women who can think both deductively and inductively."

Stephen then found that this thesis, in respect for individual differences in cognitive style, could be important and applied to all kinds of situations and people. He also reported our discussion to his wife who felt that it made sense.

Two evenings before our next discussion, another familiar dissonance had occurred. Evelyn had an important personal issue in her school teaching that would come up the following day and she wanted to discuss the problem and get his opinion. Stephen agreed, and canceled his plans for the evening. Evelyn said she would take their daughter up to bed and then she could talk to him. She went upstairs with the child and Stephen settled himself with reading, until he became aware that two hours had passed, and Evelyn still had not returned. He found the child fast asleep, and Evelyn working at a simple chore, and he exploded, "I cleared the evening for you to talk with me about something important, and now you are spending the time with a simple task you could have deferred, as I have done," and stalked away. She didn't come down, didn't apologize, they both went angrily to bed, and she was sullen all the next day. "I'm baffled again, and can't understand why she became angry at me."

From Stephen's prior descriptions, the probable explanation presented itself. "Does Evelyn have a problem judging the accurate passage of time?" I asked. He laughed. "She is punctual with routine time schedules, but with an unexpected time appointment, she can get absorbed in some activity, have no idea how late she is getting, and then rushes away to meet the person, profuse with apologies. It's so well known that if the event is important, the family or friends will remind her to be on time."

"Well, if that's the case, when you noticed twenty minutes or so had passed, why didn't you call to her and remind her of the time?"

Stephen admitted sheepishly, "I became busy reading while waiting for her to come down and forgot the passage of time myself—then I totally forgot her *time problem.*"

This led to a discussion of Stephen's blind areas due to his arrogance. People like him, who have gone through life with unbroken success during childhood and adolescence, who then achieve a very impressive career, and who are highly respected by others, can develop the occupational hazard of arrogance. "You become justifiably proud, and don't accept the faults of other people, and at the same time shrug off any faults of your own."

With his arrogance, Stephen is intolerant of his wife's time problem. His own time problem is acceptable since it is labeled as "persistence." Similarly, he saw her difference of cognitive style as inferior in comparison to his. "In principle, I'm sure you believe that individual differences do not mean inequality. But in your arrogance, this inner feeling becomes evident. Your wife is justifiably resentful and angry."

I then summarized for Stephen how the goodness of fit concept applied to his relationship with Evelyn. Out of the myriad quarrels that had become a dominant feature of their daily life, Stephen had in fact selected two representative areas. First were their different styles of problem solving. Stephen's method was to examine facts as he viewed them, explaining his conclusions as stepwise logic. He dismissed Evelyn's contrary conclusions because she could not and did not wish to explain her thoughts in similar steps. Stephen assumed his method to be the standard acceptable method. In the particular departmental issue of racism under consideration, both Stephen and Evelyn were in harmony in considering it to be of importance and in need of action. Yet, despite Stephen's awareness that, in the past, Evelyn had been right in her judgement on similar questions, it did not occur to him to give credence to her opinion now. Instead, his whole focus had been to persuade her to accommodate to his thinking style and to judge her own as inferior. Not only did he fail to recognize that, in this instance, his style was a poor fit for planning strategic action, but also he neglected to include in his report of the quarrel the fact that his strategy had bombed. This turn of events was reported only when I asked directly what had been the result of the next day's faculty meeting. Despite Stephen's logic, in his arrogance he had selected to consider only those facts that fit with his own style of cognition. When asked to explain Evelyn's accurate prediction that his strategy was a poor fit for this problem, he could only term it a "fluke" or "feminine intuition," despite his statement of disapproval for such sexist terms.

It is of interest that Stephen did recognize that his own contribution to the marital disharmony needed to be explored, as was shown by the fact of his seeking a consultation. The genuine nature of his commitment to his marriage was to be seen in his readiness to become aware that he did fail to respect his wife's style of thinking. He now provided several examples of instances when her style had been more fitting, such as in understanding their child's feelings and needs.

The problem of differences in time awareness was another example of the usefulness of the concept of goodness of fit. This had arisen in the course of a mutual attempt to help Evelyn solve one of her work problems. Having cancelled his own commitments to be available to discuss her problem with her, he was outraged when she became distracted and oblivious to the passage of time. Stephen's report was accurate enough to make it evident that he, too, had become engaged in activity, so that the fact of time going by had escaped him for several hours.

As soon as the focus was placed on the fact that Stephen and Evelyn had a mutual purpose, a joint desire, the real task could proceed. The real task was Stephen's desire to understand and change the behavior and attitudes that were threatening the stability of his marriage. In fact, despite Evelyn's absence from the interviews, Stephen had been discussing each office visit with her, listening with growing respect to his reactions. A good fit had been attained for both.

Stephen was fascinated by this discussion, pursued the logical implications of the concept of goodness of fit in general, and specifically identified what was required to modify his attitude toward his wife's cognitive style and time perception. He was so clear about the solution of the marital problem, after three sessions I felt he could go along on his own. I suggested we postpone any further appointments for six months, then follow up at that time, unless he needed a prior discussion before that. He agreed emphatically.

After six months, we reviewed events. Having adapted our discussion to his deductive style, the necessary changes were clear. He had relapsed several times, but Evelyn had reminded him and by now Evelyn's anger had practically disappeared. "We will always have disagreements, that is life, but now we know how to comprehend them." Six months later Stephen called to report the continued smooth and positive relationship with his wife.

☐ Comment

I have detailed Stephen's case report at length because it was an unusual application of the goodness of fit concept in marital therapy. First, the marital therapy occurred with only one of the partners present to discuss the facts and interactions. Such a situation is usually far from ideal and often a bad fit from the standpoint of reaching successful resolution.

Yet in this case, there was the counterweight of Stephen's scientific training that enabled him to describe events accurately. The information presented made it possible to identify the cause and cure of the problem. When it became clear he was primarily responsible for the poorness of fit with his wife, he did not become defensive; rather, he was delighted to find the answer, and ready with confidence and success to embrace his necessary changes in attitudes. And when he changed so genuinely, his wife responded and the problem became soluble.

Such an ideal case does occur in some marital therapies, but many others are difficult and take more to resolve the disturbed marital situation. The facts of the problem may have been distorted by the husband, wife, or both in their complaints colored by subjective antagonistic interpretations. If the therapist is patient, a special incident, though reported highly subjectively, may serve to clarify the significance of the pertinent facts.

☐ A Difficult but Successful Case
Another Successful Case

Mr. and Mrs. G. came to me describing their serious and increasingly destructive marital relationship. Both in their middle thirties, the husband and wife had successfully achieved professional careers in different fields.

For both of them, their childhood, adolescence, and college years were uneventful. Each obtained a positive beginning in their separate career choices after graduation, and over the next ten years worked well, were promoted regularly, and achieved senior status. They met each other in their mid-twenties in an informal social party arranged by a mutual friend. They were immediately attracted to each other, and dated frequently, as they found each other very congenial with respect to basic social and personal values, and cultural and political interests. They married after two years and now had two children who were in their middle childhood years.

To begin, they had no substantial disagreements over financial issues, over personal decisions, or over their parental functioning with their children. Their sexual life was highly satisfactory.

But after their first few years of marriage, they began to have short quarrels and disagreements. And with each succeeding year their conflicts became more frequent, longer, and more heated. By their middle thirties, they realized that their marital problems had become serious, and their marriage was indeed endangered. They were bewildered, could not pin down any explanation for the transformation of a happy to an unhappy relationship. They realized they needed professional help and were referred to me (A.T.).

For the next few sessions, they recounted the details of their quarrels over the previous weeks. Some of them were even explosive, but I could not catch a clue as to the dynamics of their destructive interchanges. In the next session, they began to hurl accusations, one to the other, he or she, "did so many things to deliberately hurt me." This comment rang a bell for me. I jumped in, and said, "Give me an example." The wife hesitated and then charged, "He insists on opening the window on a cold night and freezing me." With that the husband chimed in, "But she insists on closing all the windows and I can hardly breathe in the hot, stuffy air." I turned to Mrs. G., "Are you sensitive to cold weather and rough clothing?" She exclaimed, "How did you guess? If the temperature hits below 60 degrees, I need a coat or sweater and a heavy pair of pants. As to clothing, I can't stand any wool fabrics, including blankets. I'm only comfortable with smooth cottons, synthetics or silk. I've been that way since my childhood. My brothers and sisters always teased me that I babied myself. I began to believe it, and still do, and I am ashamed at myself." I turned to Mr. G., How about you?" He laughed, "Cold doesn't bother me, I don't need a coat until the weather is freezing. I'm sort of proud of this, being tough. As to rough clothing, that doesn't bother me at all. I can wear a woolen or silk shirt, and couldn't tell the difference."

The very pettiness of the example given above concerning the opening or closing of windows in cold weather might have been a clue in the exploration of the source of excessive stress. Mr. and Mrs. G. had just described a long known and acknowledged difference between them in cold toleration and in skin sensitivity to the texture of warm clothing. On the face of it, one would presume that such a couple would find a common sense solution themselves. Instead, this intelligent and presumably compatible husband and wife dedicated themselves to charging malicious motivation in their disputes.

I said to them that this apparently minor grievance suggested the possibility of an important problem, namely the poorness of fit of their differences in one or more of their temperamental conflicts. I then went along to explain to them the concepts of temperament and goodness or poorness of fit. They listened to me intently, then peppered me with specific questions, and with my answers, they began to grasp these concepts, and also a new beginning.

However, the temperamental variability in sensor threshold level to temperament and to skin irritability did not seem to be an adequate answer, as this had not been the only one of their temperamental differences.

With that, I raised the question, "Possibly, you may have a conflict in other temperamental differences. Think about it." They nodded, for a few minutes thought carefully, and simultaneously both burst out.

Mr. G. said, "I love to go to cocktail parties or other social events, but after a few minutes my wife begins to pester me, insists on leaving, and spoils my pleasure. Sometimes, I go alone, give an excuse that she has a headache, or had a special appointment, etc. Is that a good solution?" Mrs. G. responded, "I've always been shy. Even when I was a child or teenager, I felt miserable when I had to go to a new school or birthday party, and now I am the same way with a new job or social party. I grit my teeth and do it. But my husband thinks I'm just not normal."

I nodded and turned to Mr. G., "I think you respond positively to new situations and places and also adjust quickly to most new or different issues. With these traits, you are sociable, which is usually desirable in this world. Your sociability came from your innate temperamental characteristics, and not from any special talent."

I then turned to Mrs. G., "It sounds as if you were born with the temperamental traits of responding negatively to new situations and adapting slowly to most new or different issues. We call that combination slow-to-warm-up or shyness. If your parents had noticed this style of behavior when you were a young child and consulted a good counselor or therapist, he or she would have outlined a simple guidance strategy that would gradually markedly diminish your problem of shyness." I then briefly described the method of parent guidance used to help a child with slow-to-warm-up temperament like hers. "Unfortunately, I have to speculate that for some reason, when you were a child, your parents ignored your shyness or had bad advice from someone. Had you learned a parent guidance strategy, your marked shyness would have been controlled (if not cured) and you would not have been bedeviled by it throughout your life. However, even now we can work out a simple strategy of improving your shyness. This program would actually be very similar to the one used for parent guidance with a child who is slow-to-warm-up."

I then addressed them as a couple, "The problem you face because of your differences in sociability versus shyness is exactly the same type of issue as your differences in sensory threshold. The first need is to respect the temperamental uniqueness of each other. Only from this stance can you agree on a course of action that can be sustained." To clarify this proposition, I repeated the details of the first discussion (of sensory threshold) and related this to the issue of level of sociability. I concluded by stating that both of them had absorbed a great deal of information concerning individual differences, and suggested that they now think about these issues during the week and try to apply them to resolving their conflict over opening or closing their windows at home. "That is a tough assignment, but do your best. I will see you next week."

At the next appointment, Mr. & Mrs. G. appeared, and both looked sheepish. Both of them chimed, "We thought we understood the concepts you spelled out last week. The next evening, we sat down with your assignment and started to figure out a reasonable solution for our differences in sensory threshold, as you labeled it. In a few minutes, we began to argue and criticize each other for misinterpreting your concepts. It took only a few more minutes till we were shouting at each other, and all our knowledge went out of the window. Excuse the pun. It looked hopeless."

I smiled at them, "I'm not surprised. You have been conditioned over the past few years toward immediate quarreling when one or the other has a disagreement over any issue. Let's now tackle the window issue together right here, starting by setting up some basic ground rules. We can save your marriage even if you may be pessimistic. I will write them out for you so you won't forget."

Here are the rules I helped the couple outline:

Rule 1. You are determined to save your marriage, for the sake of your-selves and your children. That's why you consulted me for help.

Rule 2. Whenever a disagreement arises in your marriage discuss it, but above everything, *don't quarrel.* You can't avoid the prob-lem—you have to discuss it rationally until you resolve it. You may not resolve it in a single discussion. The moment you start to quarrel, or one or both begins to blame the other, shout, or feel victimized, you are then on the road to disaster. You lose the real discussion, you can't resolve the problem, and are left with another source of resentment towards each other. Once a disagreement arises, you must recognize this as a danger signal and keep saying to yourself, 'I can disagree but I must not quarrel.' If one of you starts to quarrel, the other must raise his or her hand, and say decisively, 'stop quarreling, we have to go back to a discussion.' This rule that you can't quarrel is a cate-gorical imperative, a *sina qua non*, or whatever similar term you may prefer. I am sure that on your jobs, when policy disagree-ments arise with your superiors, colleagues, or staff members, you must discuss the problems objectively until they are re-solved. If you or the others start quarreling on the job, you know the policy can't be implemented, and your organization will be endangered. It's the same issue in your marriage.

Rule 3. In your discussion when one or more disagreements arise, you have to clarify the reasons for the disagreement. Whatever your differences may be, both of you have to respect each other's style of behavior and imperatively avoid a pejorative label, such as malice, stupidity, self-indulgence, etc. You have an example of this issue from our discussion last week. You charged your dispute over opening or closing a window as de-liberate maliciousness. But it turns out that this disagreement was due to a poorness of fit in a temperamental trait regarding high or low threshold sensitivity, perfectly normal for both, and to be respected. I'm sure that the more you learn about your normal individual differences in temperament, or other differences, such as energy level, number of hours needed for sleep, etc., the more you will respect each other's style of functioning.

"There may be a special reason for your individual differences, which are normal and should be respected, but it still may be important enough to try some modification. For example, Mrs. G., your extreme shyness has really made you suffer. As you have put it, you have had to face important difficult situations such as in school or on a job, and sweated out your distress, gritted your teeth, and coped successfully. But social situations are different. Gritting your teeth in your distress doesn't make for enjoyment at those occasions. They are not essential, you could avoid them, but you are being denied possible enjoyment at social parties. Your joint attendance, with your husband, would be another positive experience in your marriage. Also, thinking ahead, when your children become adolescents, you may want to enjoy some new social events of teenagers that they would want to attend with you and their father. Think about it, over the week. If you are willing, I can set up a specific program for you to significantly reduce your shyness. It is not difficult; the program would be very similar to the one we have used to counsel parents in helping their children with slow-to-warm-up temperament to successfully, overcome shyness.

"You couldn't succeed at all with the problem of opening or closing the window. Let me give you a head start with a few suggestions. This is wintertime and the air will be cold. Here's an analogous situation. Suppose, one of you suffered a mild handicap due to a chronic illness or an accident. Both of you care deeply for each other. The one with the handicap needs help or an adjustment to function completely normally. In such a situation, each of you would certainly pitch in gladly even if it requires some inconvenience. High or low sensory threshold is normal, and not basically a handicap, but I suggest that both of you consider the problem of opening or closing the window as analogous to a real handicap. Suppose you decide to open the window only partly. Mrs. G., you will not freeze, but have a mild discomfort, which should be acceptable, or you might even be glad that you, Mr. G., would not suffer because of a very stuffy atmosphere. Mr. G., you on the other hand, will not be severely distressed with the window only partly open, but might suffer a mild discomfort, which should be acceptable, or you might even be glad that your wife will not suffer from a freezing atmosphere. Beyond that, you could minimize even your mild discomforts if Mrs. G. dresses in warm clothes, and Mr. G. wears very light clothing, which both of you would, in any case, prefer."

As I talked, the husband and wife were very thoughtful. Mr. G. explained. "It's amazing. Last week, you discussed the concepts of the significance of temperament and goodness of fit, and applied them to our quarrel over the opening or closing of a window. We sort of understood what you had said, but really didn't grasp the concepts. So, we went on quarreling the same way. But now, as I listen to you spelling out the meaning of your three rules, and add the two specific suggestions as to how we could cope with our window, it all makes sense and becomes clear. It is a revelation!" Mrs. G. nodded vigorously, "I agree completely with what Henry just said. Now, I'm sure that both of us can readily tackle our problems."

I smiled and congratulated them. "You have grasped quickly a set of new concepts in the mental health field that have taken many professionals a long time to understand. Now, I am confident that this coming week you will come to grips with the beginning of your healthy interaction regarding specific disagreements. And always remember, quarreling is dangerous and forbidden. Once you stop quarreling, you have the answer for a different approach. I will see you next week, the usual time."

Mr. and Mrs. G. came on time the next week, as usual. When I greeted them, they beamed at me and bubbled with excitement. They began to report, alternating. "The next day, after last week's session, the weather was cold. We followed your suggestion and didn't quarrel. We opened the window partially, and wore appropriate clothing. We checked with each other. Each felt a slight discomfort, but it was no problem. And beyond that, we knew we understood each other's need. We felt good that we were helping each other—a wonderful sense we had in the first years of our marriage, which we lost and are now recovering. Also, we felt so good that the following evening, we realized that we could further implement the solution of the cold air issue on our own. One or two evenings a week usually one or the other of us has to go to some professional meeting separately. Furthermore, some evenings we watched television together with the children, but on some other evenings, one of us had to work on paperwork in our study, and the other one would read or watch television in the living room. With this schedule, we realized that on two, three, or four evenings a week, one of us was alone in the living room without the other, either in the study, or out attending a meeting, and could close the window or open it fully, depending on the preference.

"And believe it or not," Mr. G. reported, "during the week some disagreements came by over a minor or large issue. Whenever one of us started to quarrel, the other lifted a hand and said, 'remember, we can't quarrel,' and the first said, 'OOPS, my mistake,' and we went back to a reasonable discussion, with a quick, sensible, joint decision." Then Mrs. G. added, "This is such a revelation. With that I realized how long I have been tortured by my extreme shyness, and how bad it has been for the whole family. When you said, last week, that you could help me with the problem, I am sure you must be right, and I am eager to take up your offer. Can you give me a separate appointment as soon as you can?"

Of course, I was delighted at this spectacular success. I suggested that they continue on their own and let us set our next appointment for four weeks ahead. I assured them, if something were to happen during those weeks, so as not to lose the right track, they should call me immediately and I would set up a special appointment, review the details of the relapse with them, and clarify the problem. Also, I set up a separate appointment to devise a program for Mrs. G.'s shyness problem.

I met with her and started by asking her whether she could identify two community programs in the suburban area where they lived that met regularly and frequently, and that might be interesting and useful to her. She nodded, thought for a few minutes, and then said, "Yes, I can indeed pick at least two of the kind of program you describe. The suburb is full of community activities. I had even thought of joining them but didn't. With my shyness problem, I gave myself the excuse that I was too busy. I would certainly be welcomed by these groups, and I can arrange my time to participate." With that, I spelled out a program for her. To summarize, I set up a simple clear schedule for her. She should meet with the one in charge of each group. "Identify yourself, describe your credentials, experience, and your interest in volunteering. Then, be frank and clear that you have avoided joining the group because you have a problem of shyness, but are now eager to participate. A good counselor has advised you to solve your shyness problem by attending the first meeting for thirty minutes, the second meeting for one hour, and then the full time for the subsequent meetings. Promise each one that you will be reliable, and arrange your schedule to be free for each meeting. There's no guarantee, but I am confident, that the leaders of the groups and their members will welcome this schedule as long as you are frank, direct, and not apologetic. Call me after your first meeting, and tell me what happened."

To her surprise, but not to mine, when Mrs. G. called, she reported that when she met with the group leaders and several of the committees, all of them welcomed her, sympathized with her shyness problem, and accepted her schedule for adjusting to the group. She called the next week and described her first meeting. For the half-hour period, she was quite distressed and tense and glad she had arranged to leave early. She called the following week, excited, and reported that for the next meeting, everyone was pleased to see her, she kept her commitment, stayed for an hour, began to participate in the discussions, and was amazed that her distress was so much less than at the previous meeting. She was able to stay easily for the whole hour, but still glad to leave. I predicted, and she agreed, that with her change in this second meeting, she would be able to stay for the next full meetings, be involved actively in the activities with only mild discomfort. Inasmuch as the next session with me had already been scheduled jointly with her husband, she could then tell me about her next meetings.

At the next session, Mr. and Mrs. G. came in. I greeted them, and they burst out, "We have so much to tell you." First Mrs. G., reported that at the next full meeting she had no difficulty in staying to the end, accepted several assignments, and left with mutual, friendly good nights to the members. "I only had very mild distress and even forgot about that most of the time because I enjoyed the discussions, not only seriously, but also with social chit-chat exchanges with a number of members. Now I have also found a whole new set of friends among them." Both her husband and I congratulated her, and she nodded with a bright smile.

With that, we turned to their description of their joint interchanges in the past four weeks. They exclaimed, alternating and agreeing, 'It's amazing. We haven't had a quarrel in that whole month. We've had several minor disagreements, but we always resolved them. Either we came to a joint agreement, or compromised, or agreed to maintain our minor differences which were no big deals." They described the specific conflicts and how they handled them. Mr. and Mrs. G. were completely on the right track. This included tackling the big problem: the husband's pleasure in being sociable at parties, and his frustration over his wife's intense discomfort, pressuring him to leave the party after a few minutes. She had now taken the initiative. "I've learned, with your help, how to cope with my shyness in community activities. I realized that I could use the same strategy with cocktail parties or other special social occasions. Henry was delighted, and so was I. We worked out a schedule for this project along the same lines with which I have done so well, thanks to you, in adapting to the community meetings. We decided to accept the next social occasion to which we were invited and to tell our host that we would be glad to come, but could only stay for a half-hour or an hour. The first party occurred last week. We gave the host a reasonable excuse, and he understood. Henry enjoyed himself hugely, without my nagging. I felt quite distressed, but I was determined, and wandered around, exchanging pleasant, simple, short conversations with several of the other guests. After 45 minutes or so, I told Henry it was time to go. He nodded, excused us to our host, and we went home both feeling happy. It was a real landmark. Our next special social occasion is scheduled for next week. I'm sure at that second party, my discomfort will be less, and we can stay longer. I will call you after the party and tell you how it went." (She did call me, and reported that the party turned out exactly as she had predicted.)

Finally, both of them communicated that their successful resolutions of bitter, quarrelsome conflicts were not only important for their lives together, but also for their children. The couple noticed that now that the quarrels had disappeared, both their son and daughter appeared more cheerful and lively. They asked the children whether their quarrels had bothered them. Both reported that they had been very worried, afraid that they would lose their mother and father as their fights got worse and worse. Now that their parents were so happy, they were relieved and didn't have to worry any longer. With that report, Mr. and Mrs. G. began to berate themselves for being, "so self-indulgent when we ignored how the children were suffering over our stupid quarreling." I laughed, "A little guilt won't do you any harm. Your commitment to raise your children in a healthy family environment is another incentive to make sure you always keep on the right track."

With that, I told the couple we didn't need further regular appointments. They were well on their way, and so if anything went wrong, they should call me. If everything went well, they should write me a short note after three months.

They thanked me effusively; I congratulated them on their ability to grasp the complex concepts of temperament and goodness of fit so quickly, and on their ability to apply their implications in action so quickly.

Since then, I have received a Christmas card from them every year, with a note, "We are fine." And they also reported the accomplishments of their children over the years.

We should respond to a possible question. Here are a husband and a wife who start their marriage with highly compatible values and standards, who are both highly intelligent, and who have no significant problems in their professional, social, or child-caring aspects of their lives. In such a potentially successful marriage, how could small disagreements fail to be resolved? How could their problems have escalated to the point where their marriage was endangered?

Even in successful marriages, small disagreements inevitably come up in the course of daily living, and most of these are resolved quickly and easily. However, if there is some special and substantial underlying problem which goes unrecognized and unresolved, the marital course is different. The stress and conflict catalyses the significance of the simple disagreements until they become magnified and distorted. In this case, Mr. and Mrs. G. were conflicted by an unrecognized serious poorness of fit due to dissonance in two of their temperamental characteristics—sensory threshold and approach in social situations.

☐ Comment

These two cases illustrate the value of the application of the concept of goodness of fit to marital problems. But, this approach is not a panacea. Some couples are entangled in a series of situations of profound poorness of fit and, for a variety of reasons, cannot respond successfully to a therapist's goodness of fit approach.

One of our colleagues, after reading the case of Mr. and Mrs. G., commented that all they had really needed was some common sense advice about opening or closing windows in cold weather. Why then all the fuss? Had they, in fact, ended their consultation by adopting some arbitrary window rules, this would not have helped. A single illustration of disagreement does not in itself contain the full pattern. To solve this single problem in isolation would be similar to telling a child how to spell a single word correctly but failing to identify the child's dyslexia and its multiple consequences. In the case of Mr. and Mrs. G., it was only when they had identified and rectified their temperamental difference and poorness of fit that their positive actions became common sense and a goodness of fit.

Of course, there are a host of other reasons why marital dysfunction may occur beyond the issue of poorness of fit. The voluminous professional literature spells out these issues and their therapeutic strategies.

Physical and Mental Handicaps

In Chapter 10, we report how Drs. Engel, Eisenberg, and Lerner have challenged health professionals to extend their responsibilities for patients' physical and mental handicaps to the full breadth and scope, taking into account the biological, psychological, and social (environmental) pathogenic influences.

We fully endorse these cogent formulations. In the preceding chapters we have discussed the importance of the application of the goodness of fit concept to individuals with various types of psychological problems. But when we come to the cases of such physical handicaps as blindness, deafness, or hemiplegia, for example, or mental handicaps, such as schizophrenia, manic-depressive illness, autism, or malignant personality disorders, the major therapeutic strategy must involve the biopsychosocial model.

However, while a goodness of fit cannot play the major role in the prevention or treatment of severely handicapped individuals, the application of the goodness of fit model can lead to a significant amelioration of the undesirable or even crippling consequences of their handicap.

☐ The Role of the Application of the Goodness of Fit Model

How can the goodness of fit concept provide modest, and sometimes even substantial, therapeutic help to the severely physically or mentally handicapped? The term handicap presumes that the expectations and demands of the normal environment cannot be successfully coped with by an individual, because of a specific or general chronic incapacity. Such a limitation in adaptability, the handicap imposes a poorness of fit with the various unfavorable consequences to the sufferer. However, if the environmental demands can be ameliorated, and/or the person's handicap diminished by specific measures, then the poorness of fit can be counteracted, and its undesirable consequences mitigated. A poorness of fit becomes partially transformed to a goodness of fit.

☐ To Take Two Examples

Diplegia

Diplegia is a paralysis of the legs due to an accident or a neurological disease. A handicapped person with severe diplegia is unable to walk, and in the past would have been imprisoned in a crude wheel chair at home, with very limited mobility. In recent years, however, two technical advances have dramatically expanded the range of functional activity by a diplegic. With an attached motor, the wheel chair becomes much more mobile. With various technical mechanisms and modifications of architecture, the use of the electric wheel chair can assure accessibility to public buses and many public buildings. With these modifications, the previous limit of the range of the diplegic's mobility and activity is now enormously expanded. A poorness of fit is changed to a substantial goodness of fit.

Chronic Schizophrenia

The ravages of this illness have traditionally crippled the lifestyle of education, work, talents, social relations, and self-respect of the victims of this still-mysterious disorder. In the 1940s, a voluntary group organized by and for chronic schizophrenics was established in Manhattan in a rehabilitation clubhouse called Fountain House.

Here, the members learned to work at routines of daily living, and practiced ways to socialize actively. Beginning in the 1960s the members were trained and given opportunities to work in commerce and industry at regular wages in nonsubsidized jobs. "Staff work alongside members at the same tasks to reinforce member dignity and equality" (Isaac & Armat, 1990, pp. 289–290).

☐ Deafness: Its Consequences and Management

Case Vignettes

For the non-handicapped child, all five senses are available to explore the horizons and limits of the immediate landscape. For the deaf child of deaf parents, development and increasing mastery generally goes smoothly. If hearing parents learn to sign, communication provides a good fit for smooth development. If the child is capable also of learning to lip-read and to vocalize, functioning in hearing society is attained. Hearing impairment is, like any handicap, not always straightforward. Jim is an example of such a puzzle.

Jim, age 9, was brought to me (S.C.) for consultation because of a group of escalating symptoms of a year's duration. At home he had increasingly shown bewilderment at changes in the days events or cancellation of plans. He had gradually acquired a set of repetitious actions that were interfering with his previously competent functioning, such as checking and rechecking of plans, homework assignments, and the chores assigned to him. His bedtime routine had become lengthy and repetitious and he laid out clothing and other articles in what was described as compulsive and obsessive style. Although Jim was in the proper grade and a good student, his teacher had reported that he had become inattentive and often disregarded instructions. When reminded, he complied but was upset.

History of his birth and early development was entirely normal. His pediatric history was unremarkable, although descriptively, Jim fulfilled the criteria for childhood obsessive compulsive disorder. We could find no trauma in the history that might be causative.

In my playroom interview, Jim was pleasant and quickly at ease. He was very attentive and faced me as we talked. His enunciation and content of speech were excellent and he talked of a range of age appropriate interests, friends, and hobbies. He tried out my darts, punching bag, drew pictures—all with coordination and interest. There was no ritualistic activity. But there were two behavioral features that seemed not to fit with the rest: one was Jim's hypervigilence that resembled behaviors that were often characteristic in children with significant degrees of deafness. He stopped activity to fix his gaze on my face when I talked. Also, he frequently turned briefly to check my face when I had not spoken. Yet, Jim had replied when I had spoken with my face lowered. Also, several times he had turned toward a noise from the outside.

My question to myself was whether this behavior might have been adaptive at some time in the past when he might have had an unrecognized hearing loss. A direct question to Jim, "Did you ever have trouble hearing what people say?" brought a denial. But this very attentive boy had been brought to me because of inattentiveness.

I now had found a focus for further exploration of Jim's prior behavior and health. Specifically I raised the question with the parents of possible fluctuating hearing loss. If this were the case, Jim would have only been aware of being scolded for *forgetting* instructions and plans when in fact *he had not heard them.* His growing compulsions might then have been his attempts to return to the good fit of his former circumstances. The pediatrician consulted his records and did find that there had been a tendency for middle ear infections to follow upper respiratory infections. The treatment here that restored Jim's functioning to a good fit was (1) to inform him that he was not to be blamed for his failure to hear at times; (2) that his hearing would be monitored more frequently; (3) that he would have his ears checked for infection each time he had a cold, (4) no one would be impatient when he verified plans; and (5) his school teacher would be alerted so that she would make certain he was hearing her teaching sessions and homework instructions. On both the three weeks and the six months follow-up, visits all rituals had ceased.

Children often hide handicaps to avoid censure. They use both compensatory and diversionary tactics to achieve the outward appearance of a good fit. It is scarcely the child's responsibility to realize that his self-protective maneuvers interfere with outward recognition of real difficulties that need redress. On the adult side, utilizing the framework of goodness or poorness of fit enhances our recognition of areas needing exploration before closing options of diagnosis. Behaviors seen in Jim's case—from reports from Jim's parents and teacher, and watching Jim himself—were all adaptive to his own concept of adaptation. Only when all converged into a meaningful pattern and the descriptive discrepancies were explained, could a useful strategy be developed. In this case, Jim's competence as a hearing child was affirmed.

☐ Comprehensive Discussion of Deafness

The case report of Jim, above, indicates the usefulness of the biopsychosocial paradigm of a chronic physical handicap, interrelated with psychiatric treatment based on the goodness of fit concept. This same approach had been pointed out briefly at the beginning of this chapter using two examples of serious handicaps—one neurological (diplegia) and the other psychiatric (chronic schizophrenia). The same approach could be applied to a host of other physical and mental illnesses.

The description of Jim's case had been useful in demonstrating the strategy of obtaining the correct diagnosis and treatment. Beyond the level of reporting the clinical data of this single case, a comprehensive discussion for the etiology, prevention, and treatment of a wide variety of physical or mental handicaps for health professionals, parents and caregivers is needed. Fortunately, a number of useful books on these topics have been published. We have been able to compile a condensed comprehensive body of data on the issue of deafness, and this is presented here as a model for the exposition of many other handicaps.

☐ The Rubella Birth Defect Evaluation Project at NYU-Bellevue Medical Center

I (S.C.) directed the study of the psychiatric consequences of congenital rubella, the behavioral aspect of the Rubella Birth Defect Evaluation Project at NYU-Bellevue Medical Center. In 1964, there was a worldwide epidemic of congenital rubella. The rubella virus is teratogenic (causes birth defects). Throughout the United States there was an estimate of 20,000 to 40,000 handicapped children born as a consequence of this epidemic. The rubella virus can pass through the placenta and grows in fetal tissues. All organs forming in the fetus at the time of infection and thereafter may, consequently, have distorted development. The earlier the infection, the greater the number of organs at risk for malformation. There was a group of these children whose mothers had had rubella late in pregnancy, whose sole consequence was deafness. The behavioral project followed these children from infancy through early adult life. From this study, it was possible to ascertain the areas of excessive stress and poorness of fit in social and educational areas. In addition, I (S.C.) acted for 10 years as psychiatric consultant to a school for the deaf.

The major area of poorness of fit for the rubella deaf children was communication. Because deafness in children of hearing parents is usually not suspected at birth, these deaf babies' lack of hearing was frequently not diagnosed until the infants' babbling failed to incorporate a social component. And often the defect is not investigated until age 18 months or even later, when words fail to appear. Should there have been effective treatment or operative cure, as in middle ear infection, the restoration of communicative pathways would be a goodness of fit. Speech would then need to be taught, as well as the social and safety rules for that age group. At the time of this study, there was no operative or other technique available to restore any type of hearing in rubella deafness.

When the cause of the deafness is congenital, as in rubella, in the vast majority of cases the failure to hear is due to nerve damage. The two measures of help would then be the wearing of a hearing aid, should there be some degree of residual hearing ability, together with the learning of a means of communication not requiring hearing. To hearing parents and to their pediatricians, often *normalcy* means looking like a normal person in public. Hence, recommending a program of lip reading and word vocalization for the deaf child may be the only advice acceptable to such parents. At their most restrictive, methods of oral training which forbid the use of of gestures while talking to the deaf baby are advocated in the belief that this would enforce vigilance toward lip movements. However, gestures are a normal component of speech. Gestures and games using gestures—such as 'this little piggy went to market'—or playfulness during dressing and bathing normally utilize both gestures and vocal language simultaneously. To interdict gestures adds a further element of pathology and limitations to child–caregiver interactions. The option of the alternate language of American Sign Language is, with few exceptions, now used in schools for the deaf, together with instruction in lip reading and speech. Until a few decades ago, sign language of any sort had been erroneously considered by most hearing educators not to be a true language. Hence, the obvious public display of hand signals was discouraged and even socially sanctioned.

Sign language is, however, a true language with all that this means for learning and abstract thinking. In a review of research studies on the acquisition of language, Moskowitz put the issue well:

> Children who are deaf before they can speak, generally grow up with the handicap of having little or no language. The handicap is unnecessary: deaf children of deaf parents who communicate by means of the American Sign Language do not grow up without language. They live in an environment where they can make full use of their language-learning abilities, and they are reasonably fluent in sign language by age three, right on the development schedule. Deaf children who grow up communicating by means of sign language have a much easier time learning English as a second language than deaf children in oral-speech programs learning English as a first language (1978, p. 108).

Total Communication is the way language is taught now at schools for the deaf. It is to be contrasted to the former Oral Schools in which lip reading and vocalization of words were the communication mode.

Total Communication includes sign language; American Sign Language (ASL) or the National Sign Language of the country, together with lip reading, vocalization, generous use of hand gestures, facial expressiveness and body movements. The latter supply the nuances and emphases of the meaning and add to the richness of communication and in a way, supply its grammar. With the exception of England, sign originated in Spain, was further refined in France and is to a large extent an international language.

By the use of Total Communication, the deaf child's visual and motor abilities can be harnessed to compensate for his auditory deficit in learning language. It is the capacity of the brain for plasticity of development that makes possible this utilization of these alternative pathways to language mastery by the deaf child. Using sign language, lip reading, facial and body expressiveness, she can argue, push limits, understand why and when safety rules are necessary, learn social necessities, express emotions clearly, explore ideas, and master abstraction and symbolization.

☐ Mainstreaming

In the past, handicapped children were assigned to special schools. This was justified by the idea that a youngster who was different from the majority, who had some physical or mental defect, would be prevented from learning adequately in a regular classroom with non-handicapped children.

To no surprise, separate schools for the handicapped, with few exceptions, were never given the special budgets they needed to properly educate handicapped children. When the children failed to learn, the answer was usually given that this was due to the handicap itself rather than inadequate teaching approaches.

This attitude was finally challenged by Public Law 94–142 of Congress (Education for All Handicapped Children Act of 1975). This act asserts that the handicapped child has the same right to education as any other child, and that this right is best achieved if the handicapped child attends a school with the least restrictive setting. This means that such a child, whatever the handicap, should attend a regular community school wherever possible rather than a special school. Furthermore, to achieve this objective the handicapped child attending a regular community school should have special resource teachers and other aids available to him to minimize the effect of his handicap. Thus a deaf child who cannot hear the teacher's explanations or assignments, or a blind child who cannot see what is written on the blackboard, or a neurologically impaired child with a tremor who cannot write easily, should all receive special assistance to overcome these serious handicaps to learning in a class with non-handicapped children.

This policy has been labeled "mainstreaming." When first established as official government policy, the concept of mainstreaming was greeted with enthusiasm by most parents, educators, and community agencies concerned with the proper education of the handicapped. It was hoped that by placement in regular schools, with help from special resource teachers, the handicapped youngster would benefit from the educational resources available to other children. Also, his social contact in school with non-handicapped children would presumably give him the experience to live and work in the real adult world, experience he could not get in a special school. Finally, he would avoid the social stigma so often attached to attendance in special schools. A good fit was anticipated.

However, serious problems have also arisen in those communities and schools where mainstreaming has been attempted. In all too many cases, handicapped children were placed in regular classes with little attempt to provide the special resource teachers and other aids needed by the disabled child. In many schools, teachers were not given preliminary orientation and training sessions for dealing with a handicapped child. For example, in a class with a deaf child, the teacher who is explaining material on the black board often had not been trained to turn to face the class so that his deaf pupil could lip-read a teaching unit.

But the handicapped child all too often finds the regular classroom highly stressful and a poor fit. He quickly perceives that he is different and that peers and adults in school react to his handicap. He may see other children ignoring or avoiding him, calling him names like "retarded," ridiculing him. All this will affect his self-esteem. His exclusion and loneliness will still hurt him. Besides the isolation, the handicapped child will often be behind academically, and this always carries the danger that the child will think of himself as "stupid."

In our own congenital rubella group, a number of the deaf children were mainstreamed. In some cases, the results were a good fit, highly positive, with a big leap forward in the educational and social development of the child. In other cases, the results were unfortunate with either no improvement or even deterioration in the child's overall functioning. A few case vignettes can illustrate these differences and suggest some of the reasons for success or failure in mainstreaming.

Changing Needs, Changing Solutions

At age thirteen Julie had superior language skills, was an avid reader and writer, and enjoyed learning new words. She used complex sentences with fine nuances of meaning and correct grammar. She had a number of hobbies and kept herself occupied. She was extremely persistent in all undertakings. Julie was at grade level in school, was accelerated in English, and was average to superior in all other subjects. She did superior work in any independent academic project. Her goal was to be a writer. Her oral speech had pronounced deaf intonation and was difficult to understand for unfamiliar people. She understood spoken language only if able to visualize the lips in motion.

Julie's family situation and relationships were basically harmonious. Her mother spoke frankly of the special stresses and demands on the family presented by her profoundly deaf daughter, but met them in a constructive and accepting manner. The family members helped Julie cheerfully with special situations such as telephone conversations. The family appreciated Julie's positive qualities, and she, in turn, was grateful for their help and direct in asking for it when she needed it. She and her mother both shared a realistic view that she could be part of hearing society to a limited degree and must develop activities in and relationships with deaf groups. Toward this goal, her mother had encouraged her to attend a deaf young adult social group, which she enjoyed. She was also learning sign language for the first time.

Of great importance in attaining this good fit was the emergence of Julie's superior language skills and interests. She became extraordinarily adept at lip reading, and her oral communication was adequate almost until adolescence. Mainstreaming was academically effective because her teachers were responsive to her eagerness and quickness to learn; they were patient with her hearing difficulties, and a special resource teacher was provided. At home, Julie occasionally expressed frustration over problems of comprehension in school. Her mother listened, soothed, and referred her back to school where her teachers repeated lessons as needed until Julie understood and responded with adequate and often superior comprehension.

Unfortunately, Julie's social relationships with hearing peers became increasingly stressful and dissonant. In contrast to earlier age periods, she found that rapid verbal communication was essential in teenage social groups. Lip-reading, at which she was adept, was now not adequate for this purpose. Her own speech was difficult for other youngsters to comprehend. She was increasingly socially isolated outside of the home and her deaf social group. Some of her classmates were sympathetic, but others mocked and teased her. As she put it in a beautifully written and poignant autobiographical story about a girl named Andrea, "Often, the other children teased and tormented Andrea of being deaf and talking differently, sometimes with an unusual, squeaky high pitch." Her solution in this story was to have Andrea make overtures to a socially isolated boy with normal hearing. After a period of tumultuous interchanges, "there shone the love and respect of friends."

Perhaps Julie will experience in real life the hopeful dream of her written story. However, she and her mother were facing the realities directly, as they always have. If her social situation continued to deteriorate, they were considering a transfer to a high school for the deaf when Julie finished junior high school. At that time, mainstreaming was no longer a good fit for Julie.

At no time had Julie been considered to have a behavior disorder. Stressful environmental demands were always mastered effectively in childhood. Her social frustration in adolescence had a realistic basis, and she and her mother were struggling with the issue directly and objectively. After finishing high school, she attended Gallaudet College for the Deaf, a top academic college in Washington, D.C.

A Happy Story

Mainstreaming also was academically successful for Wally, age thirteen and a half, though he had not approached Julie's intellectual accomplishments. His school made extraordinary efforts to give him special tutoring and emotional support. He was in the sixth grade, which was behind for his age; he was also not up to age level in mathematics. However, his teachers reported that he caught on to concepts quickly, though he still found it difficult to shift easily from one procedure to another and he required repetition. A special resource teacher was used effectively to supplement his regular class instruction.

Wally's social adaptation in adolescence was less frustrating than Julie's. He had been somewhat protected from the qualitatively different stresses and expectations of this age period by his small stature and placement in a sixth-grade class. He was shy in new situations and with new people and preferred younger playmates. He did join neighborhood ball games and attended hockey games with the one hearing friend he had. He had an active, positive relationship with his father which was also centered around sports, with joint participation in golf, fishing, and spectator sports. A special bridge to social relationships developed through his mechanical talents. He fixed neighborhood children's bikes and various items of school apparatus. He also built his own bicycle from spare parts. His speech teacher taught him sign language; his lip reading ability had only been fair. With instruction in Sign, his mastery of language and grammatical construction accelerated markedly. In addition, the school set up a Sign club for those pupils interested in learning this skill, whether hearing or deaf. Wally became the leader of this club, and this special status had been valuable in stimulating a positive self-image.

Years earlier, Wally's parents and the school for the deaf he was attending had decided when Wally was nine that he was ready for mainstreaming, and he was enrolled in a regular community school. Initially, this decision proved disastrous. No special resource teacher was provided, no transition program was planned, and the teacher resented having a deaf child in her class. In this highly stressful and frustrating situation, Wally developed tantrums and oppositional behavior at home. At school he kept running around and out of the classroom and began hitting other children. The diagnosis of moderately severe reactive behavior disorder was made.

The parents then combed the other schools in the community until they found a principal ready to make a strong commitment to Wally's education. The boy transferred to this school at age ten and his developmental course changed dramatically. His disturbed behavior disappeared, his mechanical skills blossomed, and he began to learn effectively.

Wally was planning to attend the National Technical Institute for the Deaf, a college-level institute in which hearing students and deaf students attend integrated classes. If he continued the progress of recent years, this appeared to be a realistic goal.

A Failure

By contrast to Julie and Wally, mainstreaming was a failure in every sense for John, age thirteen. At early adolescence he was virtually friendless and had little capacity for social interaction with peers. He was at least two years behind in reading and mathematics and could not write a full sentence; little academic progress was made. He engaged in solitary play activities and shared a woodworking hobby with his father.

As happened with many congenitally deaf children, John made only limited progress in oral communication. His lip reading skills were inadequate and his speech, defective. When he was nine, the school recommended that he learn sign language, but his parents rejected this suggestion. Instead, they felt he could develop oral skills if he were mainstreamed. They were able to gain his transfer to a general community school. Here his academic progress was markedly retarded. Even a special resource teacher was ineffective because of John's poor mastery of oral communication and his parents' refusal to allow sign language. John was eager to please his schoolmates, but was always on the sidelines and withdrew quietly when rebuffed. In school, he also sat quietly, unable to follow the verbal interchanges of teacher and pupils, hoping that his good behavior would bring him some measure of social acceptance. Most of the time even his family couldn't understand him, and he had only pantomime and gesture to fall back on, as his writing skills were also deficient. Unfortunately, due to parental refusal, our research team was unable to do a follow-up of John's subsequent development.

A Parent's Dilemma

Barbara, suffering from congenital rubella, was born with a severe hearing loss in one ear, and moderately severe loss in the other. Her intelligence was above average, and as she grew, she became a physically attractive girl. As to temperament, she was always a difficult child, with intense negative reactions to any new situation and with slow adaptation. With the combination of her hearing problem and difficult temperament, she had periods of loud fussing and occasional tantrums, at home, nursery school, and the early grade years in school. Once adapted to the situation, she was a pleasant, cooperative child. Fortunately, her parents and teachers understood the meaning of her periods of frustration and occasional brief outbursts and waited them out patiently.

With the severity of her hearing handicap, Barbara was placed from the first grade in a good school for the deaf. With her high intelligence and sensitive, supportive teachers she adapted successfully and mastered her schoolwork. In a Total Communication curriculum, she learned lip reading and also American Sign Language.

In her fifth grade, the teacher offered the mother the option for Barbara to move to a mainstream, regular school and class. Instruction in words would make high demands on Barbara's oral skills, but this school did already have a resource teacher for deaf children. The parents were troubled over the decision. Mainstreaming potentially gave the opportunity for a better education and social exposure to the non-deaf world, giving wider latitude for later educational choices. Barbara, with her good intelligence, could cope with a more demanding curriculum in a regular school. But could she master behaviorally all the new situations in such a change—a new building, new classmates, new teacher, and new type of curriculum—with her difficult temperament? Beyond that, Barbara would have to take a special bus to school and back home, whose driver was notorious as an irritable personality with strict rules of order for the children so as to maintain her concentration on driving.

With this dilemma, the parents consulted me (S.C.). I had previously done a consultation with the parents when Barbara had difficulties as a preschooler. The clinical evaluation revealed that her problems were due to a rather extreme difficult temperament and a poorness of fit with the parents' inappropriate demands and expectations with the child. I explained the issue to the parents and offered ongoing guidance. A few sessions only had been required. The parents understood the nature of Barbara's temperament, and changed their attitudes and handling to produce a goodness of fit. Barbara then developed with only minor problems, as indicated above. But with her difficult temperament, could she now cope with all the series of simultaneous new changes necessitated by a transfer to a general school?

The parents thoughtfully posed the details of pro and con reasons for mainstreaming. After careful consideration, I felt strongly that Barbara could not successfully cope with all the changes to a strange new general school with her difficult temperament. The stress and frustrations in the new school, or even with the bus driver, would undoubtedly trigger many outbursts, and she would be unable to benefit academically and socially from the potential value of mainstreaming. The outcome could very well become a disaster. I advised the parents to take the choice of keeping Barbara in the familiar environment of her school for the deaf. The parents were very relieved at my judgment, with which they concurred. Barbara, who had also participated in this consideration, wished to remain in her current school. She went successfully through the succeeding school years, including the high school years. The transition to a high school for the deaf was simple, because her classmates went along with her, and the school was situated in the same building as her grade school. She later attended Gallaudet College for the Deaf in Washington, D.C.

If Barbara's temperament had been easy and persistent, rather than difficult, and if she had had positive adaptation to the new, the story might have been different. Mainstreaming then would have been possible.

Requirements for Successful Mainstreaming

The requirements for successfully mainstreaming a severely deaf child: Formula for a goodness of fit.

1. Average or high intelligence;
2. Proficiency in Total Communication;
3. A teacher who learns the techniques for instructing deaf children: facing the class, slow speech, clear enunciation. These habits will, in fact, also help the hearing pupils;
4. A competent special resource teacher;

5. The alertness of the parents for sympathetic support and any needed additional help for the child.

6. The parental willingness to learn American Sign Language. This was true of the parents of Julie, Wally, and Barbara, and was of enormous positive importance. By contrast, John's parents refused to allow him to learn sign language, nor would they learn it themselves. By implication, the parents lacked encouragement and support for John in general. Sadly, they considered his silent presence in a mainstreamed classroom as the ultimate success.

7. The most serious and difficult issue is for the child to achieve active relationships with at least a few of his/her hearing classmates. Julie was an attractive girl, intelligent, superior in her academic work, talented in her language ability, in a harmonious family that was completely committed to support and help Julie in anyway they could. She had all the attributes for successful mainstreaming in junior high school, but her own speech was difficult for other youngsters to understand, and she could not achieve deep or lasting social relationships with her peers. She became socially isolated, profoundly unhappy, and her parents had to transfer her to a high school for the deaf.

Wally also achieved the assets of mainstreaming as Julie had, but with one crucial difference: He had a social bridge to his classmates by his athletic interests and mechanical talents, which minimized the impact of his speech difficulty. He did not become socially isolated, went through the mainstream high school successfully, and became ready for education at a high level integrated technical college for hearing and deaf students.

8. Compatible temperament. Barbara had the basic attributes for mainstreaming, and in her fifth grade in her school for the deaf, the teacher suggested her transfer to a mainstream school. There was only one serious liability in her choice: Temperamentally, Barbara was a difficult child. A difficult child, even without physical handicap, will be at risk when there is any special stress. Such children may be unable to adapt quickly to new situations, responding with intense emotional reactions even to the point of tantrums or screaming. With her difficult temperament, the question of whether she could cope successfully with all the series of stresses and demands of the classroom in a mainstream school became even more crucial. Barbara's consistent need for special help in the past whenever changes occurred in her environment, was an important factor in this case. It seemed unlikely that she could cope with all the changes to a strange new general school, make new friends, and communi-

cate with hearing children, in the context of her difficult temperament. The parents and Barbara agreed, and she went to a good high school for the deaf and then proceeded to one of the best colleges for the deaf.

☐ Comment

We have spelled out with four case vignettes the poorness of fit that can occur when there is a severe handicap, such as deafness. The techniques and strategies of the family, community, and government can, and should, take responsibility for working towards a goodness of fit. The requirements are demanding and our society worries that resources expended for special needs will be taken from the basic education fund for non-handicapped children. Yet, from the same society, there is often an outpouring of generosity for individual handicapped children to help them to achieve a useful and productive life.

Beyond that, history shows that periodically a handicapped individual who has special talents, determination, and opportunities, surmounts not only a partial limitation of his or her life, but goes on ahead to some dramatic success.

We now shall summarize the impressive story of a young woman who decided to become a physician, although she was afflicted by severe deafness which had its onset in childhood. As she struggled through school and medical training, her handicap brought her one problem after another, year after year. But she succeeded!

☐ The Dramatic Story of a Deaf Person

The story of Kate C. illustrates dramatic achievement in the life of a deaf young woman with a combination of intelligence, positive temperamental traits, high motivation, and many supportive individuals in her environment. The achievement was dramatic, but even with these assets, her successes did not come easily.

Kate started in life unhandicapped, with high intelligence and a supportive family. At age nine years, she began to lose her hearing. The reason was completely obscure, and no treatment was possible. Her hearing worsened year by year, but she was able to master her academic demands through high school. She learned lip reading on her own, and was determined to conceal her handicap and had no desire to transfer to a school for the deaf. "I usually was seated in the front of the classroom because I was short and because my name was at the beginning of the alphabet. That was lucky!" Beyond that, her easy and persistent temperament served her well toward her goals. She went to a good college, was determined to go into medicine, and went through her courses with excellent grades. Her classes were small, and she was able to sit at the front. She was completely frustrated in a course on the history of American Art. The professor lectured every week for three hours in the dark showing slides. Without the possibility of lip reading in the dark, she couldn't understand what the professor said, and she had to drop the course, and any other similar ones.

She was accepted to medical school, concealing her deafness, but when she started, she couldn't easily get a seat in the front of the room. One of her classmates, becoming a friend, noticed Kate's difficulty in getting a front seat, and also noticed her mild speech defect, and asked her why. She confessed her problem, which she had always kept secret previously. He promised to save her a seat every day in the front of the room, and fortunately was in the habit of taking verbatim notes. "I sat next to him for two years, and if I missed something the lecturer said, I would glance at his notes. That really saved me."

With her medical school laboratory and clinical assignments with patients, those courses were usually one-to-one tasks, and Kate's lip reading served her successfully. She couldn't participate in the operating room; all the students, residents, and attending surgeons were masked, and she was lost without lip reading. She confessed her problem to the surgical resident, who was sympathetic and helped her through all required operating room procedures.

At graduation, Kate received her M.D. degree. She then enrolled for her general internship at a good hospital. The faculty quickly detected her hearing problem. The chief of medicine tried to persuade her to switch to a pathology internship. She refused to do that, as she wanted to work with live patients. She was put on probation for several months, and then the chief of medicine was satisfied that she could function at a high level and took appropriate steps. I'm sure that some bright medical chiefs at hospitals would have forced Kate to resign medicine because "how could a deaf doctor take care of patients?" The chief was respectful of her struggles and determination (we knew his positive reputation as a humanist). The chief removed her probation because he was now convinced that no patient would be harmed by her hearing impairment. Kate concluded her service and teaching assignments successfully, and graduated after the year. She chose psychiatry as her specialty for further training. She was interested in the field, and could work effectively with patients face-to-face by lip reading and using her residual hearing. She was accepted at an excellent psychiatric training hospital. The staff was aware of her impairment and respected her achievements in spite of her handicap and she was held to the same standards as her fellow trainees. Kate went through her three-year residency without any serious problem, but always in stress. One circumstance or another inevitably came up in which her handicap interfered with her maximum talents, though her functioning was always adequate. At the completion of her residency, Kate received a staff position at an excellent clinic, and did her job at a high level of patient service.

As she matured and secured her professional position, Kate's social life also gradually became active. From a poorness of fit she had achieved a true goodness of fit.

This detailed vignette of Kate's life indicates how a handicapped person, whether deaf or with any other limitations, faces many stresses, problems, and frustrations in personal, academic, and vocational development. Kate was able to surmount these unending challenges and difficulties because of her talents and supportive family and colleagues. Beyond these favorable assets, temperamentally she was a pleasant person; adaptability to frustrations and persistence were crucial. If she had a difficult temperament, Kate could not have been able to master an academic and professional career and a diversified social life.

☐ A Facial Disfigurement

The previous case reports in this chapter have all described individuals who suffered from a serious physical or mental handicap. This last case is presented, by contrast, of a girl with no physiological dysfunction. But she was born with a large port wine birthmark (angioma simplex) on her right cheek that produced severe guilt feelings on the part of her parents, feeling that they were responsible for their daughter's ugly facial appearance.

The parents, Mr. and Mrs. Smith, were referred to me (S.C.) to deal with their guilt and the threatening negative self-image of the girl, Vivian.

According to the dermatology consultant, it would be unwise to attempt to eradicate this birthmark during early childhood. As a medical problem, there was no need for further action for several years other than monitoring the discoloration with the hope that its extent and visibility might diminish spontaneously. The parents were, however, devastated. The pregnancy had been achieved after many years of infertility. Desiring another child, their first concern was whether this birthmark was a genetic likelihood. Despite no family history, the mother's fears bordered on the obsessive. It soon emerged that Mrs. Smith's concern for her daughter's comeliness had multiple roots. She herself had been a plain child with a very attractive older sister. She voiced both personal guilt that she was responsible for producing a "monster," and grief for the social rejection she anticipated for her daughter. And, in truth, she admitted that she herself was repulsed by her daughter's face. By contrast, Mr. Smith, while initially upset by the cosmetic handicap, had had a childhood friend with a similar birthmark. He recalled that, in the multiplicity of mutual activities, awareness of the birthmark had receded to the background. Thus he could easily accept a postponement of remedial action, and did not feel that his daughter's appearance was any personal reflection on his own or his wife's personal worth. A sensitive and compassionate man, his enthusiastic pride in his daughter dampened the extent of Mrs. Smith's grief.

The child, Vivian, herself became a positive factor in the balance of good versus poor fit. The magic of watching infant development itself took over. Experiencing Vivian's increasing competence in social recognition, motor accomplishments, and general maturation produced a growing mother–daughter bond, which was increased by the father's spontaneous and unreserved joy and participation in infant caregiving. And of crucial importance was Vivian's easy temperament. Her reaction to visitors, to new foods, to exploration of toy gifts, and experiences in general made child care fun. She adapted to new circumstance easily. And her mood was mostly positive, so that the cause of her crying could usually be interpreted quickly so that each specific need could easily be met, such as hunger, or a soiled or wet diaper. Analysis of the areas of goodness versus poorness of fit determined that the focus of intervention should be (1) helping Mrs. Smith to come to terms with the causes of her catastrophic reaction to the presence of this particular handicap; (2) helping her to create the groundwork for her daughter's later coping; and (3) working toward consonance and openness in both parent's expressed attitudes, neither with denial nor undue focus. Planning for the future, it would be necessary to help Mrs. Smith to anticipate that older developmental periods, such as adolescence, would bring different meaning to the handicap, necessitating different coping approaches for herself and her husband and for Vivian.

In another setting, the degree and type of parental reaction to the same birth defect would have been different, with its own set of prior attitudes and values bringing their existence to the problem and to the solution. Had Vivian been a temperamentally difficult child, her own tempestuous behavior might have intensified her mother's adverse reactions to the facial mark, and complicated the measures needed to create a goodness of fit in Vivian's development.

PART

IV

CLINICAL
APPLICATIONS

Prevention and Early Intervention of Childhood Behavior Problems

Parental Guidance is an important tool in both the prevention of behavior disorders in childhood, and early intervention when a behavior problem has occurred. The attitudes of parents and primary caregivers are high on the list of the forces dominating a young child's own attitudes and actions. Excessive pressures on the child produce poor fit and undermine his accommodative powers for mastering the environmental features of his daily life. A powerful tool would be to reverse this poor fit by transforming the inappropriate attitudes of the caregivers. Then the constancy of new and appropriate pressures, in the context of a good fit, enhances the child's enjoyment of daily life and increases his sense of empowerment.

We shall first give an example of a therapeutic situation that provided an unexpected psychological insight, namely the power of motivation under extraordinary circumstances, to bring about behavioral change. In the case history that follows I (S.C.) was referred to a psychologically distressed mother who was correctly convinced that her own distorted perceptions and deep anxieties were harming her three-year old son, Tom. Her very severe anxiety neurosis had led to a restrictive life for herself and had been the cause of her divorce and her present social isolation. She had hoped that enrolling her son in nursery school would provide a normalizing influence.

Mrs. S. had gone through several years of psychoanalysis in an effort to cure her anxieties, with no positive results. The nursery school director, noting strengths in the child and the desperate struggle of the mother, had sent her for psychiatric consultation to me.

School policy was that a parent might remain in the classroom to help a new child feel comfortable and familiar. Usually this meant for the duration of a week, with a gradual diminishing period each day as the pupil made friends and became absorbed in activities. Tom's mother had remained in the classroom for the entire morning for a full three weeks with every evidence that she intended to stay indefinitely. Tom had, in fact, become absorbed in activities and seemed to pay little attention to his mother. When Mrs. S. wanted to leave, she would make sure to get his attention to say good-bye. In response, Tom started to cry and cling, and she stayed longer. The director finally insisted that Mrs. S. leave the classroom but permitted her to remain within earshot in her own office. To Mrs. S.'s amazement, Tom quieted down immediately after his mother vanished and was clearly enjoying himself. Mrs. S. now became concerned that she was inhibiting Tom's healthy development and might be dooming him to become an anxious individual like herself.

In my consultation, it immediately emerged that Mrs. S. had what at that time, 30 years ago, was classified as an anxiety neurosis. She had severe claustrophobia and frequent panic attacks. In recent years, a new anxiety syndrome, a biologically based panic disorder, has been identified. Mrs. S.'s symptoms correspond with the current diagnosis of panic disorder, and would now be treated by medication without psychoanalysis (Klerman, 1989). She had tried psychoanalytic treatment before that medication was available, but this had not helped and she was unwilling, almost panicked, at the suggestion that she try psychotherapy once more. I had never had the experience of giving guidance successfully with a mother with a fixed, deep-seated anxiety. I had no idea whether there was any possibility of success. But, unwilling to abandon this self-disparaging but highly-motivated mother, I embarked on a therapeutic program by trial and error.

There were no abnormalities in Tom's birth, and he had had an early, healthy developmental course. He was intrigued by the playroom, and I settled Mrs. S. in an adjoining room with the door ajar—to minimize her anxiety. Tom behaved as a competent, interdependent three-year old with good verbal skills. Temperamentally, he was adaptive, of positive mood, an approacher—an easy child. Due to the nursery school director's acumen, Tom had already had the experience of visiting classmates after school. This had been achieved by sending Tom on the school bus with his friends, to be called for later by his mother. Several times, a happy visit had had to be aborted because Mrs. S. had phoned in response to a panic attack, needing reassurance that he was safe. As soon as Tom realized that his mother was on the phone, he had begun to cry and demand that she come at once. On these occasions, Mrs. S. felt that she was a malignant influence, but felt helpless to change her pathologic feelings.

A program to attack this problem was worked out collaboratively. On the positive side was the fact that Tom was developmentally normal and had an easy temperament. There was also a knowledgeable and supportive nursery school director and teacher. Parents of other children liked to have Tom visit because he was a pleasant companion. On the negative side, there was Mrs. S.'s anxiety-driven actions. The plan was to desensitize Mrs. S. to specific types of events in increments that she could tolerate, utilizing her strong and genuine motivation to allow Tom to achieve healthy maturity.

The first step was to have Tom become used to taking the school bus to and from school without his mother at his side. This was easy to achieve because Tom had already asked for this. He saw the bus ride as a social occasion. For her own reassurance, Mrs. S. was permitted to phone the school for confirmation that he had arrived safely and was functioning well. When this had become an established pattern, we focused on extending Tom's afternoon visits to classmates' homes. It was arranged that Mrs. S. should phone during the visit but the other mother would refrain from identifying her caller. Thus, Mrs. S. could receive her reassurance and hear her son's contented voice as he played without interference from her. It required several months to achieve this degree of good fit.

Tom himself initiated the next step toward independence. He had noticed that some classmates were not met by their mothers, but were escorted by the doorman into the building. He obtained his mother's promise that she would allow this and boasted to the other children that he was now a "big boy." He got off the bus on the day arranged and waved triumphantly. Turning, he saw his mother, who just "happened" to be returning from food shopping—a maneuver impelled by her own anxiety state. With that, Tom had a mammoth tantrum, screaming, jumping, angry and despairing—actions totally out of character. He and his mother were both devastated by the event. In our next discussion, Mrs. S. was desperate to find the strength to restore Tom's dignity. Fortunately, her apartment was at the front of the house. We arranged that she would be at the window—but hidden from sight—so as to watch the bus arrive and witness his being escorted into the lobby. She would then descend to meet him. The success of this maneuver was double: It restored Tom's self-esteem and prestige with his friends, and it had very positive repercussions for Mrs. S. It reassured her that she was not, at least at this time, poisoning her son's well being. Even more important, she declared herself reassured by his tantrum as a demand for independence. She now felt, no matter what errors of judgment her panic states might bring, that Tom's own commitment to independent functioning would prevail. She remained a prisoner of her own psychiatric problems, but it was clear that her son would not allow her to have a pernicious effect on his development.

☐ Comment

We started our NYLS in the 1950s because we had begun to doubt the dominant psychiatric thesis of that period, that the role of the parents, and especially the mothers, was always the primary causation of the development of psychopathology in their young children, and that this influence extended into adolescence and adult life. From our clinical experiences, we were convinced that the "blame the mother" concept was just wrong. Our NYLS findings have provided extensive documentation of the equal importance of the child's qualities in symptom formation.

The vast majority of parents do want their children to prosper physically and psychologically. Many of them are able to parent wisely and effectively on their own, with only the inevitable minor difficulties arising in the course of their children's psychological development. Other parents may be caught up in antagonistic interactions with their youngsters, confused and bewildered as to how to handle their child, and may misinterpret their child's behavior by introducing a motivational element inaccurately. These parents search for answers that will be able to be helpful for their child's welfare. They are willing and even eager to accept the consultation and advice of a competent professional who can identify the cause or causes of the antagonistic parent–child interactions and provide helpful answers.

Mrs. S. was representative of a minority of parents whose severe and chronic psychological problems were overwhelming enough to be causal of the child's symptoms. She was able, through her own exceedingly strong motivation, to learn how to inhibit her outward reactions selectively. When this achievement on her part released her son's own healthy capacities, she was able to become an active participant in a joint program toward the child's successful mastery of three-year-old independent behavior.

While ideally, early intervention should be aimed at removing unhealthy parental attitudes, at times this is not possible with our present-day tools. The huge complexity of personality structure, however, can sometimes be tapped in unexpected ways. We have been consulted in other situations in which the pathology of one parent seemed overwhelming at first account, yet the positives were none the less more dominating. I recall a situation in which a mother had a circumscribed paranoid system in which she believed her child's food to be surreptitiously poisoned by an unknown person she referred to as "the joker." Other than this, her ideas and behavior were not only normal, but she was an intelligent and sensitive individual. Loved by her husband, both acknowledged that her belief was impossible and pathological. Yet her paranoid system had been impervious to treatment and its origin was unknown. By the time the parents came for consultation, when their daughter was age ten, it was clear that they had worked out very effective normalizing strategies. Mother was allowed her declared "silliness" of covering over the glass of milk between sips, for example, and Helen, the child, thought this very funny, even joked about it with her friends. Helen had a circle of friends and led a normal life. Evaluated thereafter at six-month intervals, at age 15 when last seen, she had shown no pathology.

With these known situations in which severe pathology has been successfully prevented from becoming a dominant malignant force on healthy child development, I can only conjecture that there must be many such circumstances of which we are ignorant. Human ingenuity should be sufficient so that no clinical problem should be summarily prejudged as hopeless of correction, and decided as such only after a thorough attempt.

But, that does not mean that there are *never* parents who are harmful for their children's development. We have cited the case of Norman, in Chapter 9, whose father had a major responsibility for his inexorable tragic life course.

☐ Parent Guidance

Whenever our clinical evaluation of the cause of a child's behavior problem was clarified, this gave the parents and us the specific answer for the amelioration or even cure of the behavior problem, with the great majority of the parents willing and eager to accept our diagnostic evaluation and therapeutic advice.

In this parental orientation and counseling, with regard to their problem children, we have used the goodness of fit concept, and labeled this approach as *parent guidance*.

The parent guidance program of our NYLS project rested on the commitment to an *individualization* of the treatment strategy for any child and set of parents. With this commitment, counseling in general global terms was considered inadequate and even counterproductive. What was necessary, rather, was the identification of the specifics of the poorness of fit in each individual case, and this varied qualitatively from one child to another.

The initial parent guidance session in each case started with our affirmation of a common concern of the parents for their child's welfare, and a joint interest in eliminating the symptoms that were jeopardizing the youngster's happiness and functioning. We urged that both parents participate in the guidance discussions, and in most cases this was achieved. With both parents present, if conflict and disagreement between them became evident, compromise could often be achieved. Even if differences remained, it could be emphasized that they were still both committed to their child's interests and needs.

The rationale of the guidance program was explained to the parents in terms of the concept of a goodness of fit between the child's characteristics and the parents' functioning as the essential basis for the youngster's healthy psychological development. The specific area or areas in which a poorness rather than a goodness of fit existed were then identified. This involved a description of the child's temperament, or any other child attributes that were pertinent, and of the particular parental behaviors and attitudes which, in interaction with the child's characteristics, were producing excessive stress. Other relevant factors where they existed, such as inappropriate school expectations, were also defined. In a few situations the poor fit was traced to parental under-expectations that ignored the extent of the child's abilities or interests.

Throughout this discussion the parents were assured that the poorness of fit formulation in no way meant they were "bad parents," and that the same behavior on their part with a child with different attributes might have been positive rather than negative in its consequences. It was also emphasized that the child's disturbed responses to their well-meaning efforts did not mean that the youngster was "sick," "bad," or "willfully disobedient." This focus helped to clarify the basic thesis that the necessity for parental change in attitudes and behavior did not mean that they had wanted to harm the child. It was a question of lack of knowledge, misinformation, and/or confusion, rather than motivation that had led to undesirable consequences for the child.

Reference to concrete incidents in the child's life was made to illustrate each recommendation. For example, the initial intensely negative responses to new situations and slow adaptability of a temperamentally difficult child were documented by details of the child's history with new foods, new people, new activities, new school situations, etc. These reactions were distinguished from anxiety or motivated negativism. The recommendations for parental change then followed logically, in terms of the goal of quiet, firm, and consistent handling, with patient expectation that positive adaptation would occur after a number of exposures to the particular new demand. It was also emphasized that whenever possible the youngster should be exposed to only one or two new situations at a time, so as not to overwhelm his capacity for adaptation. At the same time, shielding the child from *any* new demands and experiences to avoid the turmoil and tension these produced in child, parent, and bystander was highly undesirable, for it left the youngster overprotected and unable to transform new stressful circumstances into familiarity and mastery on his own initiative.

This review, which was done in detail, was usually required for the parents to become adept at identifying those situations in the child's daily life in which modification of their techniques of management was required.

I applied the principles of parent guidance developed in our NYLS equally successfully with the parents in my private consultative practice, the child psychiatric-pediatric liaison clinic at Bellevue Hospital, and in our PRWC longitudinal study parents. Parents have been able to grasp the parent guidance issues effectively, irrespective of class or ethnic identity. The length of the period of guidance depended on the severity or complexity of the problem.

Inevitably, the guidance sessions revealed defensiveness, anxiety, or guilt in a number of parents, in addition to misconceptions, misinformation, and confusion. It was often possible, in the course of clarifying the dynamics of the behavior problem development, and of pointing the way for the parents to actively resolve their child's problem, to relieve effectively these disturbed parental cognitive and affective reactions. In a few cases, these parental attitudes reflected significant psychopathology, which was not amenable to the therapeutic strategy of parent guidance.

☐ Parent Guidance Successes

Parent guidance was evaluated by qualitative clinical judgment as moderately or highly successful in approximately 67 percent of the 42 NYLS childhood behavior disorder cases. This rating was estimated both by the indication of parental behavior changed in the desired direction and by improvement in the child's behavior disorder, two factors which went hand in hand in a reciprocal relationship. When the initial efforts at change by the parents brought quick positive change in the child's functioning, this then acted as a powerful stimulus for the parents to continue and extend their altered behavior and attitudes. An average of only 2 to 3 guidance sessions were required for this successful outcome, in most cases. Several parents had difficulty in understanding the reason for the child's problem, and grasping the concept of goodness of fit. In such cases, the guidance sessions required a much larger number of discussions, some even lasting several months or longer. The parental discussions were terminated when the parents had mastered their caregiving change with the child, when they could settle themselves into habitual positive routines, with the reward of goodness of fit and a healthy self-esteem for both parents and child.

We always scheduled a six-month follow-up session for the successful cases. Most of the follow-ups were routine, but there were always a few parents who had begun to retrogress for some reason in their positive behavior. Correction of such relapses was usually simple, hence the follow-up schedule was invaluable. In an occasional case, with successful parent guidance, some unexpected and special acute experience in the family, such as the death of one of the parents, or some other crisis, disturbed the child's behavior, and the parent could not cope adequately with the child's functioning. It might be after one year or five years. The parent then called for help, unless he or she had a new counselor to consult, and I always then set an appointment immediately. This policy of providing practical assistance made it possible to be aware how often more complex demands at higher developmental levels involved similar temperamental qualities. Parents who were committed to the care of their children, and willing to modify or make a desirable change for the child's welfare were often now called upon to add a role of supporting a son or daughter's own efforts toward self understanding.

☐ Parent Guidance Failures

In approximately 33 percent of cases, parent guidance was unsuccessful, as judged by the lack of any significant change in the parental behavior and attitudes which had entered into the formation of a poorness of fit and behavior disorder development. In some cases, only one or two guidance discussions were attempted, because of the parent's fixed refusal to consider that his or her functioning was undesirable. In other instances, lip service was given to the recommendations for change, or apparently earnest efforts were made to follow the outlined program, but a number of discussions then revealed that nothing had changed. And in a few cases, a parent was willing to come for a number of guidance sessions but made it clear that this was not acceptance of our judgments and suggestions. The reader will recall the case of Norman in Chapter 10, whose father even put it that, "I know exactly what you're going to say," then proceeded to give a caricature of the discussion in the previous sessions and continued to go his own way.

Rigid parental standards, which led to excessive demands on the child, could not be influenced in the guidance sessions. Parental denial of their child's limitations also proved inflexible to change in several cases. Middle class, education-oriented parents particularly found it hard to accept mental retardation or even average intelligence in a child. The parents who failed to carry out the guidance recommendations were not prepared to face the implication that this might be due to their own psychological problems. There were others who "misinterpreted" our suggestions, minimized the problem, or simply politely but firmly disagreed with us; they just refused to participate in the guidance. It was evident that they expected the psychiatrist to take over a program of altering the child's behavior to provide a good fit for the parents. They were quite willing to consider that the child might need direct psychotherapy and make the necessary arrangements, but not that they themselves might require treatment. At least several of these parents had had extensive courses of psychotherapy in their earlier years, which they referred to openly, but this also did not facilitate any self-scrutiny in the guidance sessions. To have pressed the issue of their own problems, which we tried tentatively on some occasions, only alienated them.

Poorness of Fit: Normalcy and Vulnerability versus Pathology

Arnold K., a young man of 27 years, was referred to me (A.T.) because of his many social and corporate career difficulties. He had been treated for the same symptoms by a competent therapist for the previous entire year. As his treatment proceeded, Arnold was increasingly dissatisfied. The psychiatrist appeared concerned and thoughtful, but his interpretations and suggestions gave Arnold no real insight as to the cause and nature of his problems. With this year of unsuccessful treatment, he decided to terminate any further sessions with the psychiatrist. Arnold hoped that a new therapist, who had a different approach, might prove successful in helping him. After some inquiry, one of his good friends, who had a successful course of psychotherapy, gave him my name. Arnold called me for an appointment.

Arnold came promptly on time and introduced himself. As soon as we sat down, he immediately launched into his frustrating experience with psychotherapy, detailed his symptoms clearly and precisely and then looked at me, adding, "I'm hopeful, but skeptical." He impressed me as a thoughtful, well-organized person, with a pleasant, rather soft voice, who sat quietly, and physically was not tense. However, he emphasized his anxious and bewildered feelings at his difficulties with his personal and professional life. I told Arnold I was willing to arrange a series of therapeutic sessions with him: "My sense is I am optimistic, but cannot guarantee success. If, after three or four months, nothing should change, we should terminate. We should not drag on for many months without progress." Arnold nodded, and we arranged for a regular weekly schedule of appointments.

Arnold was a "good" patient, in that he answered my questions clearly and concisely, and responded to my suggestions thoughtfully. If my comments were unclear, he asked for specific explanations, and, if he disagreed, he promptly rejected my idea amicably but firmly. I spent the first month gathering information as to the details of specific unhappy episodes of his behavior in the routines of his daily life. He answered my inquiries cooperatively, but kept asking, "Why don't you ask me about my early childhood memories? The other psychiatrist did, and I thought all psychiatrists always do that."

Then, after another month, a sudden simple experience occurred that served to make him appreciate my approach, and to begin to examine the nature of his behavior differently. Arnold was always on time for each early appointment, but for this one, he was late. I waited, and after twenty minutes, he burst into my waiting room panting, and apologizing that he overslept past his proper subway station. I nodded, ushering him into my office. As soon as we sat down, he blurted, "I have to find the reason I overslept. Somehow, I either had a reaction of hostility or anxiety to our last session discussion. I must have overslept so as to avoid the next discussion, but I cannot find the answer. Can you?" "Yes, I think I can, but first let me ask you a few questions." "Did you actually feel any anxiety, hostility, or resistance in the last session?" "No," he shook his head, "I can only remember the discussion as rather innocuous. That's why I'm confused that I overslept this morning." "During your sessions with your other psychiatrist, did you ever feel distressed at his interpretations?" I asked him. He nodded vigorously, "Plenty. Many times I felt confused, or even angry because he seemed to be on the wrong track." "When you felt that way, did you avoid his next appointment, by forgetting, oversleeping, or canceling by some excuse?" "No," he shook his head, "I took pride in my responsibility for any appointment, socially, at work, or for any other reasons, to always be on time, whether it was a pleasant or unpleasant occasion." "That's why," he repeated, "I can't understand today's lateness." I nodded, "One last question. Did you wake up this morning sleepily for some reason?" Arnold stared at me for a moment, "By God, I was certainly sleepy. My father had a serious heart attack, and I visit him every night for several hours after work. His outcome is very precarious, the doctors still cannot reassure us. I spend a great deal of time trying to reassure him and my mother. Every night I come home exhausted and late and have to get up early to get to my job. However, this morning, I could barely get out of bed, I was so sleepy and tired. Nevertheless, I left for our appointment on time. That is my responsibility. But I was so exhausted, I fell asleep on my train."

I answered, "Fine, the answer is clear. Your oversleeping and being late was perfectly normal, considering the serious problem of your father's illness. And you were bedeviling yourself with all kinds of pathological reasons—hostility, anxiety, etc., etc." Arnold spluttered, "You're right. But with my other therapist, if I ever did something "wrong," by a slip of my tongue, an unpleasant dream, or an unpleasant argument with a friend or co-worker, he immediately jumped at me and searched to find some unconscious abnormal reason for my behavior. He always figured out some such answer. I was really unconvinced by most of his answers, then he called my reaction *resistance*. How could I argue, he was the doctor." He kept shaking his head.

I broke in and explained to Arnold that all too many psychologists and psychiatrists have a one-track mind and goal. If a patient comes to the therapist with a set of symptoms, any of the patient's deviant behavior and feelings must have been created by one or another unconscious pathological cause. It then becomes the therapist's job to probe and uncover such a "cause." Unfortunately, it is always found possible, by various therapeutic maneuvers, to find some pathology, and ignore other possibilities of the normal. Unearthing pathology is an interesting task, but is all too often the search for a "fool's gold." I quoted to Arnold the wise comment of Dr. Lawrence Kolb, Professor of Psychiatry at Columbia University, lamenting that psychiatric training always tends to emphasize the liabilities of individuals and their psychopathology, rather than their healthy assets (1978).

This incident, with his lateness and the discussion, was a breakthrough in Arnold's therapy. In the previous sessions, I had tried to pin down the clear details of the factual report of any specific distressing episode he mentioned, as I always did with any patient. However, Arnold was wary and held back on many details. He wanted a new approach to his treatment, but after his disastrous experience with his former therapist, he could not trust me. If I had tried to press him, and interpret that he was "resisting," it would appear to be a repetition of his previous unfortunate experience. I had to go on gently, collecting the crumbs of facts he doled out at each session. Now with the lateness episode, I had demonstrated a different approach, and made sense to him.

I re-emphasized my basic therapeutic approach, Arnold understood it completely and was happy to proceed cooperatively. From then on, at each session, I obtained a detailed and clear factual story of each episode of disturbed behavior, whether in a social or work setting. It then only required four further sessions for me to formulate a definitive analysis of the cause and nature of his problem.

To summarize, Arnold's special temperamental characteristic was *extreme persistence* that was evident in his life-course from middle childhood to adult life. His persistence was a valuable asset in many of his life situations. He was intelligent as well as persistent. Whenever he was faced with a difficult problem, academically, socially, or on a job, he plugged away at the task, no matter how long it took, and avoided any distraction, until he completed the project successfully. With these accomplishments, teachers, employers, and friends welcomed him. He had also gone through post-graduate study with high marks, was promoted to increasingly responsible career positions, and had active and positive social relationships.

But, this successful life-course with goodness of fit was not benign. His persistence was an asset, but his *extreme persistence* was another matter. This created a poorness of fit in many situations, with unfavorable consequences, and brought him to the need for psychotherapy.

In many situations, he could not complete a task, even with persistence. His teacher would say, "Your time is up, you've done enough, you have to go on to the next classroom and topic. Tomorrow, you can return to this task and probably finish it then." Another person, with moderate persistence, would reluctantly leave the project unfinished, and respond to the teacher's direction. However, with Arnold's extreme persistence, he refused to quit, tried to continue the task, and ignored the necessity to move on to his next classroom assignment. Several times such a confrontation with his defiance of his teacher's order led to an explosive eruption by both. Sometimes, the outburst simmered and Arnold finally left to his new classroom, with simmering anger and frustration. Sometimes he was disciplined for his behavior. These incidents were the models for all too many frustrating and even disrupting episodes.

One day, when he was absorbed in working out a complicated company program, the supervisor rushed in, told Arnold that there was a special deadline for another of the firm's special projects, and that all the junior staff, including him, had to meet at the conference room immediately to work together. Arnold said he could not come, since he had to finish the job he was doing. The supervisor repeated, "drop what you are doing, your program can wait." Arnold refused. The supervisor stormed out, outraged. Two days later, the boss called Arnold in. "Arnold," he said, "I should have fired you. You were obstructive, you were not concerned for the company's urgent program. However, you are talented, imaginative, and productive. I will keep you on as a queer duck, and let you work by yourself in your little office. With your behavior, do not expect to be promoted. For God's sake, if you get some sense in your brain, you could have a great career ahead."

He and his girlfriend, Sandra, love each other and want to get married. She said, "Arnold, you're my dream man, you're a wonderful person, except you're a tyrant. When you have your own idea, whether it is where we should go for the weekend, or what kind of car we should buy or whatever, you won't listen to my objections, and insist that your idea is better and we have to do it your way. I can't marry you if you don't respect my opinions."

As the data was gathered, and the horrendous incidents were spelled out in detail, I first began by explaining the concept of temperament, and how different children's or adults' behavior were influenced by their temperamental characteristics. I summarized the nature of the category of persistence, a prominent feature of Arnold's temperament, how it was an asset for him, but how it became a threat when it was extreme. Arnold listened intently, and asked pertinent questions. I answered, he nodded and asked, "Am I abnormal? How can this extreme persistence ever be changed?" "You are absolutely normal, we believe all the categories of temperament, whether mild, moderate, or extreme, are normal. As to how to correct it, I have given you a very big chunk of information. Think about it, I will set up a special appointment tomorrow and we will tackle the answer together." He began to ask more questions. "That is your extreme persistence." "This is the first lesson," I said. "The discussion was highly informative and enough, and, whether you like it or not, we are finished now."

Arnold was back the next morning promptly with more thoughtful questions. I answered them, then said, "That's enough, let us go on to how to solve your problem." He looked at me, "I understand, but I am baffled." To summarize, I told him, he understood how much harm extreme persistence does to him; There is no answer with a magic pill, but understanding would enable him to control his behavior. I gave him several examples of how he could apply self-control.

"Basically, you have to learn to really listen when someone is asking or expecting you to stop what you are doing for a good reason. Your impulse will be to say 'No, leave me alone,' and that is a danger signal, a reminder to listen, to understand, and to change your behavior. In the same way, if you are intent on persuading Sandra and she begins to object, your impulse is to brush away her objections because you feel you must persuade her. That impulse is also a danger signal. You have to stop and think seriously about her objections. She may be right." Arnold stared, "Is it that easy?" "No, it is very hard. It may be easy to start, but it is also very hard for a person who leaves food, when he has to go on a diet for a serious health issue. If you think it is going to be easy, you will not change. However, it is tough, and remind yourself you have to do it. Applications of these suggestions will save your career, your pending marriage, your friendships." I know I was giving him a "pep talk" but it was the only answer for him. Arnold thought silently for five minutes, then nodded, "Doctor, I hear you. It is up to me. I have one request. Postpone our next appointment, make it two weeks from now." I suspected what he planning to do, but I was not sure, and I agreed immediately. He left amiably, but walking slowly.

He came in at the two-week appointment, walking briskly, sat down immediately and launched his lively report at once. "When I left the last session I understood your analysis of temperament, the reason for my behavior, and what I had to do. However, it shook me up, it was a revelation and a big demand on myself. I had the sense it was a life or death issue."

"The first week, I took a long walk every evening, rehearsing our discussion, pondering on its meaning, and what I had to do. At the end of the week, I made a few basic decisions. The next day, at work I spoke to my boss. I apologized for my behavior, thanked him for keeping me, and admitted I had made a terrible mistake. I promised it would never happen again. He smiled, jumped up, shook my hand telling me, 'Arnold I do believe you. Keep your promise and your future will be fine.'

"In the evening I waited until Sandra came in. I asked her to sit down and listen to me. I gave her the whole story of my sessions with you, and your interpretations of my obnoxious behavior that now made good sense for me. I told her, 'I understand why sometimes I acted as a tyrant, but that is the last thing I want, especially with you. The doctor gave me the red light signals that could warn me and control by behavior. I am determined to do that, and you can even help me. If I start to press you obnoxiously, say 'Red light' and I will understand at once. I will guarantee I will never be a tyrant, I will prove it, and in three months I will be ready to say, now, we can get married.' Sandra stared at me, then jumped at me with a scream of joy, shouting 'I believe you, I understand, in three months we can get married!'

"I spoke to my best friend, who had been distancing himself from me, because of my distasteful blow-ups. I told him basically the same story I told to Sandra. He jumped up, embraced me, saying, 'Arnold, it is great. My friends and I were mourning at losing your wonderful companionship, because of your blow-ups. I have to tell our friends the good news, and we will all celebrate next week.'"

Arnold said, "That's it. It was a life or death issue, and you gave me the answers clearly. I had to do it. What amazed me, I was on the way to being a pariah with everybody. And everyone, my boss, Sandra, and my friend, all immediately responded with delight and enthusiasm when I told them the reason for my terrible outbursts, and my determination to change my obnoxious behavior."

I responded, "I am also amazed in one way, but not really. Very few patients of mine have grasped your basic issue and applied the solution as effectively and quickly as you have. Congratulations! As to the impressive positive response of your important people, I can offer an explanation. Basically, you were an impressive person—talented, intelligent, highly responsible, and sociable. You must be attracted to people easily, and distressed when you spoil your relationships by your unexpected and bewildering episodes of self-indulgent, disagreeable outbursts. As your friend put it, they are mourning at the danger of losing their positive relationships with you. Once, you came to them, enlightening the reason for your intolerable misanthropic episodes, and determined to change them, naturally, they were all delighted.

"I have only one caution. I am very optimistic at your future. The healthy changes you are making will be reinforced by the positive responses of others. However, life is unpredictable and if anything happens such as an unexpected stressful experience in your life, you may possibly relapse to your former extremely persistent, undesirable behavior. If so, call me, and it can be corrected quickly."

Arnold responded, "I understand, but in any case, Sandra and my friends will warn me." We said good-bye, and every year I received a New Year's card from Arnold and Sandra, saying, "Everything is fine, thank you."

☐ Comment

We have detailed Arnold's case history for a reason. In Chapters 2 and 3, we presented the two alternative conceptual models as explanations for a patient's pathological symptoms of lesser psychiatric disorders.

One concept assumed that such symptoms must be based on one or another unconscious pathological structure consequent on early life traumata and conflicts. With that formulation, the therapist's task involved probing at a patient's every incident of deviant behavior for clues to uncover the presumed unconscious pathological structure.

The other alternative postulated, in most cases, that the patient's disturbed functioning was the consequence of the development of a poorness of fit. The basic pathology would not lie in the patient's presumed unconscious pathological structure. Rather the pathology would be created in the patient–environmental interactional process. The patient would be normal, with exceptions, and vulnerable to one or another stressful environmental demand or expectation. With this approach, the therapist's task involved probing for the detailed, factual history of one or more of the specific incidents of the patient's disturbed functions.

From these data, the therapist could then formulate the dynamics of the vulnerability of the patient's interaction with the environmental stress. The formulation, as in Arnold's case, could clearly indicate the specific change or changes of the patient's behavior and/or the environmental stress needed to transform a poorness to a goodness of fit.

Arnold was a test case. Two therapists treated him, each used a different conceptual model. The outcomes of the two models were qualitatively different.

☐ Poorness of Fit: Pathology of the Interaction

This concept—the pathology of the interaction—was formulated in Chapters 1 and 2, and dramatically demonstrated in the history of Arnold's case, above.

We do not have to repeat the formulation. But, it would be useful to discuss several variations in the nature of a person's vulnerability and the uniqueness of the pathology of each interaction, citing some of the clinical vignettes described in earlier chapters.

The case of Howard, cited in Chapter 8, is a vivid example. He was a normal boy, with normal parents and brother. The family was harmonious, and the parents were highly committed to the healthy physical and psychological care of both sons. What was Howard's vulnerability? Both parents and the elder son were very high achievers, but Howard was average in most ways—intelligence, athletics, etc.—and had no special talents. As he reached adolescence, the gap of accomplishment compared with the rest of the family was very wide. He was truly the "ugly duckling." The parents and older brother devoted themselves to encouraging Howard, but the facts were inexorable. He became depressed, self-denigrating, and hopeless. Therapy, which was aimed at restoring self-esteem, was a failure. He finally drove his car on an icy highway, skidded, crashed, and was killed. Whether it was an accident or suicide was never known.

A different type of an individual's vulnerability and the pathology in the interactional process is cited in the case of the young actress, Joyce H., in Chapter 3. She was basically normal, but was suffering with severe anxiety symptoms, demoralization, and felt threatened by the possible destruction of her career. Her vulnerability consisted of a power issue. The leading actor on her cast attempted to sabotage Joyce's chance for acting success. When she defied the actor's sabotage, with the help of the therapist, her vulnerability disappeared, her symptoms vanished, and her career blossomed. Her temporary period of severe disturbance was not due to some intrinsic pathology, but rather to her vulnerability as a beginning professional. The pathology was due to the malignant actress–actor interaction, and was resolved by the actress's action.

Another variation can be cited in the case of Norman, in Chapter 10. Again, he was a normal young boy, but his vulnerability was his temperamental characteristics of distractibility and low attention span. He was vulnerable because the dominant, hard-driving father interpreted his son's temperament as "laziness, lack of character, and willpower." The father refused to accept Norman's temperament as normal, in spite of many discussions and explanations by one of us (S.C.). His father hammered away at Norman's denigration year after year as the boy's self-esteem and functioning deteriorated progressively. Norman was helpless with his vulnerability, could not defy the father in any way. He finally developed a severe, chronic, narcissistic personality disorder by early adulthood and several attempts at psychotherapy by competent psychiatrists were failures.

Another special variation, not yet mentioned, occurred with a girl, Claire, who developed the rare illness of lupus erythematous at age two. The internist, given the absence of treatment at that time, predicted the girl could only live to the age of eight, at the best, and recommended to her mother that she give Claire everything she wanted, so the girl could at least be happy for the few years of her life. Despite her basic good sense, the mother followed this advice and Claire became a spoiled, demanding, and tyrannical child. Fortunately, a medication for the effective treatment of this illness was discovered soon and her lupus became asymptomatic. The very reasonable mother consulted the pediatric-psychiatric clinic which I (S.C.) headed, for advice as to how to deal with Claire's unhealthy functioning. I prescribed an appropriate schedule for handling the girl's various undesirable items of behavior. The mother followed the advice faithfully and Claire changed bit by bit until she became a much more adaptable youngster. In this case, the girl started as a normal child behaviorally until she developed this vulnerability of a life-threatening physical illness. The psychiatric pathology developed in the interaction, in this case, the reaction of the child to the unhealthy handling by the mother.

The variations of a poorness of fit in the normality and vulnerability of a patient, and the development of pathology in the interaction with the environmental stress, have a multiplicity of combinations. This conceptualization has provided an important and useful element in the overall goodness/poorness of fit concept and its clinical applications.

V

CONCLUSION: THE BASIC STRUCTURE OF GOODNESS OF FIT

19

CHAPTER

The Clinician's Guidelines for the Applications of the Goodness of Fit Concept

In the previous chapters, the clinical vignettes have illustrated the range and scope of the usefulness of the application of the goodness of fit concept in different age-periods. Many varied patterns of the development of a poorness of fit and its consequences, and the specific therapeutic therapies devised to transform the poorness to a goodness of fit have emerged.

Now, from the examples of these vignettes and our numerous case experiences, in this chapter we will formulate a series of generalizations and guidelines for use in clinical practice.

☐ The Clinical History and Observations

When a clinician has a referral of a child, adolescent, or an adult suffering with psychological distress and/or deviant behavior, the first task should be to obtain a succinct but comprehensive clinical history of the patient's life course. If the history is obtained from the adolescent or adult himself or herself, simultaneously the clinician can note any significant observations of the patient's behavior or language. If the patient is a child, the parents or other caregivers will give the history and a similar observation of their behavior or language is pertinent.

The clinical history should then move to obtain the details of the patient's symptoms: specific characteristics, time of origin, and nature of the course of the symptoms until the current period. For a child patient, a play interview is necessary.

☐ Differential Diagnosis

For an experienced therapist this description of the first steps of a clinical history and observation are not essential. But not all therapists take histories routinely. The next step, after obtaining the data described above, is a consideration of possible differential diagnosis. Is the patient suffering from a severe mental illness? For example, in Chapter 14, Mr. Bruce S., a musician, had recently developed bizarre behavior. His friends and colleagues were convinced that Bruce's behavior was due to addiction to drugs and alcohol. This might have been due to some special environmental event, which had created a poorness of fit. If the bizarre behavior had been diagnosed as addiction consequent upon stress, treatment plans would be predicated on that basis. Bruce denied any problems, but finally agreed, under pressure from his friends, to see a psychiatrist and was referred to me (A.T.). In the clinical interview, his behavior was first coherent. Within an hour, his abnormal speech and manner convinced me that Bruce was suffering from manic illness. I prescribed lithium, a specific medication for this illness, and within a month, his deviant behavior and drug abuse disappeared. With that, I was able to complete his clinical history. This revealed an additional and separate diagnosis, severe, comprehensive, promiscuous homosexual behavior. I treated him for this for two years, without success, and the outcome was tragic. The use of the organized history had expedited the identification of the full range of problems.

The next question in taking a history is whether the patient suffers from any biological or physical disorder. For example, in Chapter 13, a six-year old boy, Carl, was referred to me (S.C.) by the parents, because of the teacher's report of the boy's bizarre behavior in the classroom. From the clinical history obtained from the parents, complemented by my play period with Carl, the diagnosis was clear: the biological developmental disorder of dyslexia, namely difficulty in reading. Carl's bizarre behavior was the expression of a defensive mechanism designed to hide his deficiency in reading from his classmates. Having identified the nature of the poorness of fit, the treatment focused on remedial training with a skilled professional. The training was successful in teaching him reading by methods appropriate for dyslexia and bringing him up to grade. No longer needing a defensive mechanism, his odd behavior disappeared, and his succeeding life years were positive, with only very minor residues of his dyslexia by adolescence.

An occasional case of psychological disorder is created by a physical illness, and if this diagnosis is identified or suspected the patient should be immediately referred to an appropriate physician. If the clinician is uncertain as to the possible diagnosis of a serious mental illness, he or she should refer the patient for further investigation.

☐ The Next Step: The Diagnosis and Treatment of Poorness of Fit

If the clinical evaluation of the patient's psychological disturbance has ruled out the possibility of a significant mental or physical illness, or developmental problem such as dyslexia, the diagnosis may appropriately indicate a lesser psychiatric disorder. Examples would be an adjustment disorder, mood or anxiety disorder, conduct disorder, personality disorder, or sexual dysfunction (DSM-IV).

For clinicians with patients suffering with one or another of these lesser psychiatric disorders, an evaluation and treatment of a poorness of fit is appropriate. The consideration of some other types of psychological problems are also appropriate, such as socio-cultural issues (Chapter 12), educational issues (Chapter 13), and marital problems (Chapter 15).

The Identification of Poorness of Fit

This identification is achieved by analyzing the data gathered by the clinician's systematic clinical history-taking and the observations of the patient's behavior and manner to formulate a hypothesis of the patient's particular poorness of fit. This would include conceptualizing of the development of the patient–environment interactional process, and its unhealthy behavioral consequences.

The clinician is indeed faced with an essential but challenging step; identifying of the nature of the patient's poorness of fit. The task *cannot* be facilitated by processing the accumulated data through some routinized template or blueprint for all cases that will give the appropriate answer of the patient's person–environment interactional process. This analysis has to be *individualized* by the clinician, through an inductive formulation by carefully scrutinizing the accumulated data. The clinician has to sift through and identify the relevant data, and organize those items to construct a plausible pattern of the patient-interactional process. The clinician must then explore with the patient, and gather evidence to validate the formulated pattern. In some cases, the successful analysis of the data may be achieved quickly and easily. At the other extreme, in a relatively small number of cases, the analysis will require lengthy discussions and probing for additional descriptive reports of the patient's behavior and reactions and/or further environmental descriptions of influences of specific persons, groups, or community and cultural choice.

Specific Suggestions for the Clinician

We have tabulated here a number of suggestions exemplified by the many case vignettes in previous chapters. These may be helpful for the clinician's analysis of the individualized formulation of the interactional process and the patient's poorness of fit.

The nature of the patient's symptoms may be a valuable clue suggesting the source of environmental stress. For example, Joyce H., the young actress (Chapter 3), came for help with severe anxiety and demoralization, together with specific difficulties on her job in her television program. This suggested the need for an exploration of the details of the daily events of her work on her job. The source of her severe and excessive environmental stress proved to be the behavior of the leading actor sabotaging the nature of Joyce's pattern of work.

Another example is Robert D., the young man who came for help with severe anxiety and bewilderment at his apparent failure on his first promising staff position at a big corporation. His report led to focusing on a detailed story of his work, which revealed that his two supervising executives had confronted Bob with presumed evidence that he had made two serious, careless errors. They had threatened him with losing his position. He could not understand how this happened, hence he was unable to correct his assumed malfunctioning. This had led to his becoming anxious and bewildered.

Mrs. Phyllis G., a young mother with her first child, a six-month old boy, Eddy, had also come in for help under severe stress, sobbing and berating herself, "I'm a failure," (Chapter 4) as she detailed a list of her caregiving inadequacies. From her history, I (A.T.) deemed, it was Eddy who, despite a normal development, possessed the typical behavioral pattern of difficult temperament. We call this temperament difficult because many mothers or other caregivers will need special understanding and patience to accomplish the infant's daily routines of caregiving successfully. For some mothers, handling such a child may create excessive stress, as had occurred here. In this case, a previous consultation provided continuity of insight. I had treated her six years before when she was an unmarried young teacher, for an obsessive personality disorder. Excellent in actual teaching, she was extremely sensitive to the maintenance of order in her classroom, with unrealistic demands of decorum, reacting strongly even to minor misbehavior. There was an inevitable backlash, and periodically she lost control of her class. Treatment had been successful, she went on as a good and relaxed teacher, then married, and had her first child who turned out to have difficult temperament. Her perfectionism recurred, she pressured Eddy to be a "perfect" infant, and then experienced the inevitable caregiving difficulties which lead to excessive stress for her.

Validating the Poorness of Fit Hypothesis

In each of the three cases above—Joyce, Bob, and Phyllis—the clues for a plausible hypothesis for excessive stress and poorness of fit were generated. The next step required a validation of the hypothesis by additional information. The suitable strategy devised to obtain the information again had to be individualized. In some cases, the clinician might be able to tap specific sources of information, such as parents, teachers, friends, medical reports, and psychological tests. For children with a behavior disorder, a structured play interview could often provide valuable information, as in the case of Carl, with dyslexia (Chapter 13).

In many of the cases, additional information could be obtained by devising a specific change in the patient's functioning or the environmental influence.

This was true in the three cases cited above. With Joyce, it appeared that the leading actor was sabotaging her performance. She was directed to defy the actor's orders at the next program, and act in her own style. She was fearful and reluctant to follow this advice, "It was a big gamble." However, after a short discussion, she agreed with the logic of this necessary change. She made the change successfully at the next rehearsal. The actor's sabotage was revealed as the cause of her excessive stress, and she also gained an understanding of the reason for the actor's sabotage. She saved her career and her symptoms disappeared. With Bob, the threatening charge of incompetence was very stressful, but as to the basic reason Bob was completely bewildered. He was advised to pick one of his trusted, experienced friends or acquaintances at the office, tell him the details of his terrible problem and ask for his response. Bob nodded and understood what he should do. He came back at his next session, no longer anxious but now angry. At the dinner meeting his friend had revealed to him that these same two supervising executives were monstrous characters who worked hand in hand together to destroy any promising young staff member who might threaten their entrenched positions. The friend described his own strategy with which he had circumvented the two executives' machinations, and urged Bob to use the same tactics. Bob thanked his friend fervently. The information was crucial but he decided that he had no taste to live in a jungle, and changed his career to a more socially useful and personally satisfying profession. Bob's choice was wise, his poorness of fit was transformed into a goodness of fit, and his career and personal life prospered. As to Phyllis, the validation of the formulation that her caretaking expectations created excessive stress and a poorness of fit with her infant's functioning fit in well with my prior awareness of her obsessive perfectionism. Faced again with what she interpreted as her own inadequacy in controlling her infant's reactions, she had resurrected her obsessive perfectionism, an exceedingly poor fit for an infant with difficult temperament. Using the same therapeutic strategy that I had used successfully in my earlier treatment with her, I reminded Phyllis of the dynamics of her attempt to achieve unrealistic perfection and its poor consequences with her pupils. Now the same pattern had recurred with her own infant. The therapeutic strategy was similar for dealing with her caretaking practices. She had to reshape her attempts at perfection and replace them with responses necessary for a normal, healthy child with difficult temperament. I gave her a copy of an excellent book, written specifically for advice to parents with a temperamentally difficult child (Kurcinka, 1991). She understood quickly the gist of my explanation and advice, felt relieved, and said she would read the book immediately. She returned at her next session, after ten days, and burst out, "I followed your advice and the author's to a *T*. Really, her specific rules were very similar to yours, so it was no problem. Eddy is now like a new person, he is no problem and he is happy. And so am I. How could I have behaved so crazy again, when I learned so much from your treatment with me before. I just have to watch myself." She did, but, inevitably, she slipped again, but not strongly, when new issues arose as Eddy matured in the following three to four years. She came back each time.

The discussions and advice were basically the same, she followed the same appropriate approach, and each "crisis" was resolved quickly.

☐ The Next Step: A Therapeutic Strategy and its Application

The clinician has now determined the valid formulation of the individual–environment interactional process leading to a patient's poorness of fit and its symptomatic consequences. With that analysis elaborated, the clinician is ready to launch a therapeutic plan toward the transformation of a poorness of fit to a goodness of fit, with the amelioration of the patient's psychological disturbance. The first step in the formulation of the therapeutic strategy is to identify the specific maladaptive behavior of the patient's functioning, and/or the dissonant, excessively stressful environmental demands or expectations. With the identification, the clinician can then shape the specific strategy and treatment toward the creation of an effective *change* in the maladaptive dissonance. The aim is to utilize productive elements already nascent in the patient's behavioral repertoire, as well as alterations in the current environment, that promote an adaptive and consonant interactional process and a goodness of fit.

In some cases, as with Joyce, Bob and Phyllis, the tactic used to validate the hypothesis of the cause of the poorness of fit serves actually to change the specific pathogenic element in the dissonant individual–environment interaction, and to transform the poorness of fit to a goodness of fit. With that, no further treatment is necessary since constructive functioning and the self-confidence which it produces reinforces its own continuation. Routine follow-up for assurance, usually after six months or a year, is wise.

Other individuals, such as Carl, the boy with dyslexia and bizarre behavior due to a defensive mechanism, will require specific, relatively long treatment to produce a goodness of fit. In Carl's case, the appropriate treatment, targeted to his disability, was specialized training in remedial reading. Other cases may require a long, arduous period of treatment. For example, Janet, a 13-year old, was referred to me (S.C.) with a moderately severe social problem (Chapter 13). She had no lasting friendships, constantly fought with her two younger sisters, her parents, and her teachers and schoolmates. I took a comprehensive history from her parents who were objective, thoughtful, and deeply concerned for Janet's welfare. They were able to describe in detail episodes of Janet's disturbed behavior which they had witnessed. With this extensive and pertinent information, I was able to judge that she fit the extreme but normal pattern of difficult temperament, combined with both high persistence and high intelligence. This formidable combination of attributes, particularly in combination with her intelligence and intensity of mood, was postulated to be an important element in her behavior. Typically for Janet, when the teacher differed from her judgements, she persisted in her arguments. Becoming increasingly frustrated she often blew up with disagreeable tongue-lashings and tantrums. By age 13, these episodes were more violent, and increasingly alienated her in her social and academic relationships. With that, she became more firmly fixed in a defensive conviction that "everybody is picking on me." I judged that psychotherapy was essential, the parents agreed, and Janet was willing to come to regular sessions. In the first sessions, I was given the opportunity to experience typical samples of Janet's behavior. In place of sympathizing with Janet over her reported ill treatment by others, I asked her to give a blow by blow account of each incident. This questioning of the accuracy of her perception of herself as victim led her to assign me a role as one more of her tormentors. Because Janet was essentially a truth seeker and because I failed to join the fray, eventually the child began to listen to her own accounts. Once I succeeded in mutually agreeing that our prime goal was to help Janet become an effective proponent of her own opinions, the poorness of fit of her current approach became evident. In her typical, contentious fashion, she was able to eventually comprehend that my suggestion that she use different debating tactics was not an attack, but rather was aimed at making her more effective. It helped that, in fact, Janet's opinions were worthy of respect and her causes were of high morality.

In another case, a poorness of fit was transformed into a goodness of fit by a chance series of fortuitous events. Nancy also had difficult temperament. The father made rigid and unrealistic demands on the girl, and the mother was inconsistent and uncertain in her handling. The parents were unresponsive to our parent guidance. The father flatly stated, "She's a rotten child." With this pathogenic parent–child interaction, Nancy developed a severe behavior disorder in her early school years. The parents arranged for psychotherapy, but the results were only slightly favorable. The girl's prognosis appeared to be ominous, but a totally unexpected transformation developed when she was nine years old. She suddenly blossomed out with moderate dramatic talents, not stupendous but impressive in comparison to her classmates. Now, the parents began to hear praise of their daughter, instead of the previous years' complaints. Fortunately, the parents had a high regard for these talents. Now the father, in place of calling Nancy "a rotten kid," approved her temperamental attributes, saying, "She's just like Maria Callas." The mother was also delighted. With that, literally, within a year Nancy's behavioral symptoms melted, and she proceeded with a goodness of fit with her family, academic, and social relationships. She had brief stormy periods with new situations and people, but adapted more quickly as she passed through adolescence. In adulthood, Nancy undertook demanding academic training, and then went on to have a satisfactory career and social life.

The clinical applications of goodness of fit were mostly gratifying, but inevitably, there have been some failures. There was Norman whose history had been an inexorablly tragic course. Our attempts to utilize the goodness of fit strategies we have outlined proved to be a failure (Chapter 10) with Norman. He had been temperamentally distractible, with a short attention span from infancy to adulthood. Though his attention was short, in his early school years he concentrated well for brief periods and learned easily and quickly, even with these short spurts of attention. However, his father was a hard-driving professional, with high persistence and long attention span. His temperament and behavioral pattern was, unfortunately, exactly the opposite of his son. The father treasured his own characteristics, and denigrated with contempt Norman's quick shifts of attention, "dawdling," and "forgetfulness" (his father's terms) at his homework and family chores. With these stated problems, the parents asked me (S.C.) for a consultation. After a clinical evaluation, I gave my conclusion that Norman's behavior pattern was not pathological, although inconvenient. Derogative terms were misjudgments of the nature of his temperamental attributes. Norman was doing well at school, was cooperative at home, and did well socially. His prognosis was excellent—if the parents accepted his temperament and behavior patterns and worked constantly with them. The mother hesitantly agreed, but the father, the dominant figure in the family, absolutely refused to agree with this judgment and advice. The concept of temperament was "nonsense," and he exploded with a condemnation of Norman's behavior as "irresponsibility and a lack of character and willpower. He has to shape up." With this destructive poorness of fit, Norman's self-confidence slipped and his academic achievement and responsible work diminished year by year. I made several efforts to alter the father's malignant attitudes with the boy. He was friendly and polite and said he knew I was trying to assist. As the reader may recall, when I started to talk about Norman, he interrupted with, "I know exactly what you will say," repeated my judgment with my exact words quite accurately and ended pleasantly with, "You are entirely wrong." With Norman's continuing downhill course, when he was 18, the parents finally decided that he needed psychiatric care. They were referred to a very competent psychiatrist, but the treatment was a complete failure. As an adult, Norman was nonfunctional, lodged with his parents, lived by "borrowing" money from parents and other family members and friends. He developed sequential grandiose fantasies of incipient careers as a musician and song composer, actor, or some other new career. These were expected to blossom in the near future, but he took only token action. His diagnosis was narcissistic personality disorder, severe.

In addition, in Chapter 17, we described the program of parent guidance as an important tool of both prevention and early intervention when a behavior problem had occurred. Most parents were willing and even eager to accept the guidance advice, and with this a poorness of fit was changed to a goodness of fit. A minority of parents could not accept the guidance advice for one reason or another. If the dissonant parent–child interaction was severe, as in Norman's case, the child's life course was substantially unfavorable. If the dissonance was mild, the long-term, unhealthy effect was variable. In some cases, the youngster developed a mild to moderate behavioral problem, but not severe enough to prevent the development of a productive life-course. Some youngsters, when they were adolescents, were able to take their lives into their own hands and look to somewhere other than their parents for their guidance. With positive life functioning under their own control, they were enabled to ignore undesirable parental idiosyncrasies.

☐ Summation

In this chapter we have elaborated the highlights of a systematic and comprehensive clinical schedule, for use by a clinician, for a patient suffering with a psychological disturbance. The sequence of steps: First, a comprehensive clinical history and observations; for a child this would be a play session. Next, a review of the diagnostic possibilities, given the information obtained. Then, an identification of psychiatric, neurologic, or somatic symptoms requiring special, additional diagnostic study. Finally, the time is appropriate for the clinical application of the goodness of fit concept. This involves the identification of the patient's pattern of behavior which expresses the maladaptive individual–environment interactional process, and poorness of fit. Emphasis is now placed on the specific elements in this interactional process that are critically responsible for the maladaptive pattern. The next necessity is to formulate the *change* of the person's behavior and/or environmental factor required to convert the poorness of fit to a goodness of fit and pursue the discussion with the patient until he or she understands and implements the necessary specific therapeutic change.

This schedule is not useful if it is applied as a routinized blueprint, but requires an individual approach. For every patient, the content of the history may be different, the nature of the person–environment interaction may be different, the identification of the critical issues requiring a change in patient or environment are unique, the ease or difficulty in making it possible to achieve the change will most certainly vary. In addition, this therapeutic strategy is plausible, but not guaranteed. Failures are inevitable in a minority of cases, as happens with any other system of theory and practice.

To complete this chapter we will comment on one more issue pertinent for the clinician's guidelines: the depth of treatment.

☐ The Depth of Treatment

Some psychiatrists, especially among psychoanalysts, have criticized the therapeutic application of the goodness of fit as "superficial." Namely, because this approach does not attempt to identify the presumed basic underlying cause of the patient's problems. Even if such "superficial" treatment was successful, the critics would say, it has only served as an incomplete task because the symptoms must have reflected some deep, unconscious, pathogenic basis; if a thorough treatment has been ignored another symptom will replace the one superficially eliminated. (See Chapter 3 for a review and critique for the concepts of early childhood determinism.)

How do we define unhealthy symptoms either as "superficial" or showing depth? Let us take the case of Joyce, the young actress. She came for help with considerable anxiety, demoralized, losing her self-confidence, and concerned that her career as an actress was threatened. She had decided on this goal in adolescence and worked with deep motivation to achieve this desire. Her symptoms were indeed deep. Her whole persona was threatened by severe anxiety, her self-esteem shaken, and her lifestyle and goal under attack. How could this be called superficial, just because her symptoms had originated and escalated over the course of a few months. The cause of her deep and threatening symptoms was not due to some early childhood trauma or conflict, but was the creation of a destructive environmental situation (the leading actor's vengeful behavior). And how could the therapy be "superficial" when a single change—the resumption of her true acting style—dramatically ended her troubling symptoms, restored her to successful functioning, and established the basis of a satisfactory life-course?

Our argument with the controversy of deep versus superficial therapy is bolstered by the New York Times report of an interesting discussion at a meeting of a large group of psychoanalysts in New York City in March 1998. Their agenda talked about "what deduction, trauma and fantasy meant to them" (Boxer, N.Y. Times, 1998). The newspaper reporter commented that, "Many of the analysts at the meeting sounded doubt-ful that they could even get a firm grip on historical reality, the factors of their patients' lives and traumas. And the strange thing was, many of them didn't seem to think that this mattered all that much." At the meeting, Dr. Robert Michels, Professor of Psychiatry at Cornell University, and a senior psychoanalyst, put it that, "We are experts not in helping patients learn facts but in helping them construct useful myths. We are fantasy doctors, not reality doctors. We don't help patients decide what is true . . . they can become more comfortable not about what happened in the past but about uncertainty and ambiguity."

From the newspaper reporter, it appears that most of the psychoanalysts at the meeting agreed with Dr. Michel's assertion (Boxer, N.Y. Times, 1998). His formulation would strongly imply that psychoanalysis is not a scientific field that searches for verifiable facts, but is a special religious field, concerned with myths and fantasies.

We have the deepest respect for Dr. Michels and some other psychoanalysts whom we know personally as highly ethical and talented professionals in their commitments to the care of their suffering psychiatric patients. However, the advocacy for the "construction of useful myths" is a dangerous therapeutic goal. People may become comfortable with "useful myths," but all too often harsh reality may explode such a myth, with tragic consequences.

Another recent series of reports has further undermined the assertion of the importance of "deep" therapy. A major emphasis of this ideology, starting with Freud, contends that deeply repressed memories in early childhood—whether of the conflict of the id and superego, the Oedipal conflict, penis envy, etc.—are one source of the repressed memories which are responsible for the psychopathology suffered by individuals in succeeding years. Therapists committed to this theory logically search and probe to expose these memories together with their patients.

Now, a series of reports have exposed that many of these repressed memories, unearthed by therapists, are actually *false*. A spectacular incident is described in a report of a lawsuit in which a patient sued her therapist who had convinced her that she had memories of being part of a satanic cult that sexually abused numerous men, and that she had even abused her own two sons. None of this was true. The insurance company settled the suit by paying her 10.6 million dollars. Apropos of that lawsuit, the newspaper reporter stated that, "recently the tide had been turning away from accepting the validity of these recovered memories. Three years ago, the American Psychiatric Association cautioned that such memories were not true" (Belluck, N.Y. Times, 1994). The comment of the reporter is confirmed by the documentation of several books that many reports of repressed memories elicited by therapists are untrue (Loftus & Ketchum, 1994; Ofshe & Watters, 1994). Daniel Schacter in his scholarly study of memory, comments on the tragic results of eliciting false repressed memories: "The psychological toll on those involved is massive and often irreversible" (1996, p. 249).

To conclude, above we have expressed our profound skepticism of the validity of the concept of "deep therapy."

20
CHAPTER

Overview and a Look to the Future

In the series of preceding chapters in this volume we have explicated and documented the details of the positive clinical and theoretical applications of the goodness of fit concept.

To summarize, the clinical assets of this concept have comprised flexibility, individualization, and comprehensiveness. The application of the goodness of fit model can be applied to the psychotherapeutic treatment of a person with psychological dysfunction at any age-period, from early childhood to adult life, with the exception of severe mental illnesses or panic disorders.

A successful treatment requires no *a priori* time deadline. In some cases, for a successful course of treatment, a few discussions may suffice, in others, several months of therapy may be necessary. In a few difficult cases, more intensive and extensive months of therapy may be required. Failures also may occur. In some cases, a few discussions may reveal the inevitable unfavorable outcomes. In others, a lengthy and laborious therapeutic process may be attempted without felicitous results.

Flexibility of treatment strategies may require modifications at different ages for different and disorders, due to differences in the level of psychological development and the variability of environmental locales and stresses.

Individualization has required the rejection of any fixed blueprint of any therapeutic system used as a template for all similar cases. Rather, the therapist has to take into account any individual patient's structure

206

of assets, talents, motivation, and dysfunctional patterns. Further, the therapeutic strategy may shift and need modification should there be a significant change in the patient's symptoms and/or in the environmental status.

As to comprehensiveness, the application of the goodness of fit concept prescribes the gathering of the pertinent data from all sources, including the patient's psychological and biological characteristics, and the range of environmental influences and stresses. Only with such a comprehensive data collection can a satisfactory diagnosis and treatment plan be elaborated for each individual case.

The theoretical basis for the formulation of a goodness of fit has included the involvement of the organism–environment interactional model (Chapter 2) and the biopsychosocial model (Chapter 11). As indicated in those chapters, these two theoretical formulations have been developed by a number of psychological and psychiatric developmentalists.

However, in very recent years, we have ourselves conceptualized another significant aspect of the goodness of fit model, namely normalcy and vulnerability versus pathology and the dictum that the pathology is in the interaction (Chapter 18). This formulation, with an emphasis on the concept of vulnerability, has been our first elaboration of this idea in this book. We had emphasized the importance of the normal basis of an individual's behavior problems or the parental functioning in a number of clinical vignettes described in various chapters of this book. However, only now we have systematically spelled out the concept of vulnerability.

☐ Why is the Concept of Vulnerability Important?

Take the case of Arnold K., detailed in Chapter 18. He went for help to a previous therapist, needing to solve his severely dysfunctional psychological behavior in his personal, social, and work activities. His behavior was threatening to prevent a marriage with a close, intimate girlfriend, alienate his circle of good friends, and endanger his promising career development. Beyond his severe anxiety at the risk of these disastrous consequences, he was bewildered. He had too much self-respect to seize upon some irrational explanation, such as "its bad luck," or "its everybody's fault."

Traditionally, in such a situation, the therapist would assume that the cause of the patient's dysfunction must be in some devious pathological element in his personality. Skillfully, the therapist seized on any clues in Arnold's deviant behavior, and assumed them as evidence of pathology; he then accepted these interpretations and expected that they would explain Arnold's serious, dysfunctional behavior. However, none of these interpretations served to clarify and help Arnold's problem. He was increasingly dissatisfied with the therapist's effort, had to search for another therapist, and found me (A.T.).

The lesson from the history of Arnold's case history, and from others in our experiences, is clear. If a person is suffering from substantial dysfunctional behavior and other symptoms, and is found to be basically normal psychologically, the probe for a pathological causation will become the search for a "fool's gold." The genuine gold will be found in the patient's *specific vulnerability* and the interaction with the *specific environmental stress*. The pathology will not be in the person's psychological structure but *in the interactional process*.

We are not the first to have proposed the issue of normalcy and vulnerability. Werner and Smith, in their long-scale longitudinal study of the children of Kauai, Hawaii, found that many of the children suffered severe behavioral or learning problems. However, they reported that some of the children were, *"vulnerable*—exposed to poverty, biological risks, and family instability, and reared by parents with little education or serious mental health problems—who remained *invincible* and developed into competent and autonomous young adults *who worked well, played well, loved well and expected well"* (1982, pp. 2–3). Their report is indeed dramatic.

The Vaillants created another impressive epidemiological longitudinal study of vulnerability at Harvard Medical School (Vaillant & Vaillant, 1981). Their study, in many respects, was similar to the Kauai, Hawaii project (Werner & Smith, 1982). The Vaillants followed a sample of 237 inner city men in Boston, with severely disadvantaged childhood, including chaotic families. In adult life, there was found a several-fold difference between 138 men who enjoyed robust mental health and capacities for meaningful interpersonal relatedness and the 119 men who were found to be emotionally impaired by a number of objective ratings. The one significant difference in the outcomes of the two groups was located in the ratings of the ability to find employment at age 14 years. The 138 men with positive work histories had healthy developmental courses in adult life. By contrast, the 119 men with poor capacity for work went on to unhealthy and even pathological outcomes.

A third similar epidemiological longitudinal study of vulnerability is summarized in a recent book by Michael Rutter and his wife, Marjorie Rutter, a Clinical Nurse Specialist. Their volume is a comprehensive review of psychological development from infancy to old age (Rutter & Rutter, 1993). The authors included a follow-up study of a number of British women who spent most of their childhood years in a group foster home because their parents could not cope with bringing them up.

The majority of the institution-reared women had an unfavorable life-course in adult life. They married deviant men, due to their tendency to marry on impulse. In general, the women did not plan ahead in life decisions. By contrast, the other girls were characterized by their ability to foresee their life contingencies successfully as adults regarding marriage and work. As to the explanation for the development of self-organization in the latter group, the Rutters reported that "the findings showed that part of the answer lay in positive school experiences" (p. 58).

These three studies, in Hawaii, Boston, and London, all emphasize that a significant number of disadvantaged, vulnerable youngsters could develop basically normally and, as they grew, could cope successfully with their new environmental demands and expectations.

☐ Further Reviews of Vulnerability Studies

In order to identify still other studies of vulnerability, we obtained a computer search of the psychiatric and psychological literature over the past ten years, using the key term *vulnerability*. The printouts comprised 142 articles, with authors, institutions, titles, and detailed abstracts.

We have tabulated the data of these 142 articles, and have been disappointed by their findings. The range of the individual patterns of vulnerability are widespread—social disadvantage, neurochemical dysfunction, physical or psychiatric illness, suicidal risk, drug abuse, complications of aging, positive HIV findings, aberrant genetic factors, etc. The basic theoretical model of the analysis of the individual research and clinical reports consist of interactive qualities and are static, rather than possessing interactional and dynamic features. In other words, each author reports a simple, additive, interactive effect. For example, drug abuse increases vulnerability, or being a vulnerable individual increases the risk of drug abuse; complications of aging augment the vulnerability of the aged, or being a vulnerable aged person leads to a greater risk of complications of aging. By contrast, we are convinced that an interactionist approach is essential. For example, the issue of drug abuse and vulnerability, or the complications of aging and the vulnerability of aged individuals should be analyzed by the two factors in a dialectic process in which opposites interact with each other to produce an organic unity of opposites. (See our discussion of interactionism in Chapter 2.)

Also, in the 214 articles, there is very little noted to the importance of vulnerability in contraposition to normalcy, in contrast to the emphasis placed on normalcy in the longitudinal studies of Hawaii, Boston and London, and in our individual case reports.

The Clinical Application of the Goodness of Fit Model is Not a Panacea

The previous pages of this chapter have summarized the clinical applications of the goodness of fit concept. The assets and therapeutic value of the model have been illustrated in many of the clinical vignettes in previous chapters. I presume no psychotherapeutic system has a 90–100 percent success rate. This is true for our goodness of fit concept. Three tragic failures in our attempts to change a poorness to a goodness of fit are described: Howard in Chapter 8, Norman in Chapter 10, and Bruce in Chapter 14. In Chapter 17, the value of parent guidance in the prevention and early intervention of childhood was noted. However, a small minority of parents would not or could not change their negative approach to a positive one with their children (Norman's father is an illustration) for one reason or another.

Usefulness and Limitations of Other Theoretical and Clinical Systems

In Chapter 3, we briefly emphasized the limitations of the other major theories and clinical approaches to contrast the theory and clinical applications of the goodness of fit concept. By now, we have explicated the breadth and scope and special usefulness of the goodness of fit formulation in the successive chapters of the book.

With that, we should return to the numerous theoretical and clinical assets of other systems. For example, behavior therapy is often helpful in treating specific phobic symptoms, often more effectively than a goodness of fit approach. The same is true for the usefulness of cognitive therapy, with its structured clinical approach to the treatment of depression. As to Piaget's concepts of "assimilation" and "accommodation," their clinical value has yet to be proven. However, his developmental formulations of "adaptability" and "equilibrium" are more likely to work out pertinent concepts with regard to the dynamics of the goodness of fit application. As to the theory of attachment, its central formulation is very controversial, its basic measurement device, the Ainsworth Strange Situation test, has dubious scientific value in the judgement of many, and its clinical usefulness in practice is at best vague.

For the flexible psychoanalysts, the results of their clinical practice for a number of symptomatic syndromes, especially for personality disorders, are comparable, and in some cases, more useful than the application of goodness of fit. These psychoanalysts have discarded several of

Freud's ideological dicta. When they unburden themselves of the remaining weight of the discredited Freudian structure, they will approach their patients with the valid psychodynamic theory and practice applications with a higher level of success.

☐ A Look to the Future

We have been excited and stimulated by the power and importance of the goodness of fit paradigm. But we realize that the questions and issues we have raised and answered regarding this model are just a beginning.

Studies of Middle Age and the Aged

Our developmental data and case histories have been gathered and analyzed primarily in the age-periods from infancy, childhood, adolescence, and the twenties and thirties, from our longitudinal studies and clinical practice. Hence, the chapters in our book have reported those age-periods. From our clinical and personal observations, we have gained the impression that new and important changes in the normalcy–vulnerability of the individual characteristics and environmental stresses and their interactional processes occur often in the older age periods. However, our data in the upper age-periods have been only as impressions, and not enough for any clear conclusions. We suggest that a systematic and comprehensive study of the theoretical and clinical applications of the middle age and aged age-periods would be important and undoubtedly highly productive.

Family Dynamics

An extensive body of family therapists has gathered a wealth of theoretical and clinical data on the interactional process of the family structure. A study applying their data and clinical experiences to the goodness of fit model and its applications might turn out to be productive.

Group Dynamics

Similarly, a large number of group therapists, with a wide variety of group-behavior disorders, adolescent problems, drug abuse, etc., have utilized a number of clinical techniques with groups. A study, perhaps starting with a pilot study, using goodness of fit and its applications, might be applicable.

Goodness of Fit and Intelligence

Edmund Gordon, Professor of Psychology, Emeritus at Yale University and his co-authors have written two comprehensive and crucial reviews on the genesis and development of intelligence: One, *An Interactionist Perspective on the Genesis of Intelligence* (Gordon & Lemons, 1997), the other, *Culture and Cognitive Development* (Gordon & Armour-Thomas, 1991). The conclusion of the 1997 chapter is quoted, "Since human intelligence is both adaptive and transformative, it is but viewed as a dynamic, continually emergent, and protean phenomenon that cannot be explained adequately by static processes" (p. 338). In the 1991 chapter, an intensive review of the many factors that shape culture is included and concludes that, "It is the orchestration of these factors that emerges as cognition, which we see as rooted in cultural experience, and may help us understand how it is that such referents for cultural identity, like class, ethnicity, and gender, come to be so powerfully associated with developed cognitive activity" (p. 97).

Gordon's theses, as quoted above, are certainly congenial with our theoretical formulations of the goodness of fit concept. However, our clinical applications have been committed to the study and treatment of normal and unhealthy behavioral development from infancy to adulthood. We have not been experts in the field of the genesis and development of intelligence, as Gordon has been. It would be exciting to cooperate and even collaborate with Gordon's concepts of intelligence with our formulations of the behavioral clinical applications of the goodness of fit conceptualization. Such a collaboration should be productive, but it would require extensive time and energy and we leave the proposal to the younger generation of researchers.

Piaget's Concepts

As indicated in an earlier chapter, a number of talented developmental psychologists, especially in California, have been pursuing the possibilities of applying a number of Piaget's formulations to the theoretical and clinical issues of behavioral development (Cameron, 1997 personal communication). For us, a positive outcome of these studies is intriguing but unpredictable. Our semi-educated guess is that Piaget's formulations of adaptability and equilibrium appear most promising as applications to the enhancement of the theoretical structure of goodness of fit.

As a final question, we have puzzled, and not found the answers, concerning the unpredictable life courses of some of our subjects and parents. Why do some older children, adolescents, or adults with a serious poorness of fit spontaneously have insight into an intrapsychic attribute that is responsible for the poorness of fit, correct it, and go on to develop a productive goodness of fit, while others do not have this insight and go on with their poorness of fit with its pathogenic consequences in adult life?

We are confident that just as the younger generation of talented researchers and clinicians have been creatively expanding and modifying our findings on temperament, the new generation will explore imaginatively the new issues of goodness of fit we have posed and contribute additional new questions and answers.

Temperament Definitions, Categories, and Ratings

[Reprinted from sections of Thomas, A., and Chess, S. (1977), *Temperament and Development*, pp. 9–24, NY: Brunner/Mazel.]

Temperament may best be viewed as a general term referring to the *how* of behavior. It differs from ability, which is concerned with the *what* and *how well* of behaving, and from motivation, which accounts for *why* a person does what he is doing. Temperament, by contrast, concerns the *way* in which an individual behaves. Two children may dress themselves with equal skillfulness or ride a bicycle with the same dexterity and have the same motives for engaging in these activities. Two adolescents may display similar learning ability and intellectual interest and their academic goals may coincide. Two adults may show the same technical expertness in their work and have the same reason for devoting themselves to their jobs. Yet, these two children, adolescents, or adults may differ significantly with regard to the quickness with which they move, the ease with which they approach a new physical environment, social situation, or task, the intensity and character of their mood expression, and the effort required by others to distract them when they are absorbed in an activity.

Temperament can be equated to the term *behavioral style*. Each refers to the *how* rather than the *what* (abilities and content) or the *why* (motivations) of behavior. In this definition, temperament is a phenomenological term and has no implications as to etiology or immutability. On the contrary, like any other characteristic of the organism—whether it be height, weight, intellectual competence, perceptual skills—temperament is influenced by environmental factors in its expression and even in its nature as development proceeds.

In our NYLS the parents were utilized as the primary source of information on the child's behavior in infancy. As the child grew older, behavioral data were also obtained through teacher interviews in nursery and elementary school, direct observations in the school setting, and during psychometric testing at ages three, six, and nine, and direct interview with each youngster and parent separately at ages 16–17 years. Academic achievement scores were gathered from school records. Whenever a child in our study presented behaviors that might indicate that a behavioral problem was developing, a complete clinical evaluation was made. Special tests such as perceptual or neurological evaluations were carried out as indicated.

All data, whether obtained from parent or teacher or by direct observation of the child, were described in factual, descriptive terms with a concern not only for what the child did but how he did it. Statements about the presumed meaning of the child's behavior were considered unsatisfactory for primary data, though they often provided useful insights into special attitudes or judgments of the teacher or parent. When such interpretative statements were made, the interviewer always asked for a description of the actual behavior. Special emphasis was placed on the child's first response to a new stimulus (e.g., first bath) and his or her subsequent reactions to the same stimulus until a consistent long-term response was established. The sequence of responses to new stimuli, situations, and demands, whether simple or complex, provided especially rich information on a child's individual temperamental pattern.

In order to avoid bias of the data by "halo effects," different staff members were used for different phases of the data collection for any individual child. Interview protocol forms were revised as necessary to make them appropriate for succeeding age-periods. Each revised protocol was pre-tested on samples of children not included in the longitudinal study.

☐ Categories

Nine categories of temperament were established by an inductive content analysis of the parent interview protocols for the infancy periods in the first 22 children studied. Item scoring was used, a three-point scale was established for each category, and the item scores transformed into a weighted score for each category on each record. To avoid contamination by "halo effects," no successive interviews of a given child were scored contiguously. High intra- and interscorer reliability, at the 90 percent level of agreement, was achieved.

The nine categories of temperament and their definitions are:

1) *Activity Level*: the motor component present in a given child's functioning and the diurnal proportion of active and inactive periods. Protocol data on motility during bathing, eating, playing, dressing, and behavior while sitting for long periods, such as in a drive, watching TV, etc., are used in scoring this category.

2) *Rhythmicity (regularity)*: the predictability and/or unpredictability in time of any function. It can be analyzed in relation to the sleep–wake cycle, hunger, feeding pattern, and elimination schedule.

3) *Approach or withdrawal*: the nature of the initial response to a new stimulus, be it a new food, a new toy, new person, or new place. Approach responses are positive, whether displayed by mood expression (e.g., smiling, verbalizations, etc.) or motor activity (e.g., swallowing a new food, reaching for a new toy, active play, etc.). Withdrawal reactions are negative, whether displayed by mood expression (e.g., crying, fussing, grimacing, verbalizations, etc.) or motor activity (e.g., moving away, spitting new food out, pushing new toy away, etc.).

4) *Adaptability*: responses to new or altered situations. One is not concerned with the nature of the initial responses, but with the ease with which they are modified in desired direction.

5) *Threshold of responsiveness*: the intensity level of stimulation that is necessary to evoke a discernible response, irrespective of the specific form that the response may take, or the sensory modality affected. The behaviors utilized are those concerning reactions to sensory stimuli, environmental objects, and social contacts.

6) *Intensity of reaction*: the energy level of response, irrespective of its quality or direction.

7) *Quality of mood*: the amount of pleasant, joyful, and friendly behavior, as contrasted with unpleasant, crying, and unfriendly behavior.

8) *Distractibility*: the effectiveness of extraneous environmental stimuli in interfering with or in altering the direction of the ongoing behavior.

9) *Attention span and persistence*: two categories that are related. Attention span concerns the length of time a particular activity is pursued by the child. Persistence refers to the continuation of an activity in the face of obstacles to the maintenance of the activity direction.

Each category is rated on a three-point scale, high, medium, or low.

Three temperamental constellations of functional significance have been defined by qualitative analysis of the data and factor analysis. The first group is characterized by regularity, positive approach responses to new stimuli, high adaptability to change, and low or moderately intense mood which is preponderantly positive. These children quickly develop regular sleep and feeding schedules, take to most new foods easily, smile at strangers, adapt easily to a new school, accept most frustration with little fuss, and accept the rules of new games with no trouble. Such a youngster is aptly called the Easy Child, and is usually a joy to his parents, pediatricians, and teachers. This group comprises about 40 percent of our NYLS sample.

At the opposite end of the temperamental spectrum is the group with irregularity in biological functions, negative withdrawal responses to new stimuli, low adaptability to change, and intense mood expressions which are frequently negative. These children show irregular sleep and feeding schedules, slow acceptance of new foods, prolonged adjustment periods to new routines, people, or situations, and relatively frequent and loud periods of crying. Laughter, also, is characteristically loud. Frustration typically produces a violent tantrum. This is the Difficult Child, and mothers and pediatricians find such youngsters difficult indeed. This group comprises about 10 percent of our NYLS sample.

The third noteworthy temperamental constellation is marked by a combination of withdrawal responses of mild intensity to new stimuli with slow adaptability after repeated contact. In contrast to the difficult children, these youngsters are characterized by mild intensity of reactions, whether positive or negative, and by less tendency to show irregularity of biological functions. The mildly negative responses to new stimuli can be seen in the first encounter with the bath, a new food, a stranger, a new place or a new school situation. If given the opportunity to re-experience such new situations over time and without pressure, such a child gradually comes to show quiet and positive interest in an involvement. A youngster with this characteristic sequence of response is referred to as the Slow-to-Warm-Up Child, an apt if inelegant designation. About 15 percent of our NYLS sample falls into this category.

As can be seen from the above percentages, not all children fit into one of these three temperamental groups. This results from the varying and different combinations of temperamental traits, which are manifested by individual children. Also, among those children who do fit one of these three patterns, there is a wide range in degree of manifestation. Some are extremely easy children in practically all situations; others are relatively easy and not always so. A few children are extremely difficult with all new situations and demands; others show only some of these characteristics and relatively mildly. For some children it is highly predictable that they will warm up slowly in any new situation; others warm up slowly with certain types of new stimuli or demands, but warm up quickly in others.

It should be emphasized that the various temperamental constellations all represent variations within normal limits. Any child may be easy, difficult, or slow-to-warm-up temperamentally, have a high or low activity level, distractibility, and low persistence, or the opposite, or any other relatively extreme rating score in a sample of children for a specific temperamental attribute. However, such an amodal rating is not a criterion of psychopathology, but rather an indication of the wide range of behavioral styles exhibited by normal children.

The body of the NYLS quantitative scores of the nine temperamental categories for each of the first five years of life was subject to factor analyses to determine whether meaningful groupings of the categories could be derived statistically. The Varimax solutions proved to be most useful and three factors were developed. One of the these, Factor A, met the criterion of relative consistency over the five-year period. This factor included approach/withdrawal, adaptability, mood, and intensity. The scores for Factor A were normally distributed for each of the five years.

It is significant that the cluster of characteristics comprising Factor A corresponds closely to the cluster developed by qualitative analysis which identifies the Easy Child and the Difficult Child. In this qualitative categorization, which was completed *before* the factor analysis was done, the Easy Child corresponds to high Factor A plus regularity, and the Difficult Child to low Factor A plus irregularity.

It has been possible to identify each of the nine categories of temperament in each child at different age-periods in the preschool and early school years in all of the study populations enumerated above: The New York Longitudinal Study, the Puerto Rican working-class children, the mentally retarded group, the premature sample with high incidence of neurological damage, and the children with congenital rubella. In addition, these temperamental characteristics have been identified in a number of populations studied by investigators at other centers in this country and abroad (Carey & McDevitt, 1989). It is clear, therefore, that these behavioral traits occur ubiquitously in children and can be categorized systematically.

☐ Temperament Questionnaires

Our first pioneering study of temperament necessarily required lengthy and tedious formulations of their categorizations and ratings. For clinical purposes and many research projects, the repetition of our painstaking method would be impracticable. Therefore, short questionnaires, based on our findings, have been developed with psychometric standards. Dr. William Carey and his colleagues have established questionnaires for the infancy, toddler, 3–7 age-period, 8–12 age-period, and adolescence. Dr. Richard Lerner and his colleagues also have established an adolescent questionnaire with the acronym DOTS. We ourselves have developed an early adult age-period questionnaire (18–early thirties).

☐ Resources

Drs. Sean McDevitt and Robin Hegvik, colleagues of Dr. Carey, have consolidated and expanded the Carey Questionnaires and our early adult one to provide a central resource area for any requests of copies of the questionnaires—one in Scottsdale, AZ, and one in West Chester, PA. Also included are questionnaire practice manual sets for clinical, research, and instructional use.

We suggest that any request for any questionnaire with its scoring instructions and/or any practice manual sets be referred to:

SEAN MCDEVITT, PH.D.
BEHAVIORAL-DEVELOPMENTAL INITIATIVES
13802 NORTH SCOTTSDALE ROAD
SUITE 104
SCOTTSDALE, AZ 85252

☐ References

Achenback, T.W. (1988). Developmental psychopathology. In M. H. Bernstein & M. E. Lamb (Eds.). *Developmental psychology: An advanced textbook,* 2nd ed., pp. 549–591. Hillsdale, NJ: Lawrence Erlbaum Associates.

Ackerman, N. (1958). *The psychodynamics of family life.* New York: Basic Books.

American Psychiatric Association. (1994). *Diagnostic and statistical manual of mental disorder,* Fourth Edition Washington, DC: American Psychiatric Association.

Bandura, A. (1978). The self-system in reciprocal determinism. *American Psychologist, 33,* 344–358.

Beck, A. T. (1997). Cognitive therapy reflections. In J. K. Zeig (Ed.). *The evolution of psychotherapy, the third conference,* pp. 55–64. New York: Brunner/Mazel.

Bell, A. P., Weinberg, M. S., & Hammersmith, S. K. (1981). *Sexual preference: Its development in men and women.* Bloomington, IN: Indiana University Press.

Belluck, P. (1997, November 6). 'Memory' Therapy leads to a lawsuit and big settlement. *New York Times,* p. A1.

Bloom, B. S. (1964). *Stability and change in human characteristics.* New York: John Wiley & Sons.

Blos, P. (1979). *The adolescent passage.* New York: International Universities Press.

Bowlby, J. (1951). *Maternal care and mental health*. Geneva: World Health Organization.

Bowlby, J. (1969). *Attachment, Vol. 1. Attachment and loss*. New York: Basic Books.

Bower, T. (1977). *A primer of human development*. San Francisco: W. H. Freeman.

Boxer, S. (1998, March 14). Analysts Get Together for a Synthesis. *The New York Times*, pp. B9, B11.

Buss, A. H. & Plomin, R. (1975). *A temperament theory of personality development*. New York: John Wiley & Sons.

Carey, W.B. (1998). ADHD As a Disorder of Adaptation. *Journal of American Academy of Child and Adolescent Psychiatry*, vol. 37:8, pp. 787–789.

Carey, W. B., & McDevitt, S. C. (Eds). (1994). *Prevention and early intervention*. New York: Brunner/Mazel.

Carey, W. B., & McDevitt, S. C. (Eds). (1989). *Clinical and educational applications of temperament research*. Berwyn, PA: Swets North America, Inc.

Carey, W. B., & McDevitt, S. C. (1995). *Coping with children's temperament: A guide for professionals*. New York: Basic Books.

Chess, S., & Hassibi, M. (1978). *Principles and practice of child psychiatry*. New York: Plenum Press.

Chess, S., & Korn, S. (1970). Temperament and behavior disorders in mentally retarded children. *Archives of General Psychiatry, 23*, 120–130.

Chess, S., Korn, S., & Fernandez, P. B. (1971) *Psychiatric disorders of children with congenital rubella*. New York: Brunner/Mazel.

Chess, S., & Thomas, A. (1984). *Origins and evolution of behavior development: From infancy to early adult life*. New York: Brunner/Mazel.

Chess, S., & Thomas, A. (1996). *Temperament: Theory and practice*. New York: Brunner/Mazel.

Clarke, A. M. & Clarke, A.O.B. (1977). *Early experiences: Myth and evidence*. London: Open Books.

Cooper, A. M., Kernberg, O. F., & Person, E. J. (1989). *Introduction in psychoanalysis toward the second century*. New Haven: Yale University Press.

deVries, M.W. (1984). Temperament and infant mortality among the Masai of East Africa. *American Journal of Psychiatry, 141*, 1189–1194.

Dobzhansky, T. (1966). A geneticist's view of human equality. *The Pharos, 29*, 12–16.

Dubos, R. (1965). *Man adapting*. New Haven: Yale University Press.

East, P. I., Lerner, R. M., Lerner, J. J., Soni, R., Ohannessian, G., & Jacobson, L. P. (1992). Early adolescent peer-group fit, peer relations, and psychosocial competence. A short-term longitudinal study. *Journal of Early Adolescence, 12*, 132–152.

Eisenberg, L. (1986). Mindlessness and brainlessness in psychiatry. *British Journal of Psychiatry, 148*, 497–508.

Eisenberg, L. (1994). Advocacy for the health of the public. In W. B. Carey & S. C. McDevitt (Eds.). *Prevention and early intervention*. New York: Brunner/Mazel.

Eissler, K. R. (1958). Notes on problems of technique in the psychoanalytic treatment of adolescents. *Psychoanalytic study of the Child, 13*, 233–254.

Eliot, G. (1963 Ed.). *Middlemarch*. New York: Washington Square Press.

Emde, R. N. (1989). Toward a psychoanalytic theory of affect. In S.I. Greenspan & E. H. Pollack (Eds.). *The course of life, Volume 1, infancy*, pp. 165–191. Madison: CT: International Universities Press.

Engel, G. L. (1977). The need for a new medical model: A challenge for biomedicine. *Science, 196*, 129–135.

Erikson, E. H. (1959). Identity and the life cycle. *Psychoanalytic Issues, 1*, 1–171.

Eysenck, H. J. (1967). *The biological basis of personality*. Springfield, IL: Charles C. Thomas.

Flavell, J. H. (1963). *The developmental theory of Jean Paget*. New York: O. Van Nostrand.

Frank, J. D. & Frank, M.D. (1974/1991). Persuasion and healing, rev. ed. Baltimore: Johns Hopkins University Press.

Freud, A. (1960). The child guidance clinic as a center of prophylaxis and enlightenment. *Recent developments in psychoanalytic child therapy*, p.37. New York: International Universities Press.

Freud, S. (1949). *An outline of psychoanalysis*. New York: W. W. Norton.

Gordon, E.W., & Armour-Thomas, E. (1991). Culture and cognitive development. In R. S. Sternberg & L. O'Kadaki (Eds.), *Directions of development* (pp. 83–98). Mahwah, NJ: Lawrence Erlbaum Associates.

Gordon, E. W., & Lemons, M. P. (1997). An interactionist perspective on the genesis of intelligence. In R. S. Sternberg & E. Grigorenko, *Intelligence, heredity and environment* (pp. 323–340). Cambridge, MA: Cambridge University Press.

Grunbaum, A. (1984). *The foundations of psychoanalysis: A philosophical critique*. Berkeley, CA: University Calif. Press.

Hall, G. S. (1904). *Adolescence, Vol. II*. New York: Appleton.

Hess, R. D. (1970). Social class and ethnic influences on socialization. In P. M. Mussen (Ed.), *Carmichael's manual of child psychology*. New York: Wiley.

Hunt, J.V. (1980). Implications of plasticity and hierarchical achievements for the assessment of development and risk of mental retardation. In D. B. Sawin, R. C. Hawkins, L. O. Walker, & J. H. Penticuff (Eds.), *Exceptional infant, Vol. 4*. New York: Brunner/ Mazel.

Isaac, R. J., & Armat, V. C. (1990). *Madness in the streets*. New York: The Free Press.

Jensen, P. S., Mrazek, D., Knapp, P. K., Steinberg, L., Pfeffer, C., Schowalter, J., & Shapiro, T. (1997). Evolution and revolution in child psychiatry: ADHD as a disorder of adaptation. *Journal of American Academy of Child and Adolescent Psychiatry, 36*, 1672–1681.

Kagan, J. (1971). *Change and continuity in infancy*. New York: John Wiley & Sons.

Kagan, J. (1984). *The nature of the child* (pp. 62–63). New York: Basic Books.

Karen, R. (1994). *Becoming attached*. New York: Warner Books.

Klerman, G. L. (1989). Overview of the cross-national collaboration of the panic state. *Archives of General Psychiatry, 45*, 407–412.

Kohnstamm, G. A., Bates, J. E. & Rothbart, M. K. (Eds.) (1989). *Temperament in childhood*. New York: John Wiley & Sons.

Kolb, L. C. (1978, April 20). Ego assets: An overlooked aspect of personality organization. Paper presented at Menas S. Lecture at New York University Medical Center.

Kurcinka, M. (1991). *Raising your spirited child*. New York: Harper-Collins.

Lerner, J. V. (1984). The import of temperament for psychological functioning. Merrill-Palmer Quarterly, 30, 177–188.

Lerner, J. V., & Lerner, R. M. (1994). Explorations of the goodness-of-fit model in early adolescence. In W.B. Carey & S.C. McDevitt (Eds.), *Prevention and early intervention* (pp. 161–169). New York: Brunner/Mazel.

Lerner, R. M. (1991). Changing organism-context relations as the basic process of development: a developmental contextual perspective. *Developmental Psychology, 27*, 27–32.

Levy, D.M. (1943). *Maternal overprotection*. New York: Columbia University Press.

Lewis, O. (1966) *The Culture of Poverty. Scientific American*, 215, 19–25.

Lidz, T. (1968). *The person*. New York: Basic Books.

Lidz, T., Fleck, S., & Cornelison, A. R. (1965). *Schizophrenia and the family*. New York: Universities Press.

Loftus, E. E., & Ketcham, K. (1994). *The myth of repressed memory: False memories and allegations of sexual abuse*. New York: St. Martin's Press.

Lorenz, K. (1952). *King Solomon's ring: New light on animal ways*. New York: Crowell.

Marans, S., & Cohen, D.J. (1991). Child psychoanalytic theories of development. In M. Lewis (Ed.), *Child and adolescent psychiatry, a comprehensive textbook* (pp. 129–145). Baltimore: Williams & Wilkins.

Merikangas K. R., & Kupfer, D. J. (1995). Mood disorders: Genetic aspects. In H. I. Kaplan & B. J. Sadeck (Eds.), *Comprehensive textbook of psychiatry, Vol.1* (pp. 1102–1189). Baltimore: Williams & Wilkins.

Moskowitz, B. A. (1978). The acquisition of language. *Scientific American, 23*, 92–108.

Murphy, L. B. (1981). Explorations in child personality. In A. I. Rabin, J. Aronoff, A.M. Barclay, & R. A. Zucker (Eds.), *Further explorations in personality* (pp. 161–195). New York: Wiley & Sons.

Nelson, C. A., & Bloom, F. E. (1997). Child development and neuroscience. *Child Development, 68*, 970–987.

Nitz, K., Lerner, R. M., Lerner, J. V., & Talwar, R. (1988). Parental and peer demands, temperament and early adolescent adjustment. *Journal of Early Adolescence, 8*, 243–466.

Offer, D., & Offer, J. (1975). *From teenage to young manhood* (p. 161). New York: Basic Books.

Ofshe, R., & Watters, E. (1994). *Making monsters: False memories, psychotherapy and sexual hysteria*. New York: Scribner's.

Pervin, L. A. (1976). Performance and satisfaction as a function of individual-environment fit. In N. S. Endler & D. Magnusson (Eds.), *Interactional psychology and personality*. New York: John Wiley & Sons.

Rioch, D. M. (1972). Personality. *Archives of General Psychiatry, 27*, 575–580.

Rutter, M. (1972). *Maternal deprivation reassessed*. Middlesex, England: Penguin Books.

Rutter, M. (1979). *Changing youth in a changing society*. London: Nuffield Provincial Hospital Trust.

Rutter, M. (1981). *Maternal deprivation reassessed,* 2nd edition, (p. 160). Middlesex, England: Penguin Books.

Rutter, M. & Rutter, M. (1993). *Developing minds* (pp. 57–58). New York: Basic Books.

Schacter, D.L. (1996). *Searching for memory*. New York: Basic Books.

Schaffer, R. (1977). *Mothering*. Cambridge, MA: Harvard University Press.

Schneirla, T.C. (1957). The concept of development in comparative psychology. In D. B. Harris (Ed.), *The concept of development*. Minneapolis, MN: University of Minnesota Press.

Shaw, C. R. (1966). *The psychiatric disorders of childhood*. New York: Appleton-Century-Crofts.

Stern, D. (1977). *The first relationship*. Cambridge, MA: Harvard University Press.

Super, C. M., & Harkness, S. (1986). Temperament, development and culture. In R. Plomin & J. Dunn (Eds.), *The study of temperament: changes, continuities and challenges*, (pp. 131–149). Hillsdale, NJ: Lawrence Erlbaum Associates.

Talwar, R., Nitz, K., & Lerner, R. M. (1990). Relations among early adolescent temperament, person and peer demands, and adjustment: A test of the goodness of fit model. *Journal of Adolescence, 13*, 279–298.

Thomas, A., & Chess, S. (1972). Development in middle childhood. *Seminars in Psychiatry, 4*, 331–341.

Thomas, A., & Chess, S. (1977). *Temperament and development*. New York: Brunner/Mazel.

Thomas, A., & Chess, S. (1980). *The dynamics of psychological development*. New York: Brunner/Mazel.

Thomas, A., & Chess, S. (1982). Infant bonding: Mystique and reality. *American Journal of Orthopsychiatry, 52*, 213–222.

Thomas, A., Chess, S., & Birch, H. G. (1968). *Temperament and behavior disorders in children* (pp. 137–138). New York: New York University Press.

Thomas, A., Chess, S., Birch, H. G., & Hertzig, M. E. (1961). The developmental dynamics of primary reaction characteristics in children. *Proceedings of the Third World Congress of Psychiatry, Vol. 1.* Toronto: University of Toronto Press.

Thomas, A., Chess, S., Birch, H. G., Hertzig, M. E., & Korn, S. (1963). *Behavioral individuality in early childhood.* New York: New York University Press.

Thomas, A., Chess, S., Sillen, J. & Mendez, O. A. (1974). Cross-cultural studies of behavior in children with special vulnerabilities to stress. In Ricks, D. F., Thomas, A., & Roff, J. D., (Eds.), *Life history research in psychopathology* (Vol. 3, pp. 53–67). Minneapolis, MN: University of Minnesota Press.

Vaillant, G. E., & Vaillant, C. O. (1981). Natural history of male psychological health, X: Work as a predictor of positive mental health. *American Journal of Psychiatry, 138,* 1433–1440.

Wallerstein, J. S. (1985). Children of divorce: Preliminary report of a ten-year follow-up of older children and adolescence. *Journal of the American Academy of Child Psychiatry, 24,* 545–553.

Watson, J. B. (1928). *Psychological care of infant and child.* New York: W. W. Norton.

Webster, R. (1995). *Why Freud was wrong.* New York: Basic Books.

Weiss, G. (1996). Attention deficit hyperactivity disorder. In M. Lewis (Ed.), *Child and adolescent psychiatry. A comprehensive textbook* (2nd ed., pp. 544–563). Baltimore: Williams & Wilkins.

Werner, E. E., & Smith, R. S. (1982). *Vulnerable but invincible.* New York: Wiley.

White, B. L. (1975). *The first three years of life.* Englewood Cliffs, NJ: Prentice Hall.

Wolff, P. (1996). The irrelevance of infant observation for psychoanalysis. Journal of the American psychoanalytic association, 44, 369–453.

Wynne, L. C., & Singer, M.T. (1963). *Thought disorder and family relations of schizophrenia.* New York: John Wiley & Sons.

Zigler, E. (1975, January 18). [Letter to the editor]. *The New York Times Magazine,*

INDEX